4-00

Writing
English Language
Tests

Longman Handbooks for Language Teachers
General Editor: Donn Byrne

Writing English Language Tests

A Practical Guide for Teachers of English
as a Second or Foreign Language

J. B. Heaton

Longman

LONGMAN GROUP LIMITED
Longman House
Burnt Mill
Harlow
Essex
England

First published 1975
Sixth impression 1982
ISBN 0 582 55080. 7

Typeset by H. Charlesworth & Co. Ltd,
Huddersfield

Printed in Singapore by
Ban Wah Press Pte Ltd

Preface

Attitudes towards language testing have been too narrowly confined for too long. Not until recently has language testing been viewed in its proper light as a potentially powerful and progressive force in teaching. Indeed, the whole subject of testing language opens the door not only to a closer analysis of the testing and teaching methods involved but also to a better appreciation of the nature of the language being taught.

This is a practical handbook on the construction of English tests, intended primarily for the teacher in the classroom. In addition to outlining the general principles of language testing, the book shows the teacher how to construct a wide range of tests and test items and how to select those most suitable for his individual purposes. Several types of test items are described and their value assessed in relation to the particular language elements or skills which they are being used to measure. The ability to construct valid and reliable test items, however, is achieved only after constant practice. Consequently, the latter part of the book contains a carefully planned and balanced programme of work, giving the teacher practice in the different processes of constructing a variety of useful test items. It is hoped that in this way the teacher will develop a deeper insight into the fundamentals and techniques of both the testing and teaching of English as a second or foreign language.

Acknowledgements

We are indebted to the following for permission to reproduce copyright material:
John Bright and the Cambridge Examinations Syndicate for an example and possible solutions; the Education Department of Hong Kong for the reading comprehension texts and items from the Hong Kong English School Certificate Examination, 1968 and the Hong Kong Secondary Schools Entrance Examination, 1968 and the author for an extract from an article by Anthony Tucker from *The Guardian* 5th September, 1969.

It is a pleasure to acknowledge a great debt to three friends and colleagues: Albert Pilliner, Frank Chaplen and Pablo Foster. It is difficult to write any book on language testing without being aware of a debt to Robert Lado's *Language Testing*. Moreover, in drawing up several of the guidelines for writing multiple-choice items, I have made considerable use of the advice given by David Harris in his excellent book *Testing English as a Second Language*.

I also wish to acknowledge a debt to the constructors and administrators of the examinations and tests listed below. Although, for obvious reasons, I have not used any actual test items for illustrative purposes, I have nevertheless based several examples on the item *types* appearing in the following examinations and tests. Indeed, it would have been difficult to avoid doing this, since so many of these item types are now used extensively in testing: Alan Davies: English Proficiency Test Battery (EPTB); Elisabeth Ingram: English Language Battery (ELBA); the University of Cambridge Certificate of Proficiency in English; the Northern Universities Joint Matriculation Board: Test in English (Overseas); the Association of Recognised English Language Schools (ARELS): Oral Examination; the Educational Testing Service, Princeton, New Jersey, U.S.A.: Test of English as a Foreign Language (TOEFL), and the Michigan Test of English Language Proficiency.

Further acknowledgements and references (including those to individuals) are made wherever appropriate throughout the book. Indeed, if I have failed to acknowledge any item types which I have used in the book, such a fault has not been a deliberate omission on my part but simply a result of uncertainty regarding the origin of such item types.

J. B. Heaton. May, 1974

Contents

vii

9 Criteria and types of tests

10 Interpreting test scores 167

Appendix 185

Selected bibliography 189

Practical work 195

(Practice sections)

Terminology

Test criteria and types of test will be treated in detail in Chapter 9. However, the reader may find it useful to familiarise himself with a few of the terms used in this book.

Characteristics of a good test

Validity A good test should possess validity: that is, it should measure what it is intended to measure *and nothing else*. If a test does this, it is said to be valid. To what extent is an oral interview a valid test of the oral skills, for example, if the tester is influenced by the personality of the testee?

Reliability A test cannot be valid unless it is reliable. If the test puts several students in a different order of merit when it is administered a second time (provided that neither teaching nor learning has taken place in the interval), then the test lacks reliability. Furthermore, if two or more examiners award different marks for the same answer, the test also lacks reliability.

Discrimination Many classroom tests are not constructed with the primary purpose of discriminating between testees, since their aim is to assess the extent to which the class as a whole has mastered a particular syllabus. However, most other tests (e.g. school-leaving examinations) are designed to show the differences in performance of the individual testees and thus aim to discriminate as widely as possible among the testees.

Backwash The term backwash (also sometimes referred to as *washback*) refers to the effects of a test on teaching. If a test has good backwash effects, it will exert a good influence on the learning and teaching that takes place before the test.

Types of tests

Progress tests Most classroom tests take the form of progress tests, since they assess the progress which students have made in mastering the material taught in the classroom. Progress tests are often given to motivate the student. They also enable the teacher to assess the degree of success of his teaching, helping him to identify areas of weakness or difficulty.

Achievement/Attainment Tests The terms *achievement* and *attainment* are generally used to refer to more formal tests which have been designed to show mastery of a particular syllabus (e.g. end-of-year tests, school-leaving examinations, public tests). These tests are similar to class progress tests in the sense that they are generally based on a syllabus and measure what has been taught and learnt. However, they are rarely constructed by the classroom teacher for a particular class and they are designed primarily to measure individual performance rather than to act as a means of motivating the student or reinforcing learning.

Proficiency Tests Proficiency tests measure a student's achievement in relation to a specific task which he will later be required to perform. For example, does a student know enough English to follow a particular course given in the medium of English or to do a particular job requiring a use of English? Proficiency tests rarely take into account any syllabus which the student has followed, since they are concerned with future performance rather than past achievement and are often administered to students from various language-learning backgrounds.

Aptitude Tests Aptitude tests measure the student's *probable* performance in learning a foreign language, showing whether the student has any special aptitude for learning a new language. Will he experience difficulty in identifying the sounds of the new language or its grammatical structures?

Diagnostic Tests Many progress, achievement and proficiency tests can be used as diagnostic tests to some degree, enabling the teacher to identify specific areas of weakness and difficulty so that he is able to plan the most appropriate remedial programme. A diagnostic test is primarily designed to assess the student's knowledge and skills in particular areas before a course of study is begun.

1 Introduction to Language Testing

1.1 Testing and teaching

It is unfortunate that so many examinations in the past have led to a separation of testing from teaching. Both testing and teaching are so closely interrelated that it is virtually impossible to work in either field without being constantly concerned with the other. Tests may be constructed primarily as devices to reinforce learning and to motivate the student, or primarily as a means of assessing the student's performance in the language. In the former case, the test is geared to the teaching that has taken place, whereas in the latter case the teaching is often geared largely to the test. Standardised tests and public examinations, in fact, generally exert such a considerable influence on the average teacher that they are often instrumental in determining the kind of teaching that takes place before the test.

Consider the effect of the following type of test item on the teaching of English:

> Analyse into clauses, stating the kind and function of each clause:
> We cannot go until we have finished these exercises.

when compared with the effect of the following item:

> Rewrite each of the following sentences in another way but do not change the meaning. Begin each new sentence with the words given.
> We cannot go until we have finished these exercises.
> When . . . .

The former test item encourages teaching *about* the language while the latter encourages practice in using the language.

It can be argued with some justification that language examinations in the past have exerted a harmful influence on the language teacher and have considerably inhibited language learning by encouraging teachers to teach *about* the language. As a consequence, relatively few teachers sought to provide the maximum opportunity for their students to practise the language itself.

Fortunately, many external examining bodies today seek to measure the candidate's actual performance in the language, and in this way sometimes exert a beneficial influence on syllabuses and teaching strategies. Yet, however much concerned a public examining body may be about the

1

effects on teaching (i.e. the backwash effects) of its particular examination, the main purpose of that examination is to measure the candidate's ability to use the target language. The examination is thus primarily an instrument for measuring and evaluating performance.

1.2   Why test?

The function indicated in the preceding paragraph provides one of the answers to the question: Why test? But it must be emphasised that it is only one of the functions of a test and that furthermore, as far as the practising teacher is concerned, it is perhaps one of the more negative functions.

Although most teachers also wish to evaluate individual performance, the aim of the classroom test is different to that of the external examination. While the latter is generally concerned with evaluation for the purpose of selection, the classroom test is concerned with evaluation for the purpose of enabling the teacher to increase his own effectiveness by making adjustments in his teaching to enable certain groups of students or individuals in the class to benefit more. Too many teachers gear their teaching towards an ill-defined 'average' group without taking into account the abilities of those students in the class who are at either end of the scale.

A good classroom test will also help to locate the precise areas of difficulty encountered by the class or by the individual student. Just as it is necessary for the doctor first to diagnose his patient's illness, so it is equally necessary for the teacher to diagnose his student's weaknesses and difficulties. Unless the teacher is able to identify and analyse the errors a student makes in handling the target language, he will be in no position to render any assistance at all through appropriate anticipation, remedial work and additional practice.

The test should also enable the teacher to ascertain which parts of the language programme have been found difficult by the class. In this way, the teacher can evaluate the effectiveness of the syllabus as well as the methods and materials he is using. The test results may indicate, for example, certain areas of the language syllabus which have not taken sufficient account of L1 learner difficulties or which, for some reason, have been glossed over.

A test which sets out to measure a student's performance as fairly as possible without in any way setting traps for him can be effectively used to motivate the student. A well-constructed classroom test will provide the student with an opportunity to show his ability to recognise and produce correct forms of the language. Provided that details of his performance are given as soon as possible after the test, the student should be able to learn from his errors and consolidate the pattern taught. In this way a good test can be used as a valuable teaching device.

1.3   What should be tested and to what standard?

The development of modern linguistic theory has helped to make language teachers and testers aware of the importance of analysing the language being tested. Modern descriptive grammars (though not yet primarily intended for foreign language teaching purposes) are replacing the older, Latin-based prescriptive grammars: linguists are examining the whole complex system of language skills and patterns of linguistic behaviour. Indeed, language skills are so complex and so closely related to many other non-linguistic skills (gestures, eye-movements, etc.) that it may often seem impossible to separate them for the purpose of any kind of assessment. A person always speaks and communicates in a particular situation at a particular time. Without this kind of context, language may lose much of its meaning.

Before a test is constructed, it is important to question the standards which are being set. What standards should be demanded of learners of a foreign language? Should foreign language learners, for example, be expected to communicate with the same ease and fluency as native speakers? Are certain habits of second language learners regarded as mistakes when these same habits would not constitute mistakes when belonging to native speakers? What, indeed, is "correct" English?

Examinations in the written language have in the past set artificial standards even for native speakers and have often demanded skills similar to those acquired by the great English essayists and critics. In imitating first language examinations of written English, however, second language examinations have proved far more unrealistic in their expectations of the performances of foreign learners, who have been required to re-write some of the greatest literary masterpieces in their own words or to write original essays in language beyond their capacity.

1.4   Testing the language skills

Four major skills in communicating through language are often broadly defined as listening, speaking, reading and writing. In many teaching situations it is desirable that areas of the language are first presented orally before reading and writing are practised. Where this is the case, it is important for the test writer to include those types of questions which appear relevant to the ability to speak the language: e.g. questions testing the student's ability to manipulate structures encountered in the spoken language and to make the correct response to a given stimulus.

Success in traditional examinations all too often simply demonstrates that the student has been able to perform well in the examination he has taken – and very little else. For example, the precis exercise (one of the important components of many traditional examinations) measures a skill which is more closely associated with examinations and answering tech-niques than with language used in real-life situations. In this sense, the traditional examination may tell us relatively little about the student's general fluency and ability to handle the target language, although it may give some indication of the student's ability in some of the skills he needs as a student.

Ways of assessing performance in the four major skills may take the form of tests of:

(1) listening (auditory) comprehension, in which single utterances, dialogues, talks and lectures are given to the testee;

(2) speaking ability, usually in the form of an interview, a picture description, and reading aloud;

(3) reading comprehension, in which questions are set to test the student's understanding of a written text; and

(4) writing ability, usually in the form of essays, letters and reports.

It is the test constructor's task to assess the relative importance of these skills at the various levels and to devise an accurate means of measuring the student's success in developing these skills. Many test writers consider that their purpose can best be achieved if each separate skill can be measured on its own. But it is usually extremely difficult to separate one skill from another, for the very division of the four skills is an artificial one and the concept itself constitutes a vast over-simplification of the issues involved in communication.

1.5   Testing the language elements

In order to isolate the components of the language skills for both teaching and testing purposes, we should look closely at the following elements:

(i)   phonology (concerned with pronunciation, stress and intonation)

(ii)   vocabulary (concerned with word meanings and word arrange-ments)

(iii) grammar

(i) Tests of phonology

Test items designed to test phonology might attempt to assess the follow-ing sub-skills: ability to recognise and pronounce the significant sound contrasts of a language, ability to recognise and use the stress patterns of a language, and ability to hear and produce the melody or the patterns of the tunes of a language (i.e. the rise and fall of the voice).

The following is an example of a test item designed to test phoneme discrimination. Three words are spoken by the teacher (recorded on tape in the case of many public examinations) and the testee is asked to indi-cate which words are the same. Sometimes, all three words[1] are the same

(AAA); sometimes only the first and second words are the same (AAB) and so on.

(Spoken)			(Written)				
dock	dock	dock	AAA	AAB	ABA	ABC	O
bad	bad	bat	AAA	AAB	ABA	ABC	O
ship	sheep	ship	AAA	AAB	ABA	ABC	O
fairy	furry	ferry	AAA	AAB	ABA	ABC	O

(ii) Tests of vocabulary

A test of vocabulary measures the student's knowledge of the meaning of certain words and word groups. Such a test may test the student's active vocabulary (the words he should be able to use in speaking and in writing) or his passive vocabulary (the words he should be able to recognise and understand when he is listening to someone or when he is reading). Obviously, in this kind of test the method used to select the vocabulary items (= sampling) is of the utmost importance.

> [2] Put a circle round the letter at the side of the word which best completes the sentence.
>> Did you . . . that book from the school library?
>> A. beg B. borrow C. hire D. lend E. ask

(iii) Tests of grammar

These tests measure the student's ability to manipulate structures and to distinguish appropriate grammatical forms from inappropriate ones.

> [2] Put a circle round the letter of the word or group of words which best completes each sentence.
>> I'll wait here until it . . . . dark.
>> A. will be
>> B. be
>> C. is
>> D. is being
>> E. has been

Note that all three examples in this section are called *multiple-choice items*. The term *multiple-choice* is used because the testee is required to select the correct answer from a choice of several answers. (Only one answer is correct for each item.) The word *item* is used in preference to the word *question* because the latter word suggests the interrogative form; many test items are, in fact, written in the form of statements.

1.6   Language skills and language elements

Items designed to test areas of phonology, vocabulary and grammar will be examined in detail later in the appropriate chapters. The question now posed is: to what extent should we concentrate on testing the student's ability to handle these elements of the language and to what extent should we concentrate on testing the integrated skills? Our attitude towards this question must depend on both the level and the purpose of the test. If the testee has been learning English for only a relatively brief period, it is highly likely that we shall be chiefly concerned with his ability to handle the language elements correctly. Moreover, if the aim of the test is to sample as wide a field as possible, a battery of tests of the language elements will be useful not only in providing a wide coverage of this ability but also in locating particular problem areas. Tests designed to assess mastery of the language elements enable the test writer to determine exactly what is being tested and to pre-test items, carrying out statistical analyses to determine the degree of reliability and later revising them where necessary.

However, at all levels but the most elementary, it is generally advisable to include test items which measure the ability to communicate in the target language. How important, for example, is the ability to discriminate between the phonemes /i:/ and /i/? Even if they are confused by the testee and he says: *Look at that sheep sailing slowly out of the harbour*, it is unlikely that misunderstanding will result because the context, itself, provides other clues to the meaning. All languages contain numerous so-called "redundancies" which help to overcome problems of this nature. Furthermore, no student can be described as being proficient in a language simply because he is able to discriminate between two sounds or because he has mastered a number of structures of the language. Successful communication in situations which simulate real-life is the best test of mastery of a language. It can thus be argued that fluency in English – a person's ability to express facts, ideas, feelings and attitudes clearly and with ease, in speech or in writing, and his ability to understand what he hears or reads – can best be measured by tests which evaluate performance in the language skills. Auditory and reading comprehension tests, oral interviews and essays assess performance in those language skills used in real life.

Too great a concentration on the testing of the language elements may indeed have a harmful effect on the communicative teaching of the language. There is also at present insufficient knowledge about the weighting which ought to be given to specific language elements. How important are articles, for example, in relation to prepositions or pronouns? Such a question cannot be answered until we know more about the degrees of importance of the various elements at the various stages of learning a language.

1.7   Recognition and production

Methods of testing the *recognition* of correct words and forms often take the following form in tests:

      Choose the correct answer and write A, B, C or D.
        I've been standing here . . . . half an hour.
        A. since
        B. during
        C. while
        D. for

This multiple-choice test item tests the student's ability to recognise the correct form: this ability is obviously not quite the same as the ability to produce and use the correct form in real-life situations. However, this type of item has the advantage of being easy to examine statistically.

If the four choices were omitted, the item would come closer to being a test of *production*.

      Complete each blank with the correct word.
        I've been standing here . . . . half an hour.

The student would then be required to produce the correct answer (= *for*). In many cases, there would only be one possible correct answer, but production items do not always guarantee that the student will deal with the specific matter the examiner had in mind (as most recognition items do). In this particular case the test item is not entirely satisfactory, for the student is completely justified in writing *nearly/almost/over* in the blank. It would not then test his ability to discriminate between *for* with periods of time (e.g. *for half an hour, for two years*) and *since* with points of time (e.g. *since 2.30, since Christmas*).

The following example, taken from a vocabulary test, also illustrates the difference between testing recognition and testing production:

      Choose the best word to complete each blank and write A, B, C or D.
      (Recognition)
        Stand on the . . . . and tell me how much you weigh.
        A. measure   B. weights   C. scales   D. balance

      (Production)
        Stand on the . . . . and tell me how much you weigh.

A good language test may contain either recognition-type test items or production-type test items, or a combination of both. Each type has its unique functions, and these will be treated in detail later.

1.8   Problems of sampling

The actual question of what is to be included in a test is often difficult simply because a mastery of skills is being assessed rather than areas of knowledge. Although the construction of a language test at the end of the first or second year of learning English is relatively easy if we are familiar with the syllabus covered, the construction of a test at a fairly advanced level where the syllabus is not clearly defined is much more difficult.

The longer the test, the more reliable a measuring instrument it will be (although length, itself, is no guarantee of a good test). Few students would want to spend several hours being tested — and indeed this would be undesirable both for the tester and the testee. But the construction of short tests which function efficiently is often a difficult matter. Sampling now becomes of paramount importance. The test must cover an adequate and representative section of those areas and skills it is desired to test.

If all the students who take the test have followed the same programme, we can simply choose areas from this programme, seeking to maintain a careful balance between tense forms, prepositions, articles, lexical items, etc. Above all, the kind of language to be tested would be the language used in the classroom and in the student's immediate surroundings or the language required for the school or the work for which the student is being assessed.

If the same mother-tongue is shared by all the testees, the task of sampling is made slightly easier even though the testees may have attended different schools or followed different courses. The testees will all experience problems of a similar nature as a result of the interference of their first-language habits. It is not a difficult matter to identify these problem areas and to include a cross-section of them in the test, particularly in those sections of the test concerned with the language elements. The following two examples based on interference of first-language habits will suffice at this stage. The first example concerns the use of the Present Simple for the Present Perfect tense; thus, many students from certain language backgrounds write such sentences as "Television exists only for the last forty or fifty years" instead of "Television has existed only for the last forty or fifty years". A test item based on this problem area might be:

> Write down A, B, C, D or E according to the best alternative needed to complete the sentence.
> Television . . . . only for the last fifty years.
> A. exists
> B. was existing
> C. has existed
> D. existed
> E. is existing

The second example has been taken from a test of vocabulary and concerns confusion in the use of *look for*; it is directed chiefly at Arabic and Chinese learners of English. The word *fetched* has been included in the list of choices because there is no distinction in Arabic between the two concepts expressed in English by *fetch* and *look for*, while account has also been taken of the difficulty many Chinese learners experience as a result of the lack of distinction in Mandarin between *look for* and *find*.

Choices D and E might also appear plausible to other students unsure of the correct use of *look for*.

> "Here's your book, John. You left it on my desk."
> "Thanks. I've . . . . it everywhere."

> A. looked for
> B. fetched
> C. found
> D. attended to
> E. watched over

It must be emphasised that items based on contrastive analysis can only be used effectively when the testees come from the same language area. If most of the testees do not share the same first language, the test must be universal by nature and sample a fair cross-section of the language. It will scarcely matter then if students from certain language areas find it easier than others: in actual language-learning situations they may have an advantage simply because their first language happens to be more closely related to English than certain other languages are. Few would wish to deny that, given the same language-learning conditions, a French student learning English will experience fewer difficulties than his Chinese counterpart[3].

Before starting to write any test items, the test constructor should draw up a detailed table of specifications showing aspects of the skills being tested and giving a comprehensive coverage of the specific language elements to be included. A classroom test should be closely related to the ground covered in the class teaching, an attempt being made to relate the different areas covered in the test to the length of time spent on teaching those areas in class. There is a constant danger of concentrating too much on testing those areas and skills which most easily lend themselves to being tested. It may be helpful for the teacher to draw up a rough inventory of those areas which he wishes to test, assigning to each one a percentage according to importance. For example, a teacher wishing to construct a test of grammar might start by examining the relative weighting to be given to the various areas in the light of the teaching that has just taken place: say, the contrast of the Past Continuous and the Past Simple tenses (40%), articles (15%), time prepositions (15%), *wish* and *hope* (10%), concord (10%), the infinitive of purpose (10%). (It must be emphasised that this list is merely one example of the kind of inventory which can be drawn up beforehand, and it is not intended to represent a particular set of priorities.)

1.9 Avoiding traps for the student

A good test should never be constructed in such a way as to trap the testee into giving an incorrect answer. When techniques of error analysis are used, the setting of deliberate traps or pitfalls for the unwary student should be avoided. Many testers, themselves, are caught out by constructing test items which succeed only in trapping the more able student.

In the following example, the testee has to select the correct answer (C) but the whole item is constructed so as to trap the testee into making choice B or D. When this item actually appeared in a test, it was found that the more proficient students, in fact, chose B and D, as they had developed the correct habit of associating the tense forms *have seen* and *have been seeing* with *since* and *for*. Several of the less proficient students, who had not learnt to associate the perfect tense forms with *since* and *for*, chose the "correct" answer.

> When I met Tim yesterday, it was the first time
> I . . . . him since Christmas.
> A. saw
> B. have seen
> C. had seen
> D. have been seeing

To summarise, all tests should be constructed primarily with the intention of finding out what a student knows — not with trapping him. By attempting to construct effective language tests, the teacher can gain a deeper insight into the language he is testing and the language learning processes involved.

NOTES

1 This type of item is used to test phoneme discrimination in the English Proficiency Test Battery (EPTB) (Alan Davies). (The test is closed and used by the British Council overseas.)

2 Multiple-choice items of this nature have long been used in the United States by such well-known testing organisations as TOEFL (Test of English as a Foreign Language, Educational Testing Service, Princeton, New Jersey, U.S.A.) and the Michigan Test of English Language Proficiency: (University of Michigan, Ann Arbor, Michigan) to test grammar and vocabulary. Multiple-choice items are now widely used in modern language testing in Britain and elsewhere throughout the world. Robert Lado (Language Testing, Longman) was one of the first to develop the multiple-choice technique in testing the spoken language.

3 David Harris was the first to make this point in his book *Testing English as a Second Language*, McGraw-Hill, New York, 1969.

2 Objective testing

(with special reference to multiple-choice techniques)

2.1 Subjective and objective testing

Subjective and *objective* are terms used to refer to the scoring of tests. All test items, no matter how they are devised, require candidates to exercise a subjective judgement. In an essay test, for example, the testee must think of what to say and then express his ideas as well as possible; in a multiple-choice test he has to weigh up carefully all the alternatives and select the best one. Furthermore, all tests are constructed subjectively by the tester: he decides which areas of language to test, how to test those particular areas, and what kind of items to use for his purpose. Thus, it is only the scoring of a test that can be described as objective.[1] This means that a testee will score the same mark no matter which examiner marks his test.

Since objective tests usually have only one correct answer, they can be scored mechanically. The fact that objective tests can be marked by computer is one important reason for their evident popularity among examining bodies responsible for testing large numbers of candidates.

It may be helpful at this stage to distinguish between the terms *examination* and *test* since both terms are often used loosely. For our present purposes, however, the term *test* will generally be used to refer to a set of items that can be marked objectively while *examination* will be used to refer to a set of longer subjective questions (e.g. compositions).

Objective tests need not be confined to any one particular skill or element. Investigations,[2] for example, have indicated that it is possible to measure writing ability by a series of objective tests. However, while it is misleading to associate examinations solely with writing and objective tests solely with grammar and vocabulary, certain areas of language may be tested more effectively at certain levels by one method rather than by another. The following three items, for example, are designed to test the student's ability to recognise or manipulate structures containing *since*; Example A is subjective, while Examples B and C are objective.

Example A: Write two sentences containing *since*.

Example B: Complete each sentence by putting the correct word in
             each blank.
             (1) "Poor Tony's been in bed . . . . Tuesday."
                 "Oh dear! I didn't know he was still in bed."

11

Example C: Write down the letter of the word which best completes
             each sentence.
             (1) Poor Tony's been in bed . . . . Tuesday.
                 A. for   B. on   C. in   D. at   E. since

Although both Examples B and C are objective test items, Example B
tests production and C recognition. Example A, however, tests the
student's ability to use *since* in a sentence. Unfortunately, this technique
assumes that *since* will constitute the only problem for the student when
he is writing a sentence. The following answers to the question in Example
A illustrate the kinds of problems encountered in the scoring of such
subjective items. How, for instance, ought each of these six answers to be
marked?

Answer 1:   They have been absent since last week.
Answer 2:   I didn't see Bill since Monday.
Answer 3:   We've visited to Helen thrice since she went into hospital.
Answer 4:   Since last week I haven't cycled to school.
Answer 5:   No one has been to choir practice since a few weeks ago.
Answer 6:   I haven't been reading any books on the subject since
            Easter.

On the whole, objective tests require far more careful preparation than
subjective examinations. In an examination the examiner tends to spend a
relatively short time on setting the questions but considerable time on
marking. In an objective test the tester spends a great deal of time
constructing each test item as carefully as he can, attempting to anticipate
the various reactions of the testees at each stage. The effort is rewarded,
however, in the ease of the marking.

2.2   Objective tests

Objective tests are frequently criticised on the grounds that they are
simpler to answer than subjective examinations. Items in an objective test,
however, can be made just as easy or as difficult as the test constructor
wishes. The fact that objective tests may generally *look* easier is no indication at all that they *are* easier. The constructor of a standardised achievement or proficiency test not only selects and constructs his items carefully
but analyses student performance on each item and rewrites where necessary so that the final version of his test discriminates widely. Setting the
pass-mark, or the cutting-off point, may depend on the tester's subjective
judgement or on a particular external situation. Objective tests (and, to a
smaller degree, subjective tests) can be pre-tested before being administered on a wider basis: i.e. they are given to a small but truly representative sample of the test population and then each item is evaluated in
the light of the testees' performance. This procedure enables the test
constructor to calculate the approximate degree of difficulty of the test.

Standards may then be compared not only between students from different areas or schools but also between students taking the test in different years.

Another criticism is that objective tests of the multiple-choice type encourage guessing. However, 4 or 5 alternatives for each item are sufficient to reduce the possibility of guessing. Furthermore, experience shows that candidates rarely make wild guesses: most base their guesses on partial knowledge.

A much wider sample of grammar, lexis and phonology can generally be included in an objective test than in a subjective test. In an essay, for example, the student can limit the range of the sentence structures and grammatical items he uses to those which he can produce correctly. However, the fact that a test is apparently completely objective gives no guarantee that it will be a good test. It will be a very poor test if:

(i)   the wrong features of the target language are tested;
(ii)   irrelevant areas are emphasised in the test simply because they are "testable"; and
(iii) the test items are poorly written.

Indeed, it is a great pity that a number of poor objective tests have been produced for classroom use because such tests tend to bring into disrepute all new objective testing techniques.

It should never be claimed that objective tests can do those tasks which they are not intended to do. They can never test ability to *communicate* in the target language nor can they evaluate actual performance. A good classroom test will probably contain both subjective and objective test items.

Some examples of objective test items (excluding multiple-choice items) are:

(1) **Transformation**
John Brown is a very fast runner.
John Brown runs . . . .

(2) **Completion**
The time is now half . . . . ten.

(3) **Combination**
Ann did her homework. Then she went swimming. (After)

(4) **Addition** (Grammar)
YET . . . Haven't you seen this film ?

(5) **Rearrangement**
at/poor/Look/that/woman/old

(6) Correct/Incorrect (or True/False)

Put a tick if the statement is correct and a cross if it is incorrect.

The train left to time this morning.

He's doing some research on modern transport problems.

Although the examples have been confined to the testing of grammar, many of the item types can be used equally successfully to test vocabulary as well as aspects of the reading, writing, listening and speaking skills.

2.3 Multiple-choice items: general

In certain ways, multiple-choice techniques are to testing the same as perspective is to drawing: only through a true appreciation and mastery of these techniques is the would-be test constructor able to throw aside the limitations imposed by them and discover newer and improved techniques of testing. The multiple-choice item is now widely regarded as being one of the most useful of all objective item types. Although it is amongst the most difficult of all objective item types to construct, it is simple to score and administer.

The optimum number of alternatives, or options, for each multiple-choice item is five in most public tests. Although a larger number, say seven, would reduce even further the element of chance, it is extremely difficult and often impossible to construct as many as seven good options. Indeed, since it is often very difficult to construct items with even five options, four options are recommended for most classroom tests. Many writers recommend using four options for grammar items, but five for vocabulary.

Before constructing any test items, the test writer must first determine the actual areas to be covered by multiple-choice items and the number of items to be included in the test. The test must be long enough to allow for a reliable assessment of the testee's performance and short enough to be practicable. Too long a test is undesirable because of the administration difficulties often created and because of the mental strain and tension which may be caused among the students taking the test. The number of items included in a test will vary according to the level of difficulty, the nature of the areas being tested, and the purpose of the test. The teacher's own experience will generally determine the length of a test for classroom use, while the length of a public test will be affected by various factors, not least of which will be its reliability measured statistically from the results of the trial test.

The initial part of each multiple-choice item is known as the *stem*; the choices from which the student selects his answers are referred to as *options/responses/alternatives*. One option is the *answer, correct option* or *key*, while the other options are *distractors*. The task of a distractor is to distract the majority of poor students (i.e. those who do not know the answer) from the correct option.

Stay here until Mr. Short . . . . you to come. = stem

A. told
B. will tell   } = options   } = distractors
C. is telling
D. tells   = correct option/key

The following general principles should be observed when multiple-choice items are constructed:

(1) Each multiple-choice item should have only *one* answer. This answer must be absolutely correct unless the instruction specifies choosing the *best* option (as in some vocabulary tests). Although this may seem an easy matter, it is sometimes extremely difficult to construct an item having only one correct answer. An example of an item with two answers is:

"I stayed there until John . . . come."
A. had   B. will   C. would   D. has

(2) Only one feature at a time should be tested. It has long been standard practice to test only one feature at a time: it is usually less confusing for the testee and it helps to reinforce a particular teaching point. Obviously, few would wish to test both grammar and vocabulary at the same time, but sometimes word order and sequence of tenses are tested simultaneously. Such items are called *impure* items:

I never knew where
A. had the boys gone
B. the boys have gone
C. have the boys gone
D. the boys had gone

(Note that it may sometimes be necessary to construct such impure items at the very elementary levels because of the severely limited number of distractors generally available.)

(3) Each option should be grammatically correct when placed in the stem, except of course in the case of specific grammar test items. For example, stems ending with the determiner *a*, followed by options in the form of nouns or noun phrases, sometimes trap the unwary test constructor. In the item below, the correct answer C, when moved up to complete the stem, makes the sentence grammatically incorrect.

Someone who designs houses is a . . . .
A. designer   B. builder   C. architect   D. plumber

The item can be easily re-cast as follows:

Someone who designs houses is
A. a designer   C. an architect
B. a builder   D. a plumber

Stems ending in *are, were,* etc. may have the same weaknesses as the following and will require complete re-writing:

> The boy's hobbies referred to in the first paragraph of the passage were
> A. camping and fishing
> B. tennis and golf
> C. cycling long distances
> D. fishing, rowing and swimming
> E. collecting stamps

Any fairly intelligent student would soon be aware that options C and E were obviously not in the tester's mind when first constructing the item above because they are ungrammatical answers. He would, therefore, realise that they had been added later simply as distractors.

Stems ending in prepositions may also create certain difficulties. In the following reading comprehension item, option C can be ruled out immediately:

> John soon returned to . . . .
> A. work ˙ B. the prison   C. home   D. school

(4) All multiple-choice items should be at a level appropriate to the linguistic ability of the testees. The context, itself, should be at a lower level than the actual problem which the item is testing. A grammar test item should not contain other grammatical features as difficult as the area being tested, and a vocabulary item should not contain more difficult semantic features in the stem than the area being tested.

(5) Multiple-choice items should be as brief and as clear as possible (though it is often desirable to provide short contexts for grammar items).

(6) In many tests, items are generally arranged in rough order of increasing difficulty. It is generally considered important to have one or two simple items to "lead in" the testees, especially if they are not too familiar with the kind of test being administered. Nevertheless, areas of language which are trivial and not worth testing should be excluded from the test.

2.4   Multiple-choice items: the stem/the correct option/the distractors

(1) **The stem**

(i)   The primary purpose of the stem is to present the problem clearly and concisely. The testee should be able to obtain from the stem a very general idea of the problem and the answer required. At the same time, the stem should not contain extraneous information or irrelevant clues, thereby confusing the problem being tested. Unless the student understands the problem being tested, there is no way of knowing whether or not he could have handled the problem correctly. Although the stem should be short, it should convey enough information to indicate the basis on which the correct option should be selected.

(ii) The stem may take the following forms:

    (a) an incomplete statement
        He accused me of . . . . . . lies.
        A. speaking   B. saying   C. telling   D. talking

    (b) a complete statement
        Everything we wanted was *to hand.*
        A. under control   C. well cared for
        B. within reach   D. being prepared

    (c) a question
        According to the writer, what did Tom immediately do?
        A. He ran home.   C. He began to shout.
        B. He met Bob.   D. He phoned the police.

(iii) The stem should usually contain those words or phrases which would otherwise have to be repeated in each option.

        The word "astronauts" is used in the passage to refer to
        A.   travellers in an ocean liner
        B.   travellers in a space-ship
        C.   travellers in a submarine
        D.   travellers in a balloon

The stem here should be re-written so that it reads:

        The word "astronauts" is used in the passage to refer to travellers in
        A.   an ocean liner   C.   a submarine
        B.   a space-ship   D.   a balloon

The same principle applies to grammar items. The following item:

        I enjoy . . . . the children playing in the park.
        A.   looking to   C.   looking at
        B.   looking about   D.   looking on

should be re-written in this way:

        I enjoy looking . . . . the children playing in the park.
        A. to   B. about   C. at   D. on

If, however, one of the errors made by students in their free written work has been the omission of the preposition after *look* (a common error), then it will be necessary to include *look* in the options.

        I enjoy . . . . the children playing in the park.
        A.   looking on   C.   looking at
        B.   looking   D.   looking to

(iv) The stem should allow for the number of choices which have been decided upon. This is particularly relevant, for example, when comparisons are involved in a test of reading comprehension. There is no possible fourth option which can be added in the following item:

Tom was .... the other two boys.
A.   taller than
B.   smaller than
C.   as tall as

(2) The correct option

For normal purposes of testing, this should be clearly the *correct* or *best* option: thus, it is most important that each item should be checked by another person.

It can be argued that a greater degree of subtlety is sometimes gained by having more than one correct option in each item. The correct answers in the following reading comprehension and grammar items are circled.

According to the writer, Jane wanted a new racquet because
A.   her old one was damaged slightly
B.   she had lost her old one
C.   her father had given her some money for one
D.   Mary had a new racquet
E.   Ann often borrowed her old racquet

Who .... you cycle here to see us?
A. ordered B. caused C. made D. asked E. let

It is very important, however, to avoid confusing the student by having a different number of correct options for each item, and this practice is *not* recommended. Each of the two multiple-choice test items above actually comprises a group of true/false (i.e. right/wrong) items and, therefore, each alternative should be marked in this way: i.e. in the first item, the testee scores 1 mark if he circles A, 1 mark if he doesn't circle B, 1 mark if he doesn't circle C, 1 mark if he circles D, and 1 mark if he doesn't circle E (total score = 5).

The correct option should be approximately the same length as the distractors. This principle applies especially to vocabulary tests and tests of reading and auditory comprehension, where there is a tendency to make the correct option longer than the distractors simply because it is so often necessary to qualify a statement or word in order to make it absolutely correct. An example of such a "give-away" item is:

He began to *choke* while he was eating the fish.
A   die
B.   cough and vomit
C.   be unable to breathe because of something in the windpipe
D.   grow very angry

(3) The distractors

Each distractor, or incorrect option, should be reasonably attractive and plausible. It should *appear* right to any testee who is unsure of the correct option. Items should be constructed in such a way that students obtain the correct option by direct selection rather than by the elimination of obviously incorrect options. Choice D in the following grammar item is much below the level being tested and will be eliminated by testees immediately: their chances of selecting the correct option will then be one in three.

> The present tax reforms have benefited . . . . . poor.
> **A.** that   B. the   C. a   D. an

For most purposes, each distractor should be grammatically correct when it stands by itself: otherwise testees will be exposed to incorrect forms. In the above item (and in all grammar items) it is only the wrong choice, and its implied insertion into the stem, which makes a particular pattern ungrammatical. For example, option A is grammatically correct on its own and only becomes incorrect when inserted into the stem.

The following item (which actually appeared in a class progress test of reading comprehension) contains two absurd items.

> How did Picard first travel in space?
> A.   He travelled in a space-ship.
> B.   He used a large balloon.
> C.   He went in a submarine.
> D.   He jumped from a tall building.

Unless a distractor is attractive to the student who is not sure of the correct answer, its inclusion in a test item is superfluous. Plausible distractors are best based on (a) mistakes in the students' own written work, (b) their answers in previous tests, (c) the teacher's experience, and (d) a contrastive analysis between the native and target language.

Distractors should not be too difficult nor demand a higher proficiency in the language than the correct option. If they are too difficult, they will succeed only in distracting the good student, who will be led into considering the correct option too easy (and a trap). There is a tendency for this to happen, particularly in vocabulary test items.

> You need a . . . . to enter that military airfield
> A. permutation   B. perdition   C. permit   D. perspicuity

2.5   Writing the test

Where multiple-choice items are used, the testee may be required to:

> (i)   write out the correct option in full in the blank;
>   He may not come, but we'll get ready in case he . . . *does* . . .
>   A.   will   B. does   C. is   D. may

or (ii)   write only the letter of the correct option in the blank or in a box
           (which may appear either at the side of the question or on a
           separate answer sheet);
           He may not come, but we'll get ready in case he .... *B*.....
           A. will   B. does   C. is   D. may   ....

or (iii)   put a tick or a cross at the side of the correct option or in a
           separate box;
           He may not come, but we'll get ready in case he ....

           A. will   A. ☐
           B. does   B. ☒
           C. is   C. ☐
           D. may   D. ☐

or (iv)   underline the correct option;
           He may not come, but we'll get ready in case he ....
           A. will   B. <u>does</u>   C. is   D. may

or (v)   put a circle round the letter at the side of the correct option.
           He may not come, but we'll get ready in case he ....
           A. will   ⓑ does   C. is   D. may

Multiple-choice items are rarely optional in a test, for the testee would
then spend considerable time in unnecessary reading before choosing the
items he wished to answer. Moreover, unless there are good reasons for
weighting different items (using the appropriate statistical methods), it is
advisable to award equal marks for each item.

The correct option should appear in each position (e.g. A, B, C, D or E)
approximately the same number of times in a test or sub-test. This can
usually be achieved if it is placed at random in a certain position or if all
the options are placed in alphabetical order (i.e. according to the first
letter of the first word in each option). However, if the options have a
natural order (e.g. figures, dates), it is advisable to keep to this order.

           Blackwell started his career as a lawyer in
           A. 1921   B. 1925   C. 1926   D. 1932

NOTES:

1   A. E. G. Pilliner (*Language Testing Symposium: A Psycholinguistic Approach:* ed.
    Alan Davies, O.U.P., 1968, 19–21) emphasises this point in his excellent article
    on subjective and objective testing.
2   Godshalk, Swineford and Coffman, "The Measurement of Writing Ability" – an
    evaluation of the validity of the New York College Entrance Examination Board's
    English Composition Test (1966).

3 Tests of grammar and usage

3.1 Multiple-choice grammar items (1): item types

The type of multiple-choice item favoured by many constructors of grammar tests is the incomplete statement type, with a choice of 4 or 5 options. This item may be written in any of the following ways:

(a) Tom ought not to . . . . (A. tell B. having told C. be telling D. have told) me your secret, but he did.

(b) Tom ought not to . . . . me your secret, but he did.
   A. tell
   B. having told
   C. be telling
   D. have told

(c) Tom ought not to   A. tell
                        B. having told   me your secret, but he did.
                        C. be telling
                        D. have told

(d) Tom ought not to *have told* me your secret, but he did.
   A. *No change*
   B. tell
   C. having told
   D. be telling

Item types (b) and (c) are preferable to (a) because the options do not interrupt the flow of meaning in the sentence: these items present the entire sentence so that it can be read at a glance. Unfortunately, item (a) confuses the reader because of the long parenthesis (i.e. the four options occurring between *ought not to* and *me*). Item type (d) shows the correct (or an incorrect) form as part of the sentence in such a way that it cannot be compared on equal terms with the other options: a correct option, for instance, is generally easier to recognise when it appears in the framework of the sentence than as part of a list of distractors.

Another item type appears below, but it is not recommended since it requires the testee to spend time on unnecessary reading. Not only is it uneconomical but it does not present the "problem" (i.e. the options) as clearly as example (b) does.

(e) A. Tom ought not to tell me your secret, but he did.
    B. Tom ought not to having told me your secret, but he did.
    C. Tom ought not to be telling me your secret, but he did.
    D. Tom ought not to have told me your secret, but he did.

The following method is useful for testing short answers and responses:

(f) "Tom ought not to have told me."
    A. "So ought you."
    B. "Neither ought you."
    C. "Neither you oughtn't."
    D. "So oughtn't you."

Item type (g) requires the student to select the alternative which is true according to the information conveyed in each sentence. Such an item may be included either in a test of reading comprehension or in a test of grammar: a knowledge of the particular syntax is necessary for the understanding of the sentence.

(g) "Tom ought not to have told me."
    A. Tom did not tell me but he should.
    B. Perhaps Tom may not tell me.
    C. Tom told me but it was wrong of him.
    D. It was necessary for Tom not to tell me.

It may be argued that an understanding of syntactical patterning is just as necessary for the following item:

"....... was Robert late last week?"
"Three times."
    A. How much
    B. How many
    C. How often
    D. How long

Items which appear in a test of grammar and structure should be made to sound as natural as possible. The following *mechanical* test item:

This book belongs to Peter. It is ....
    A. Peter's book
    B. the book to Peter
    C. the book of Peter
    D. the book of Peter's

can be rewritten as follows:

This book belongs to Peter, but that is ....
    A. Mary's book
    B. the book to Mary
    C. the book of Mary
    D. the book of Mary's

Sometimes it is useful to construct grammar items in the form of very short dialogues or conversational exchanges. A short dialogue may help to make an item much more natural and meaningful by providing a context. In addition, such a dialogue is sometimes a useful means of ensuring that there is only one correct option, as will be seen in Section 3 of this chapter.

Note that distractors should generally be incorrect in writing and in speech. The following item proved unsuccessful when it was included in a test because many of the more able students selected option D, the reason being that they pronounced *used to* quite correctly as *use to*/ju:stə/.

> I . . . . to go to my uncle's farm every weekend.
> A. am used
> B. used
> C. was used
> D. use

3.2   Multiple-choice grammar items (2): structure recognition tests

This section attempts to show some of the broad areas which can be tested by using multiple-choice techniques. Several examples are given on the following pages for most of the areas included in the list. Three rough divisions have been made according to the ease with which the areas lend themselves to multiple-choice techniques. Generally speaking, the construction of multiple-choice items (and the writing of effective distractors) for those areas in Group A is fairly straightforward while those in Group B and C present more difficulty. It must be emphasised that multiple-choice items can be used to test *all* the areas listed, although other types of items may prove more effective for certain areas, especially those shown in the second and third groups. However, the use of a particular type of item must be largely determined by both test and course objectives. Often the teacher will wish to use a combination of techniques to assess the various factors involved in learning the language. The success of any test format and type of item used can only be determined statistically from the test performances of the students, and methods of evaluating a test are described in Chapter Ten.

A. (1) Tenses (beyond the very elementary stages)
    (2) Modals and "special" verbs
    (3) Question tags
    (4) WH-question words
    (5) Relative pronouns and clauses
    (6) Linkers
    (7) Prepositions and adverbial particles

B. (8) Adjectives and adverbs
    (9) Pronouns

    (10) Determiners
    (11) Infinitive/-ing forms

C. (12) Order of adjectives
    (13) Position of adverbs
    (14) Reported speech
    (15) Concord
    (16) Positive/negative transformations
    (17) Statement/interrogative transformations
    (18) Active/passive transformations

Examples of multiple-choice items are given for areas 1–14 listed above. When attempting to use m/c items to test such features as concord, positive/negative transformations, etc. (i.e. any feature where the choice is essentially between only two options), the test constructor is sometimes forced to introduce additional problems in order to construct 4 options. Thus, we find an "impure" item, testing not only concord (*is/are*) but also the ability to distinguish between *this* and *that*:

> Whose book . . . . over there?
> A. is that
> B. are those
> C. is this
> D. are these

Testees who select option C will still fail to answer the item correctly, even though they may have mastered the features of concord being tested here. In this sense, the item is unfair and will not offer the testee any reward for correctly opting for the form *is*. Indeed, since the choice is essentially between A and B, it might be argued that a large number of two-choice items[1] would be better than a few four-choice impure items.

(1) Tenses
1. Robert . . . . in Kenya a few weeks ago.
  A. is arriving B. arrives C. has arrived D. arrived

2. Don't talk so loudly: your father . . .
  A. sleeps B. is sleeping C. slept D. had slept

3. Where did Mr Smith go while we . . . .?
  A. talk B. have talked C. were talking D. had talked

4. I wish I . . . . the answer to that question.
  A. knew B. would know C. will know D. know

(2) Modals
1. We . . . . to hurry or we'll be late.
  A. should B. must C. ought D. had

2. Peter . . . . come with us tonight, but he isn't very sure yet.
   A. can B. could C. may D. will

3. "I . . . . to introduce you to Helen."
   "How do you do?"
   A. would like B. like C. do like D. am liking

4. Please take a message . . . . . he call.
   A. may B. will C. shall D. should

(3) Question tags

1. Your father's paying for the tickets, ...?
   A. aren't you B. aren't they C. isn't it D. isn't he

2. Mary's finished reading the newspaper, ...?
   A. isn't she B. wasn't it C. hasn't she D. isn't it

3. It'll rain soon, ...? You ought to take a raincoat.
   A. won't it B. ought it C. isn't it D. may it

4. Tom said he wasn't feeling well, ...?
   A. was he B. isn't he C. wasn't he D. didn't he

(4) WH-question words

1. " . . . . are you going?" "To London."
   A. When B. Why C. Where D. How

2. " . . . . is Dick talking to?" "John Green."
   A. Where B. When C. What D. Who

3. " . . . . does Mr Robinson go to London on business?"
   "At least once a month."
   A. How often B. How many C. How D. How long

4. " . . . . is the chair made of?" "I think it's leather."
   A. Which B. What C. How D. Who

(5) Relative pronouns and clauses

1. Is that the spot . . . . you had the accident?
   A. which B. where C. whom D. why

2. The boy's photograph . . . . you saw was taken a long time ago.
   A. who B. whose C. whom D. which

3. Have you met the woman . . . . husband is a doctor?
   A. which B. of whom C. whose D. of which

4. Are those the students . . . .?
   A. you were talking about
   B. that you were talking about them
   C. about that you were talking
   D. you were talking about them

(6) Linkers

1. We've had good weather . . . . . . I arrived.
   A. since B. for C. while D. during

2. . . . . it was very cold, neither Michael nor Andrew put on his coat.
   A. However B. Although C. But D. Nevertheless

3. The food was so good . . . . I ate all of it.
   A. but B. that C. as D. than

4. He'll never pass . . . . hard he tries.
   A. however B. even though C. despite D. yet

(7) Prepositions and adverbial particles

1. Did you arrive there . . . . night?
   A. in B. on C. at D. through

2. I live a few yards . . . . the bus stop.
   A. from B. away C. off D. for

3. Mr Smith has gone to England . . . . . . holiday.
   A. for B. on C. in D. by

4. Turn the switch off: the water is boiling . . . .
   A. out B. down C. off D. over

(8) Adjectives and adverbs

1. Those towels are . . . . for us to use to dry the dishes.
   A. so wet B. too wet C. as wet D. wet enough

2. Dick is . . . . than both Tom and Alan.
   A. fatter B. more fat C. the fattest D. as fat

3. Who is . . . . student in the class?
   A. the taller B. tallest C. taller D. the tallest

4. I'm sure you're not . . . . as Mr Lee.
   A. as strong B. strong C. stronger D. the strongest

(9) Pronouns

1. "I've forgotten my sandwiches."
   "It doesn't matter. You can have . . . ."
   A.   some of us   B.   us some
   C.   some of ours   D.   some of our

2. "Is my camera like Bill's and Ann's?"
   "Yes, it's almost the same as . . . ."
   A. them B. they C. their D. theirs

3. You shouldn't say nasty things about Jane. She's a friend of . . . .
   A. her B. you C. ours D. me

4. Mr Smith's wife was ill, so I called an ambulance to take . . . . to
   hospital.
   A. she B. her C. they D. their

(10) Determiners
1. Is that a map of . . . ?
   A. West Indies B. a West Indies C. the West Indies D. any West Indies

2. Let's listen to . . . . music on the radio.
   A. one B. those C. a D. some

3. Sociologists are concerned with the problem of man in . . . .
   A. a society B. the society C. society D. some society

4. . . . . of the boys in the room has a pen and pencil.
   A. Each B. All C. Both D. Every

The following m/c item type[2] is another way of testing the use of the
article, though it is highly artificial and should not be used too often.
Remember that the student's ability to use the language should be
tested — not his knowledge about the language.

> "Is (1) desk made of (2) wood?" "No, it's an iron desk."
> In this sentence *the*
> A.   is necessary at (1) only
> B.   is necessary at (2) only
> C.   is necessary at both (1) and (2)
> D.   is not necessary at either (1) or (2)

(11) Infinitive/-ing forms
1. I wanted . . . . the actor, but my car broke down.
   A. meet B. to meeting C. meeting D. to meet

2. Don't you enjoy . . . . television?
   A. to watch B. watching C. to watching D. watch

3. Mr Brown made Peter . . . . to the dentist's.
   A. go B. to go C. went D. going

4. You must give Audrey a lift in your car: you can't allow
   her . . . . home.
   A. walked B. to walk C. to have walked D. walk

(12) Order of adjectives
1. Tony is going on the picnic with . . . . boys.
   A.   two little other   B.   other two little
   C.   other little two   D.   two other little

2. Look smart and wear your . . . . dress.
   A.   new white cotton   B.   white new cotton
   C.   cotton white new   D.   white cotton new

(13) **Position of adverbs**

1. A. I have got just dressed.
   B. I have just got dressed.
   C. I just have got dressed.
   D. I have got dressed just.

2. A. Always the old man enjoys watching television at weekends.
   B. The old man enjoys watching always television at weekends.
   C. The old man enjoys always watching television at weekends.
   D. The old man always enjoys watching television at weekends.

The preceding items differ in format from the other items included in the list so far and require a different rubric. The following m/c item type, however, is preferable. (The testee has to select the letter showing the best position for the adverb in each sentence.)

> *always* The old man (A) and his friend (B) enjoy (C) watching (D) television.

(14) **Reported Speech**

1. "Have you passed?" I asked Bill.
   I asked Bill   A. had he passed
                   B. had you passed
                   C. if he had passed
                   D. that he had passed

2. "Is that your pen?" Mr White asked Ann.
   Mr White wanted to know   A. was that Ann's pen
                              B. is that Ann's pen
                              C. if that was Ann's pen
                              D. that was Ann's pen

3.3   Constructing multiple-choice items

Although it is not always possible to use samples of students' own written work to provide the basis for the test items, it should not be too difficult for constructors of classroom tests and school achievement tests to take advantage of the type of errors made by students in their free compositions and open-ended answers to questions.

The following extract from a student's letter is used here and in later sections to show how test items can be constructed. The letter was actually written by a student in a country where English is learnt *as a foreign language*. The errors have not been "manufactured" for the purpose of illustration, but they do represent errors made by students from only one particular language background. The mistakes, therefore, will not be typical of mistakes made by students from many other language backgrounds and thus the distractors appearing later may be useless for such students.

There is very much time I didn't write you, and now I have a little free time. Winter is behind us and therefore I hope that you wouldn't mind on such a long period between my last letter and this one. You know how is it. Sun is shining, trees become green and it's difficult to stay closed among walls. Sometimes when the weather is sunny I go to walk through the park near my lodging and enjoy looking the children playing. You know, the day before yesterday while looking through my window I saw the wet street and people with umbrellas rushing for money and prestige. I suddenly remembered last summer that belonged to us. I suppose that you were not angry to me what happened. I think that it is not good to discuss about passed feelings.

Item 1

Let us ignore the error in the first sentence for the time being and concentrate on the error of tense after *hope*.

Step 1: The first step is to reduce the length of the sentence and to correct the error (and any other errors in the original sentence). Thus,

> I hope that you wouldn't mind on such a long period between my last letter and this one.

becomes

> I hope you won't mind waiting for so long.

Step 2: Next we write out the sentence, substituting a blank for the area being tested. We write in the correct option and the distractor which the student has provided for us. However, we have to add a sentence because in certain (rare) contexts, *wouldn't* may be correct.

> I hope you . . . . mind waiting for so long. I promise to reply sooner in future.
> A. won't   B. wouldn't

Step 3: We now add another two distractors. Again, we go to the written work of our students to provide these distractors. But if we cannot locate any suitable errors without too much difficulty, we use our own experience and knowledge of the target and native languages. Thus, two useful distractors which would also balance the existing two options might be *shouldn't* and *shan't*.

> I hope you . . . . mind waiting for so long. I promise to reply sooner in future.
> A. won't   B. wouldn't   C. shouldn't   D. shan't

It may be argued, however, that *shan't* is acceptable usage amongst certain speakers, thus giving us two correct options instead of one. Though it is highly improbable that people in most areas would use *shan't*, there is a slight shadow of doubt. This is enough to make it desirable to remove *shan't* from our list of options.

Step 4: One suggestion may be that we replace *shan't* with *can't*. If students from a particular language background make such mistakes as *can't mind*, *can't* should be used as a distractor, and possibly *shouldn't* changed to *couldn't*. As can be seen at this early stage, the actual process of item writing is extremely subjective.

> I hope you . . . . mind waiting for so long. I promise to reply sooner in future.
> A. won't B. wouldn't C. couldn't D. can't

An alternative suggestion for a fourth option might be *don't* or *didn't*:

> I hope you don't mind waiting for so long.
> I hope you didn't mind waiting for so long.

Unfortunately, both *don't* and *didn't* are correct. However, in the following context, *didn't* is not acceptable:

> "How long are you going to be?"
> "About half an hour. I hope you . . . . mind waiting for so long."
> A. won't B. wouldn't C. shouldn't D. didn't

It may be argued that *didn't* stands out too much. If so — and if it is equally useful to test the use of *don't* (instead of *won't*) after *hope* — the item could be rewritten as:

> "How long will you be?"
> "About half an hour. I hope you . . . . mind waiting for so long."
> A. don't B. wouldn't C. shouldn't D. didn't

Obviously, there are varying degrees of refinement in the construction of multiple-choice items. Furthermore, some items are much more difficult to construct than others. The following two items based on errors in the student's letter are fairly simple to write.

Item 2
Error: " . . . and enjoy looking the children playing."
Item: Old Mr Jones enjoys . . . . the children playing.
    A. looking   B. looking on
    C. looking at   D. looking to

Some test constructors might be tempted to use *for* as a distractor. It can be argued, however, that *looking for* is correct: old Mr Jones might enjoy looking for the children playing (i.e. he might enjoy walking through the park, chatting to his friends, etc. while he is in the process of looking for his grandchildren, who are playing).

Note that the correct option is now in the third position, C. It is important to vary its position. Note also that the word *looking* appears in each option: in some tests the item might appear as follows (though this format is unnatural and is not recommended):

Old Mr Jones enjoys looking . . . . the children playing.
A. –   B. on   C. at   D. to

Item 3
Error: "I suppose that you were not angry to me."
Item: I do hope you weren't angry . . . . me.
        A. to   B. with   C. on   D. about

Note that *at* is also incorrect and may be used as a possible distractor. On the other hand, it may be felt that a number of native English speakers do say *angry at* a person. The decision whether or not to include *at* in the list of incorrect options is again a very subjective one.

3.4   Constructing error-recognition m/c items

The fourth sentence of the letter on Page 29 begins *Sun is shining, trees become green and* . . . The error caused by the omission of the article may be tested as follows, using a multiple-choice item:

. . . . is shining brightly today.
A. Sun   B. The sun   C. A sun   D. Some sun

It may be argued, however, that the choice here is strictly between options A and B. In such instances where the choice is strictly between two options, one useful device (still using the multiple-choice format) is the error-recognition type of item.

Error recognition[3] : item type 1
Each sentence contains four words or phrases underlined, marked A, B, C and D. Select the underlined word or phrase which is incorrect or unacceptable.

1. I do hope you wouldn't mind waiting for such a long time.
   A   B   C   D

2. I'm frightened that you'll feel angry to me.
      A   B   C   D

3. I didn't see Bill since he went into hospital last month.
   A   B   C   D

4. My car had broken down, so I went there by foot.
      A   B   C   D

Error recognition: item type 2
There is a mistake in grammar in each of the following sentences. Write the letter of that part of the sentence in which it occurs.

    A   B   C   D
1. Sun/is shining/brightly today/, isn't it?

    A   B   C   D
2. Old Mr Jones/enjoys/looking the children/playing in the park.

    A   B   C   D
3. Tony's father/would not let him/to stay out/late at night.

    A   B   C   D
4. Didn't/Susan tell you/she wouldn't mind to come/with us on the picnic?

Item type 2 allows the test writer to test errors caused by omission: e.g. *Sun is shining* and *looking the children*. This type of error cannot be tested by the first item of the error-recognition type. However, there are different ways of correcting many sentences. For example, the student may write B or C to denote the incorrect part of the third sentence above, according to which of these correct versions is in his mind:

> Tony's father would not permit him to stay out late. (= B)
> Tony's father would not let him stay out late. (= C)

For this reason, the test writer is strongly advised to avoid items of the second type.

Sometimes students are given correct sentences together with the incorrect ones: they are then required to write the letter E if the sentence does not contain any error. In practice, this method does not work too well since many students tend to regard every sentence as containing an error. Indeed, another argument against this type of item is that it emphasises the more negative aspects of language learning. It is clearly not sufficient for students simply to recognise sources of error: they ought to be encouraged at all times to concentrate on recognising and producing the correct forms. This argument is supported by many psychologists and teachers who hold that it is undesirable for students to be exposed too much to incorrect forms.

3.5   Constructing word-order items

The student who wrote the letter in 3.3 obviously experienced considerable difficulty with word order in reported speech, especially after the verbs *know* and *wonder*. Here are two of the errors he made:

"You know how is it." (3rd sentence in 1st paragraph)
"I wonder did you grow more fatter since summer."
(1st sentence in 2nd paragraph, given on page 207).

If we attempt to test the first error by means of an ordinary multiple-choice item, we are faced with the problem of being restricted to only two options: the correct option and the distractor (i.e. the error).

You know how . . . .
A. it is B. is it

As the item stands here, we cannot possibly construct other options. It becomes necessary, therefore, to lengthen the original statement to: *You know how warm it is today*. The item would then read:

"Won't I need a coat?"
"Well, you know how . . . ."
A.   warm is it today
B.   today it is warm
C.   is it warm today
D.   warm it is today
E.   today is it warm

There seems to be a danger here of confusing the testee by presenting him with the problem in such a way: a certain amount of mental juggling undoubtedly becomes necessary on his part. A preferable item type[4] is the following word-order item:

Complete each sentence by putting the words below it in the right order. Put in the boxes only the letters of the words.

"Won't I need a coat?"
"Well, you know how . . . ."
A. it B. today C. warm D. is

I wonder if . . . . since summer
A. grown B. you C. fatter D. have

Word order items are useful for testing other structures and features involving inversion.

Everyone's forgotten . . . .
A. cup B. he C. which D. used

Not only . . . ., but he took me to his house.
A. me B. he C. did D. meet

However . . . ., you'll never pass that test.
A. you B. try C. hard D. may

Leeds United should have won: just think . . . .
A. unlucky B. were C. how D. they

I don't know how long . . . .
A. going B. Bill C. is D. to be

The order of adjectives and the position of adverbs can be usefully tested in this way, as indeed can several other grammatical areas.

The police are looking for . . . .
A. big B. two C. cars D. black

Would you like to read David Brown's . . . .?
A. short B. new C. story D. exciting

Tom said . . . . cleaning his car.
A. had B. finished C. he D. just

Only . . . . been rude to you!
A. ever B. I C. have D. once

Mrs Green made Ann . . . .
A. her new pen B. to C. show D. me

Someone warned Tom . . . . thieves.
A. for B. to C. out D. look

3.6   Constructing completion items

Carefully constructed completion items are a useful means of testing the student's ability to produce the correct grammatical or structural form. They are preferable to multiple-choice items in certain test situations, since they measure production rather than recognition. Many such items appear deceptively simple to construct, but considerable time is generally spent on preparing them so that there is only one correct or appropriate word for each blank.

The error *Sun is shining* in the extract from the student's letter illustrates one (minor) difficulty of constructing satisfactory completion items. Although only one answer is possible here, this completion item would have to appear as:

. . . . Sun is shining today.

or as: . . . . sun is shining today.

The former item suggests to the testee that no determiner is necessary (since *Sun* is written with a capital letter) while the latter item suggests that a determiner is necessary (because *sun* is written without a capital).

The item can be simply re-written as a question to overcome this problem:

Is . . . . sun shining today?

Here are some other examples of completion items based on the extract.

Type 1 Write the correct word in each blank.
1. The old man enjoys looking . . . . the children playing.
2. That car belongs . . . . Bill's father.
3. I hope you're not angry . . . . me.

Type 2 Put *a*, *the*, or *some* in each blank only where necessary. If you think that no word should be placed in the blank, put a cross (X) there.
1. Can you see . . . . sun shining through the clouds?
2. I saw your uncle . . . . day before yesterday.
3. What have you been doing since I saw you . . . . last summer?

Type 3 Complete each blank by supplying the correct form of the verb in brackets.

It's a long time since I last . . . . . . (write) to you. I hope you . . . . . . (mind) such a long delay. You know how it is. The sun . . . . (shine), the trees . . . . (become) green and it . . . . (be) difficult to stay indoors. Sometimes when the weather . . . . (be) sunny, I . . . . (take) a walk through the park near my lodgings.

Type 4 Complete each of the following sentences.
1. It's a long time since . . . .
2. I hope you . . . . if I smoke.
3. When it is sunny, I . . . .

Completion items cannot, of course, be machine-marked but they are very useful for inclusion in classroom tests and for exercise purposes. The following examples of possible answers to two of the items listed in Type 4 give some idea of the subjective aspects of scoring such items:

It's a long time since *I last saw you/I wrote to you/I met you/*
summer/your last letter/
John came/the old man died/
you were here/

I hope you *don't mind/don't object/don't care/*
aren't worried/won't be annoyed/
will smoke/will stay/

Even the most straightforward completion items can cause problems in the scoring. In the following example *was preparing* and *prepared* are equally correct. It can be argued that *had prepared* is also correct if *as* is regarded as meaning *because*: i.e. people gasped because they didn't expect him to prepare for the journey — they thought he would go without preparation.

PREPARE 1. He heard a gasp behind him as he . . . . to go.

Unexpected ways of completing blanks are shown yet again in the following example:

> As soon as possible the next day I sent my story . . . . the editor . . . . the magazine . . . . which my best work usually appeared.

It is quite possible to write a story *about* an editor and send the story about the editor *to* a magazine. Although such an interpretation may sound somewhat absurd, it illustrates the lengths to which the test writer must sometimes go to make certain that testees produce only the answer he wants to be used in each blank. For class tests, such a critical attitude might well be harmful if it took the teacher's attention off more important and urgent problems in teaching and testing.

The following example[5] indicates the vastness of the range of possibilities for one completion item:

> I go to the cinema regularly, but I . . . . to the theatre for months.

The answer obviously required by the tester is *haven't been*; however, possible answers are:

haven't been	shan't be going
hadn't been	can't go
(sometimes) don't go	haven't been able to go
may not go	am not going
don't know whether I've been	didn't go
shan't go	haven't gone
won't go	haven't been going

If the aim of this particular item is to force the use of the Present Perfect tense, there are three ways of restricting the choice available to the testee (although the first two ways depend heavily on reading comprehension):

(1) by providing a context:

> Mary usually goes to the cinema about once a week but she . . . . four films already this month and it's only the 20th today.
> (Possible answers: has seen/will have seen/must have seen)

(2) by providing data:

> I go to the cinema regularly, but it's ages since I last saw a play.
> I go to the cinema regularly, but I . . . . to the theatre for months.
> (Possible answers: haven't been/haven't gone/haven't been going/ haven't been able to go)

(3) by using multiple-choice techniques:

> I . . . . to the theatre three times since I last saw you.
> A. go   C. had gone
> B. have been   D. went

3·7 Constructing transformation items

The transformation type of item is extremely useful for testing ability to produce structures in the target language and helps to provide a balance when included in tests containing multiple-choice items. It is the one objective item type which comes closest to measuring some of the skills tested in composition writing, although transforming sentences is different from producing sentences. Subjective decisions, of course, may have to be made in the scoring process: e.g. how should spelling errors be marked?

The following transformation items have been based on errors which occurred in the student's letter, an extract of which was given in Section 3.3.

> Rewrite each of the following sentences in another way, beginning each new sentence with the words given. Make any changes that are necessary but do not change the general meaning of the sentence.
>
> 1. I haven't written to you for a long time.
>   It's a long time . . . .
>
> 2. In sunny weather I often go for a walk.
>   When the weather . . . .
>
> 3. Old Mr Jones likes to look at the children playing. . . . .
>   Old Mr Jones enjoys . . . .

Other transformation items giving some idea of the range of areas that can be covered in this way are:

> 1. It was impossible to work under those conditions.
>   Working . . . .
>
> 2. I don't think it's necessary for you to stay any longer.
>   I don't think you . . . .
>
> 3. I was able to leave the office early yesterday.
>   It was possible . . . .
>
> 4. Joe can sing better than you.
>   You cannot . . . .
>
> 5. This book is too big to go on any of the shelves.
>   This book is so big . . . .
>
> 6. Frank is very good at tennis.
>   Frank plays . . . .
>
> 7. Poor Peter was bitten by a mosquito.
>   A mosquito . . . .
>
> 8. "When will you visit London?" Mr Strong asked me.
>   Mr Strong asked me . . . .

As with completion items, it is often difficult to restrict the number of possible answers. However, such restrictions are not essential·for the constructor of classroom tests, provided that he is fully aware of all the possible correct answers and of the specific area he is testing. The following examples indicate some of the alternatives possible for four of the preceding items:

> I haven't written to you for a long time.
> It's a long time *since I (last) wrote (to) you/since*
>   *you received a letter from me/* etc.

> I don't think it's necessary for you to stay any longer.
> I don't think you *need (to) stay any longer* = expected answer
>   *will find it necessary to stay any longer* =
>   possible answer

> Joe can sing better than you.
> You cannot *sing as well as Joe* = expected answer
>   *sing better than Joe* = possible answer

> Frank is very good at tennis.
> Frank plays *tennis very well/extremely well,* etc.
>   = expected answer
>   *very good tennis* = possible answer

Unfortunately, the alternatives in the last three items defeat the purpose of the tests as they stand at present. However, it is a simple matter to rewrite them as follows:

> Is it necessary for us to stay any longer?
> Need . . . . ?

> You cannot sing as well as Joe.
> Joe can sing . . . .

> Frank is very good at tennis.
> Frank plays tennis . . . .

Sometimes it is difficult to elicit the particular form we wish to test.

E.g.   I feel miserable even though I shouldn't.
       I know I shouldn't feel miserable but *I do.*

Although *I do* is the answer required, we could scarcely fault:

> I know I shouldn't feel miserable but *I certainly don't feel happy.*
> I know I shouldn't feel miserable but *I am miserable.*

In some tests,[6] testees may be required to rewrite a sentence beginning with a certain word underlined in the original sentence.

E.g.   They believed that <u>the earth</u> was flat.
The earth was believed to be flat.

This item type is a useful variation of the previous type discussed, but sometimes restricts the kind of transformation possible since the first word of the new sentence has to appear in the original sentence. Thus it becomes impossible to test the required transformation of a sentence like *Is it necessary for us to stay any longer?* (= *Need we stay any longer?*)

Transformation can also be effected by requiring testees to substitute a given verb in a sentence,[6] the new verb necessitating a change in the structural pattern.

Ten lessons *make* up the course. (consist)
The course consists of ten lessons.

I *couldn't* go swimming yesterday. (allow)
I wasn't allowed to go swimming yesterday.

NOTES

1   The True/False item is simply a variety of the multiple-choice item in which there are only two options (i.e. a pair of contrasted features). It could be set either as: Whose book . . . . over there? (*is that/are those*) or Whose book are those over there? (Right/Wrong)

2   Cairns, Peterside, and Scott, *Objective Questions in English Language*, African Universities Press, 1966, 78–80.

3   See David P. Harris, *Testing English as a Second Language*, McGraw-Hill, New York, 1969, 73–74.

4   Similar types of test items have appeared in past papers of the Joint Matriculation Board Test in English (Overseas).

5   I am indebted to Mr John Bright for this example and the possible solutions.

6   Cambridge Certificate of Proficiency in English.

4 Testing vocabulary

4.1 Selection of items

A careful selection, or sampling, of lexical items for inclusion in a test is generally a most exacting task. Many of the more traditional types of vocabulary tests are designed in such a way that they test a knowledge of words which, though frequently found in many English textbooks, are rarely used in ordinary speech situations.

The first task for the writer of the vocabulary test is to determine the degree to which he wishes to concentrate on testing the students' active or passive vocabulary. His next task is then to decide whether the lexical items in the test should be taken from the spoken or the written language. Selection of vocabulary can thus be thought of as falling into the following rough divisions according to the four major language skills:

Listening : passive/spoken
Reading : passive/written
Speaking : active/spoken
Writing : active/written

All four divisions can be included in a single test, of course, but even then careful consideration should be given to the different weighting each division will carry in the test: for example, should there be a greater concentration on those lexical items selected from the student's reading material? Generally speaking, the more elementary the level of the test, the greater the number of lexical items associated with the spoken language.

The test constructor's task is made much easier if all the testees have followed a particular syllabus. Lexical items can then be selected from:

(i) the syllabus (including a word frequency list if available);
(ii) the students' textbook (provided the items approximate to those used in natural speech situations);
(iii) the students' reading material (e.g. simplified readers, literary texts);
and (iv) lexical errors taken from the written work of the students.

The following error, however, may be one of verb patterning or simply the wrong choice of verb:

Is the government going to contribute the new industry?

41

If an error of verb patterning, the correct version would be

>   Is the government going to *contribute to* the new industry?

If caused by the wrong choice of verb, it would be

>   Is the government going to *subsidise* the new industry?

The test constructor is faced with a difficult problem if the testees have followed different syllabuses. Such a situation is generally associated with proficiency tests, in which the student's suitability and potential for a certain task are tested (e.g. university studies in the medium of English). In these cases, the tester may wish to base his selection of lexical items on those used in the tasks for which the testee is being tested. An alternative method, appropriate for all kinds of tests, is the selection of items from such well-known word lists as *A General Service List of English Words* (Michael West — Longman) and *The Wright Frequency Count*. These (and other) word lists, however, are based entirely on the written language; furthermore, no account is taken of difficulty levels (as opposed to frequency levels) and of areas where interference is encountered between the vernacular and the target language.

But testing the extent of the student's vocabulary is only one aspect of the whole problem: control of the vocabulary at his disposal must also be measured. An ability to discriminate between words is of the utmost importance at all but the elementary levels. In broader terms, this ability to discriminate may be regarded as developing a *feel* for the language.

Tests of vocabulary should avoid grammatical structures which the testee may find difficult to comprehend. Similarly, tests of grammar should contain only those lexical items which present no difficulty to the testee.

4.2   Multiple-choice items (1)

It is useful to distinguish between the following two major kinds of multiple-choice vocabulary items:

Group A   Choose the letter of the word which is the nearest in meaning to the word in italics.

>   He's been very *feeble* since his illness.
>   A. unwell B. thin C. foolish D. weak

Group B   Choose the letter of the correct or best word to complete each sentence.

>   Have you heard the planning committee's . . . . for solving the city's traffic problems?
>   A. theory B. design C. proposal D. purpose

This section concentrates on Group A items and the next section on Group B. The following item types are examples of four vocabulary recognition items which fall within the first group.

Type 1 In this type of recognition item the stem is replaced by a picture. The testee sees the picture and has to select the most appropriate word relating to the picture from 4 or 5 options. This type of item is clearly very appropriate at the elementary stages.

A. running
B. jumping
C. standing
D. kicking

Type 2 Here the stem consists of a definition: the testee has to select the correct option to which the definition refers.

> a person who receives and pays out money in a bank
> A. broker B. accountant C. creditor D. cashier

Type 3 The stem consists of a lexical item: the testee has to select the best synonym or definition.

> advocate
> A. support B. advise C. contradict D. damage
>
> dilatory
> A. growing gradually larger
> B. slow in getting things done
> C. showing care and effort
> D. heavy with drops of water

Type 4 The stem here consists of a sentence. Hence, this type of recognition item is generally to be preferred to the previous three types in so far as the "problem" word appears in context. Vocabulary is much more usefully tested in context since it is the context that gives specific meaning and relevance to a word, thus creating a situation which is as linguistically valid as possible in the circumstances.

> It's rained *continuously* for two whole days.
> A. without stopping
> B. heavily
> C. regularly
> D. at odd moments

Since subtle shades of meaning are often determined only by the specific context in which a particular word appears, it is generally advisable to provide fairly full contexts for vocabulary testing, especially at an advanced level. The fuller the context, however, the more difficult it is to find plausible distractors.[1] Few good distractors, for example, can be found for the following item:

> We've had to *put off* the meeting until next week. (postpone)

Synonyms are not always interchangeable in a context (without altering the meaning). However, where a word may be replaced by another in a particular context, testees may easily be misled into regarding synonyms as being generally interchangeable.

Guidelines for writing items

(1) If the problem area being tested is located in the options (as in Type 2), the stem should be kept simple. If, however, the problem area is included in the stem (as in Types 3 and 4), the options themselves should be simple in so far as they should contain only those vocabulary items which the testees can understand.

(2) Each option should belong to the same word class as the word in the stem, particularly when the word appears in the context of a sentence. If this rule is observed, there will be less danger of the context providing important grammatical clues for the testee. For example, although the first of the following test items is usable, options A, B and C in the second item would be grammatically incorrect when put in the context.

> contemptuous
> A. deep in thought
> B. without a sense of humour
> C. self-satisfied
> D. scornful

> Bill was *contemptuous* of the efforts of his friends to raise some money for the charity.
> A. deep in thought
> B. without a sense of humour
> C. self-satisfied
> D. scornful

(3) The correct option and the distractors should be at approximately the same level of difficulty[2]. If the correct option is more difficult than the distractors, the testees will arrive at the correct answer by process of elimination. Thus, the test may have a negative effect on the students: i.e. they will select the correct option not because they know it is correct but only because they know the other options are wrong. The following item measures the testee's knowledge of the distractors rather than his familiarity with the correct option:

> theatrical
> A. angry B. histrionic C. proud D. foolish

The converse also holds good. If the distractors are more difficult than the correct option, the item may be equally unreliable. In such a case, there will usually be a tendency for the more able student to think that the correct option is too easy and therefore wrong; he is thus tricked into selecting one of the more difficult options:

> suffice
> A. be adequate B. harass C. acquiesce D. be contrite

(4) There is some disagreement concerning the relationship of the options to the problem area being tested. Some test writers argue that the options should be related to the same general topic or area while others prefer as wide a range of associations as possible. Unless the vocabulary item being tested has a very low frequency count (i.e. is very rarely used), however, the item writer is advised to limit the options to the same general area of activity where possible[2]

Item 1	*Item 2*
apparition	apparition
A. skeleton	A. scenery
B. ghost	B. ghost
C. nightmare	C. magician
D. corpse	D. castle

If item 2 were set in a test, the student who has read a few ghost stories would probably select option B because he would associate *apparition* with the stories he had read. In item 1, however, the student is required to show a much greater control over vocabulary.

(5) All the options should be approximately the same length[2]. There is a temptation both in vocabulary and in reading comprehension tests to make the correct option much longer than the distractors. This is particularly true in a vocabulary test item in which the options take the form of definitions: the item-writer tends to take great pains to ensure that the option is absolutely correct, qualifying it at great length. However, he rarely takes such trouble over the distractors, since they are deliberately wrong and need not be qualified in any way.

> a hitch-hiker
> A. a man who makes ropes
> B. a person who travels about by asking motorists to give him free rides
> C. an old-fashioned sailor
> D. a boy who walks long distances

The student who does not know the meaning of *hitch-hiker* would clearly choose option B — and he would be correct in doing so. Consequently, if it is ever necessary to qualify a definition at some length, either one distractor or all three or four distractors should be made equally long. In this way, the correct option will be disguised a little more effectively.

(6) It is advisable to avoid using a pair of synonyms as distractors: if the testee recognises the synonyms, he may realise immediately that neither is the correct option, since there can be only one correct answer.

> The old man was always *courteous* when anyone spoke to him.
> A. polite B. glad C. kind D. pleased

Even such near synonyms as *glad* and *pleased* are sufficient to indicate to the intelligent student that the choice must be between *polite* and *kind*, since if *glad* were correct, *pleased* would probably also be correct.

It is also dangerous to "pair off" options by providing an antonym as a distractor. Options A and C in the following vocabulary item immediately stand out; again, the clever student will be able to narrow his choice down to two options once he realises that A means the opposite of C.

> ascend
> A. go up B. talk C. come down D. fetch

4.3   Multiple-choice items (2)

The guidelines given in 4.2 for constructing vocabulary items apply equally for the Group B items now being treated. In certain ways, the items shown in this section are more difficult to construct than those in the previous section. The problem is chiefly one of context: too little context is insufficient to establish any meaningful situation, while too much context will provide too many clues (both grammatical and semantic).

> 1. I saw a nasty . . . . between two cars this morning.
>   A. happening B. danger C. damage D. accident
>
> 2. I was speaking to Ann on the 'phone when suddenly we were . . . .
>   A. hung up B. run out C. broken down D. cut off
>
> 3. I should have returned this book last Tuesday: it is now five days . . . .
>   A. postponed B. excessive C. overdue D. delayed
>
> 4. Nothing had been organised and confusion seemed . . . .
>   A. inevident B. inefficient C. ineligible D. inevitable
>
> 5. Tom always tries to help people, but recently he has been . . . . . . kind and generous.
>   A. chiefly B. especially C. principally D. fundamentally

Many multiple-choice vocabulary test items of the type being dealt with in this section rely on the context itself to provide grammatical clues which automatically rule out at least one of the options. These kinds of test items are useful in many respects but may possibly belong more to tests of grammar and structure rather than to vocabulary. Nevertheless, there can be little objection to introducing, say, a few items on verb patterning in a test of vocabulary.

> 6. I'm . . . . of getting a new job: I don't like my present one.
>   A. contemplating B. thinking C. desiring D. hoping

> 7. Ann . . . . me of a girl I used to know.
>   A. recalls B. reminds C. remembers D. recollects

It is sometimes argued that many multiple-choice vocabulary tests consist largely of items such as the following and that these test only a knowledge of semantic collocation.

> 8. The television station was . . . . with letters and 'phone calls after the announcement.
>   A. drowned B. stormed C. deluged D. absorbed

Since this item ignores the ability to create unexpected collocations, it can also be argued that an imaginative use of the language is discouraged. Although there may be some truth in this argument, unexpected collocations result from a creative and intuitive handling of language, which in turn demands an implicit understanding of everyday collocations. It is usually the writer's very awareness of the degree of incongruity which makes a new collocation vigorous and meaningful.

Consequently, such items as the following can scarcely be said to exert a harmful influence on language teaching, although the collocations may be tested equally well without a context.

> 9. Dr Lee charges a high . . . . for his services.
>   A. fee B. profit C. salary D. payment
>   (Collocations being tested here, for example, are:
>   charge a fee/make a profit/receive a salary/make or receive a payment — although it is possible to charge a payment to an account.)

> 10. I don't believe you: I think you're . . . . lies.
>   A. saying B. talking C. speaking D. telling

> 11. Iron will eventually . . . . if grease is not applied.
>   A. wear B. corrode C. damage D. corrupt

> 12. My driving licence . . . . at the end of this month.
>   A. expires B. passes out C. retires D. concludes

If separated from such contexts as the preceding ones, these test items **would** read:

> 9. *charge a* fee/profit/salary/payment
> 10. say/talk/speak/tell *lies*
> 11. *iron* wears/corrodes/damages/corrupts
> 12. *a licence* expires/passes out/retires/concludes

A more telling argument against this type of item is that each context requires a "normal" reaction and takes no account of cultural differences. For example, in the following item B or D would be correct in certain societies since it is impolite to accept a gift without first vehemently refusing it.

> Ann shrieked with . . . . at the beautiful present Mrs White gave her.
> A. delight B. horror C. dismay D. anger

4.4 Sets (Associated words)

Many of the difficulties arising from the testing of collocations are avoided by the testing of word sets. In such tests the student's familiarity with a range of associations is measured. Test constructors are advised to seek a range of associations (see Type 1) instead of relying on a single one.[3]

Type 1 (Recognition)
Instructions:
Look at the word in capital letters. Each of the sets of words that accompanies it contains one word associated with it. Underline the words that seem to you most closely connected with the main word.
(Note that the first example is more appropriate to the elementary levels while the second example shows the application of this item type to more advanced levels.)

TRAFFIC	(a) journey	c̲a̲r̲s̲	people
	(b) luggage	station	l̲o̲r̲r̲y̲
	(c) v̲e̲h̲i̲c̲l̲e̲s̲	mile	path
EQUIP	(a) f̲u̲r̲n̲i̲s̲h̲	defend	lend
	(b) launch	present	a̲r̲m̲
	(c) purchase	attack	s̲u̲p̲p̲l̲y̲

Type 2 (Production)
Write in each space one word for each of the following groups of words.

chair	table	cupboard	bed	(= furniture)
cars	buses	lorries	trams	(= traffic)

It is sometimes argued that such a test is appropriate only at the most elementary levels, but it can be used as a very subtle means of testing word associations at a more advanced level:[4]

> Each group of words is related to a particular subject. Write down the particular subject which is connected with each group of words.

hand	theatre	volume	nursery
wrist	sister	track	lift
dial	bed	head	slope
face	ward	spool	snow
(= watch)	(= hospital)	(= tape-recorder)	(= skiing)

4.5   Matching items

Type 1 of the following test items suffers from testing together lexical items from different word classes while Type 2 tests a mixed bag of tense forms, etc. The result is that for both types of test items grammatical clues assume great importance, since they are instrumental in limiting the range of choices facing the testee for each blank. For example, although there may appear to be 20 words for selection for blank (1) in Type 1, in practice there are only 3 which would fit grammatically: *turned (down), broken (down), knocked (down).* Similarly, in the first sentence of Type 2 there are only 2 options (*pull through, get away*), since all the other options are either past tense forms or participles. Both items need to be rewritten, therefore, if a higher degree of reliability is to be obtained.

Type 1 Write the correct word from the following list at the side of each number on your answer sheet. Use each word once only.

road	accident	travelling	turned	side
broken	know	knocked	middle	looked
lorry	policeman	pavement	running	hurt
lying	crossed	left	forgot	talk

Poor Tom Wright was (1) down by a (2) last week when he was crossing the (3). He was quite badly (4) and he had to go into hospital for a few days. His left leg was (5) and both his arms were cut. While he was (6) in bed in the hospital, a (7) came to (8) to him.

"Was the lorry (9) very quickly?" he asked Tom.

Tom told him all about the (10).

"I was (11) home from school and I (12) the road. I (13) right but I (14) to look (15). In the (16) of the road I suddenly saw a lorry. I didn't (17) what to do, so I began to run to the other (18) of the road. The lorry (19) but it hit me when I was near the (20).

Type 2 Complete the following sentences with the most suitable verb phrase from the list.

came about	pull through	broken out	falling out
running into	brought up	get away	browned off

1. "Did the prisoner manage to . . . .?" "Yes, the police are still looking for him."
2. Most of the pupils were . . . . . . with the dull talk.
3. The doctor thought Mr Benson would . . . . after the operation.
4. The couple are always . . . . and causing a disturbance.
5. And so it . . . . that we eventually parted.
Etc.

It is much more efficient to test words from the same word class (e.g. nouns only in Type 1), or parallel tense forms (e.g. the Past Simple tense in Type 2). Thus the Type 2 item could be rewritten as follows:

came about   ran into   pulled through   got away (etc)

1. "I hear the prisoner . . . . yesterday and the police are still looking for him."
2. "We were all relieved that Mr Benson . . . . after the operation."
Etc.

Type 3 From the list of words given, choose the one which is most suitable for each blank. Write only the letter of the correct word after each number on your answer sheet. (Use each word once only.)

A. completely   C. busily   E. quickly
B. politely   D. carefully   F. angrily

"Write (1) . . . .," the teacher shouted (2) . . . . "Hurry up; you must get used to working (3) . . . ."
"Please, sir," a student said (4) . . . ., "I've finished."
"No, you haven't," answered the teacher. "You haven't (5) . . . . . . finished until you've ruled off."
Meanwhile, the boy sitting next to him was (6) . . . . engaged in filling his pen.

This type is satisfactory in many ways because all the lexical items tested are adverbs. However, like the other two types, this type gives the student too little choice. For instance, there will be only one word left for the last number. Thus, it could be improved considerably by the addition of a few other adverbs. The list might then read as follows:

A. completely   E. deliberately   I. quickly
B. heavily   F. busily   J. hardly
C. ably   G. hastily   K. angrily
D. politely   H. carefully   L. suitably

The first attempt to construct this list included the adverbs *silently* and *already*, but it was then found that either of these could be used at (6) instead of the correct option *busily*. This illustrates one of the dangers of this particular testing device: clearly the more distractors there are, the greater is the chance that one of the distractors might be a correct option for at least one of the other items.

The following items provide two other examples of matching items:

Type 4 Find the correct meaning in List B for each word in List A. Then write the number of the meaning in the space at the side of each word.

List A	Answer	List B
gloomy	12	1. very important
momentous		2. dark and obscure
barren		3. over-crowded
fleeting		4. friendly and loyal
parochial		5. close and familiar
intimate		6. too poor to produce crops
		7. passing very quickly
		8. naked and cold
		9. narrow, limited
		10. penniless
		11. as soon as possible
		12. sad and miserable
		13. connected with the sea
		14. religious and holy

Type 5 Choose one word from the list on the left, and put it after the word on the right.

bus	Fire	alarm . .
bomb	Hair	. . . .
gun	Traffic	. . . .
cut	Telephone	. . . .
shave	Post	. . . .
office	Atom	. . . .
alarm		
queue		
jam		
bullet		
exchange		
headquarters		
centre		

The rubrics and the lay-out of both these item types are confusing. Apart from the novelty of their appearance, the item types have very little to recommend them over the ordinary multiple-choice item. Indeed, the multiple-choice item type is generally to be preferred, for it at least ensures that each "problem" word has 4 or 5 good options: E.g. *Atom – bullet/bomb/shell/rocket.* In the present form of the test items, the number of useful distractors varies considerably from each lexical

item: e.g. *Hair – cut/shave*, but *Telephone – office/alarm/exchange/
centre/headquarters*. Again, care must be exercised, since a distractor for
one word might prove to be the correct option for another: e.g. the word
station, though a useful distractor for *Telephone,* cannot be included in
the list because it could be used after *Fire* (thus giving *Fire* two correct
options). Such item types, therefore, are best limited to class progress
tests – and then only when novelty and variety are badly needed.

Type 6 The most useful type of matching item is undoubtedly that based
on a reading comprehension passage. The student is given a list of words at
the end of the passage and required to find words of similar meaning in the
passage. Since a detailed context is provided by the passage and little
additional material is required, this is an economical method of testing
vocabulary. The chief risk here, however, is the duplication of questions: if
one of the reading comprehension questions depends for its answer on a
knowledge of the meaning of a particular word, care must be exercised *not*
to test that word again in the vocabulary section.

4.6   More objective items

This section contains examples of types of vocabulary items which have
appeared in certain tests. While Types 1 and 2 are useful for classroom
testing, Types 3 and 4 are rather artificial, and should be avoided where
possible.

Type 1 Word formation test items
Write a word in each blank. The word you write must be the correct form
of the word on the left.

    (i)   CARE   Be . . . . when you cross the road.
    (ii) CRUEL   To mistreat animals is a form of . . . .
    (iii) INTEREST Do you think this book is . . . .?
    (iv) ENTER   Can you show me the . . . . to the cave?

Type 2 Items involving synonyms
(a) Write in each space the best word to replace the words underlined in
each sentence.

    (i)   Tom went <u>at once</u> to the doctor's.   immediately
    (ii) <u>All of a sudden</u> there was a loud cry.   . . . .
    (iii) <u>I came across</u> an interesting book.   . . . .
    (iv) The boat is over fourteen feet <u>in length.</u> . . . .

(b) In each space write one word that means almost the same as the word
on the left. The word you write must rhyme with the word on the
right.

    Example: early *soon* moon

(i) purchase . . . . . . die
(ii) miserable . . . . . . bad

A similar item may be constructed so as to involve antonyms rather than synonyms. The phonological element (rhyming) in 2(b), however, may only confuse the testee instead of helping him. Words are tested in isolation, so, apart from its sheer novelty, the item serves little purpose.

Type 3 Rearrangement items
Rearrange the following letters to make words.

PLEAP	ROLRY	CELPA
SUHOE	IRACH	EGURA

As can be seen, this item is little more than a crossword puzzle. It may, perhaps, be of some use in an intelligence test, but it is of doubtful use in a language test.

Type 4 Definitions
(a) Use each of the following words in a sentence so as to show the meaning of the word.

economy   politics   industrious   etc.

(b) Explain the meaning of each of the underlined words in the following phrases.

an archaic word   a fortuitous event

These item types are of very little use. They test writing ability in addition to a knowledge of word meanings. It is extremely difficult even for native speakers to produce sentences "to show the meaning" of words — and it is certainly not a useful task. A student may be familiar with the meaning of a word and may use it correctly, without being able to express this meaning in a sentence (under test conditions). Furthermore, there is a high degree of subjectivity in the marking of each of these item types.

4.7 Completion items

Several types of completion items can be used for the testing of vocabulary. Again, tests which incorporate such items in a context are generally preferable to those which rely on single words or on definitions.

Type 1
(a) Make each of the following words mean the opposite by putting either 2 or 3 letters in the brackets in front of the word.

(IM)possible	( )usual	( )obedient
( )important	( )legal	( )lawful
( )covered	( )liked	( )pleased
( )satisfied	( )convenient	( )frequent

(b) In the following sentences every word beginning with OVER is incomplete. Complete each word in the space provided.

> Example: I'm late this morning because I OVERSLEPT.

>> 1. Tom feels certain he'll win, but I doubt it simply because he is OVER . . . .
>> 2. Bill has been standing too long and is OVER . . . .

Similar types of items can be constructed for suffixes.

Type 2 The following are perhaps more useful than Type 1.

(a) Complete the following blanks. Words and phrases similar in meaning are given in the brackets.

Every year several thousand new words come into the English language. Since the m—j————y (most) of them disappear after a short time, we may en————e (ask) who actually d—t————nes (decides) which words are r—t————d (kept) and which words are dis—————— (thrown out). Certainly not a s—l——t (carefully chosen) group of scholars as some people think . . .

(b) Read through the following passage containing a number of incomplete words. Write each completed word on your answer sheet at the side of the appropriate number. (Each dash represents one letter.)[5]

Snakes are one of the (1) d—m—n——t groups of (2) r—pt————: there are at least 2,000 different (3) sp—c——s of snakes (4) sc—t————d over a wide area of the earth. Not all snakes are (5) p——s—n——s: in fact, the (6) m—j————y are quite harmless. Contrary to (7) p—p—l—— belief, a snake's (8) f——k—d tongue is not (9) d—ng—————— to human beings: it is merely for touching and smelling (10) s—bs——n——s. Snakes (11) in——ct poison into their (12) vi————'s body by (13) b—t——g him with their (14) f——gs.

The latter test item comes close to a type of item sometimes used to test reading comprehension (described in Chapter 7). Clearly, a large degree of comprehension is necessary before each of the blanks can be completed. The item has been included in this chapter because clues are provided by letters in addition to those provided by the context. It rarely matters, however, whether this type of item is included in the vocabulary or in the reading sub-test in a battery of tests.

NOTES

1 Geoffrey Hutchings, *'Colourless Green Ideas: multiple-choice vocabulary tests'*, English Language Teaching, 25, 1970, 68—71

2 See David P. Harris, *Testing English as a Second Language*, McGraw-Hill, New York, 1969, 54—57.

3 Peter Strevens, *Objective Testing* in *Papers in Language and Language Teaching*, O.U.P., 1965, 97.

4 University of Cambridge Certificate of Proficiency in English: Use of English (June, 1971)

5 A similar item is used in the Davies *English Proficiency Test Battery* (although there it is intended to test reading comprehension and only the initial letter is given).

5 Listening comprehension tests

5.1 General

An effective way of developing the listening skill is through the provision of carefully selected practice material. Such material is in many ways similar to that used for *testing* listening comprehension. Although the auditory skills are closely linked to the oral skills in normal speech situations, it is frequently desirable to separate the two skills for teaching and testing, since it is possible to develop listening ability much beyond the range of speaking ability if the practice material is not dependent on spoken responses or written exercises.

An awareness of the ways in which the spoken language differs from the written language is of crucial importance in the testing of the listening skills. For instance, the spoken language is much more complex than the written language in certain ways, as a result of the large element of "redundancy" that it contains. An example can be seen in the spoken question "Have you got to go now?", the question being signalled by the rise in pitch on *go now* and by the inversion of the word order (i.e. by both phonological and grammatical features). Thus, if the listener did not hear the question signal *Have*, the rise in pitch would make him aware that a question was being asked. If the speaker slurred over *got to*, the question would still be intelligible. In addition, meaning might also be conveyed, emphasised and "repeated" by means of gestures, eye movements, and slight changes in breathing. Such features of redundancy as those described make it possible for mutilated messages to be understood, even though the full message is only partially heard. Furthermore, the human brain has a limited capacity for the reception of information and, were there no such features built into the language, it would often be impossible to absorb information at the speed at which it is conveyed through ordinary speech. Such conversational features as repetition, hesitation and grammatical re-patterning are all examples of this type of redundancy, so essential for the understanding of spoken messages.

What is the significance of these features for testing purposes? Firstly, the ability to distinguish between phonemes, however important, does not in itself imply an ability to understand verbal messages. Moreover, occasional confusion over selected pairs of phonemes does not matter too greatly because in real-life situations the listener is able to use contextual clues to interpret what he hears. Although the listener relies on all the phonological clues present, he can often afford to miss some of them.

Secondly, impromptu speech is often easier to understand than carefully prepared (written) material when the latter is read aloud. Written tests generally omit many of the features of redundancy and impart information at a much higher rate than normal speech does. Consequently, it is essential to make provision for re-stating important points, re-writing and re-phrasing them when preparing in writing material for aural tests. The length of the segments in each breath group should be limited during delivery, for the longer the segment the greater the amount of information and the greater the strain on the auditory memory. Segments of about 20 syllables are considered to be approximately the right length to allow the receiver to *digest* what he has heard.[1] The pauses at the end of each segment should also be lengthened to compensate for the lack of redundant features.

Although not always possible when auditory tests are conducted on a wide scale, it is helpful if the speaker can be seen by the listener. However excellent the quality of a tape-recorder, a disembodied voice is much more difficult for the foreign learner to follow. In practice, most tape-recorders are not of a high quality and are used in rooms where the acoustics are unsatisfactory. If the quality of the reproduction is poor, the test will be unreliable, especially when such discrete features as phoneme discrimination, stress and intonation are being tested.

Apart from the use of video-tape, however, the tape-recorder is the only way of ensuring complete uniformity of presentation and thus a high degree of reliability. It is possible, moreover, to use recordings made by native speakers and thus present perfect models of the spoken language — an important advantage in countries where native speakers are not available to administer the test.

For purposes of convenience, auditory tests are divided here into two broad categories: (i) tests of phoneme discrimination and of sensitivity to stress and intonation; and (ii) tests of auditory comprehension.

5.2   Phoneme discrimination tests

Type 1

(a) This type of discrimination test consists of a picture, accompanied by 3 or 4 words spoken by the examiner in person or on tape.

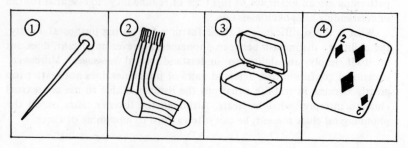

The testee hears:

1.	A. pin	B. pen	C. pair	D. pain
2.	A. shark	B. sock	C. sack	D. shock
3.	A. thin	B. tin	C. fin	D. din
4.	A. card	B. cart	C. car	D. calf

After each group of 4 words he writes the letter of the most appropriate word for that picture.

E.g.   1. A   2. B   3. B   4. A

(b) Conversely, 4 pictures may be shown and only one word spoken. In this case, it is usually better if the word is spoken twice.

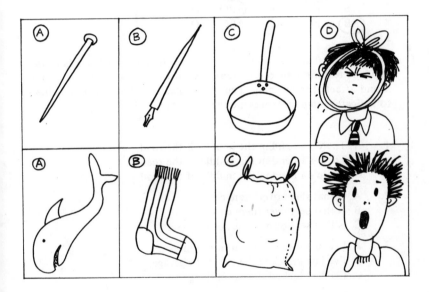

Etc.

The testee hears:

1. pain − pain (= D)
2. sock − sock (= B)
    Etc.

Type 2

(a) In this type[2] of test three words are spoken on tape: A, B and C. Sometimes all three words are the same; sometimes two are the same; and sometimes all are different. On the testee's answer sheet appear the letters

AB   BC   AC   ABC   O

The testee then hears groups of three words:

1.   A. bed   B. bad   C. beard
2.   A. road   B. rod   C. rod
3.   A. seat   B. seat   C. seat
4.   A. pick   B. pick   C. pig
Etc.

After each group the testee puts a circle round the appropriate groups of letters; if all three words are different, he puts a circle round O. Correct answers to the items above would read

1.   AB   BC   AC   ABC   Ⓞ
2.   AB   ⟮BC⟯   AC   ABC   O
3.   AB   BC   AC   ⟮ABC⟯   O
4.   ⟮AB⟯   BC   AC   ABC   O
Etc.

(b) This is a similar type of test,[3] but here the individual words in the previous test are replaced by sentences in which a single distinction in sound affects the meaning. The testees hear three sentences and have to indicate which sentences are the same, etc.

1.   A. There's a bend in the middle of the road.
      B. There's a bend in the middle of the road.
      C. There's a band in the middle of the road.

2.   A. Is that sheet over there clean?
      B. Is that seat over there clean?
      C. Is that seat over there clean?

3.   A. I've just locked the car in the garage.
      B. I've just knocked the car in the garage.
      C. I've just locked the car in the garage.

4.   A. I can see a few beds from here.
      B. I can see a few birds from here.
      C. I can see a few buds from here.
Etc.

Here is a slightly different version of the answer sheet in Type 2(a). Phoneme discrimination is also indicated by a ring drawn round the correct combination:

1.   AAA   ⟮AAB⟯   ABA   ABB   ABC
2.   AAA   AAB   ABA   ⟮ABB⟯   ABC
3.   AAA   AAB   ⟮ABA⟯   ABB   ABC
4.   AAA   AAB   ABA   ABB   ⟮ABC⟯
Etc.

Type 3

(a) In each of these items one word is given on tape: in the answer booklet three words are printed in ordinary type. (In some tests four words are given and the word on tape is spoken twice.) The testee is required to choose the written word which corresponds to the spoken word.

1. (Spoken)   *den*
   (Written)   A. ten   B. den   C. Ben   D. pen

2. (Spoken)   *win*
   (Written)   A. when   B. one   C. wane   D. win

3. (Spoken)   *plays*
   (Written)   A. plays   B. prays   C. pays   D. brays

4. (Spoken)   *coat*
   (Written)   A. code   B. caught   C. coat   D. cord

Etc.

The testee circles, or writes out, the letter corresponding to the correct word.

(b) This type of item is similar to the previous one; this time, however, the words spoken by the tester occur in sentences. The four options may then be either printed or spoken.

1. (Spoken)   I'll thread it for you.
   (Written or spoken)   A. thread   B. tread
                         C. threat   D. dread

2. (Spoken)   Did John manage to catch the train?
   (Written or spoken)   A. drain   B. chain
                         C. plane   D. train

3. (Spoken)   Put the pan in some hot water.
   (Written or spoken)   A. pan   B. pen
                         C. pin   D. pain

4. (Spoken)   The colour is very dirty, isn't it?
   (Written or spoken)   A. collar   B. cellar
                         C. caller   D. colour

(c) This item type[4] is similar to Type 3(a): one word is spoken by the tester (preferably twice). However, instead of a choice of four words, the testee has in front of him a choice of four definitions. He has thus to select the correct definition for the word he hears.

1. (Spoken)   *cot – cot*
   (Written)   A. stopped and held
                    B. a baby's bed
                    C. pulled by horses
                    D. a small pet animal covered with fur

2. (Spoken)   *threw — threw*
   (Written) A. made something move through the air
              B. not false
              C. some but not many
              D. made a picture or diagram on paper

3. (Spoken)   *bud — bud*
   (Written) A. part of a tree or a flower
              B. a creature with wings
              C. something to sleep on
              D. not good

4. (Spoken)   *watch — watch*
   (Written) A. clean with water
              B. an insect like a bee
              C. look
              D. a word used to ask questions

The test items described in this section are all useful for diagnostic testing purposes, thus enabling the teacher to concentrate later on specific pronunciation difficulties. The items are especially useful when testees have the same first language background and when a contrastive analysis of the mother tongue and the target language can be used. Most of the item types described are short, enabling the tester to cover a wide range of sounds. In certain items which test only individual words (e.g. Types 1(a), 1(b) and 2(a)), up to one hundred items can be tested in ten minutes.

Type 3(c), however, is an example of an impure test item because it tests not only the ability to discriminate between the different sounds of a language but also a knowledge of vocabulary. A testee who may be able to discriminate accurately will nevertheless find the test very difficult if he cannot understand the definitions in the options. Similarly, Type 3(a) is a test of phoneme discrimination *and* spelling ability. Type 3(b) can also result in impure test items: in this type of item, proficiency in grammatical structure will favour the testee. Thus, for example, a testee who cannot discriminate between *thread, tread, threat* and *dread* may immediately rule out the distractors *threat* and *dread* since they cannot be put in the pattern *I'll . . . . it for you.*

Each individual test item in all the types described must be kept fairly simple. Obscure lexical items should be avoided. This may seem to be a simple enough principle to observe, but the avoidance of difficult lexical items frequently makes it impossible to test all the sound contrasts that need to be included in the test. For example, the contrasts *shark, sock, sack, shock* would not be suitable for inclusion in a test intended for elementary learners of English.

Much of the material in such tests is unfortunately artificial, differing greatly from continuous speech. Frequently there is a tendency for the tester to adopt a certain tone-pattern and rhythm which may be a source of irritation to the listener or affect his concentration. However, if the tester changes pitch (e.g. live, leave, live) this will only confuse the testee. Thus, the tester must attempt to pronounce every syllable using the same stress and pitch patterns.

The ability to discriminate between certain phonemes may sometimes prove very difficult for native speakers. Many English dialects fail to make some of the vowel and consonant contrasts and thus, in addition to all the other variables (e.g. the acoustics of the room, the quality of the tape-recorder, etc.), these tests are affected by the pronunciation differences of native speakers.[5]

5.3   Tests of stress and intonation

Although features of stress, intonation, rhythm and juncture are generally considered more important in oral communication skills than the ability to discriminate between phonemes, tests of stress and intonation are on the whole less satisfactory than the phoneme discrimination tests treated in the previous section. Most tests are impure in so far as they test other skills at the same time; many are also very artificial, testing the rarer (but more "testable") features.

Type 1 The following item type[6] is designed to test the ability to recognise word stress or sentence stress. The testee listens to a sentence (usually spoken on tape) and is required to indicate the syllable which carries the main stress of the whole structure. He shows the main stress by putting a cross in the brackets under the appropriate syllable.

    (Spoken)   *I've just given THREE books to Bill.*
    (Written)   I've just given three books to Bill.
          ( )( )()()(X)(   )()( )

    (Spoken)   *My FAther will help you do it.*
    (Written)   My father will help you do it.
          ( )(X)( )( )( )( )()( )

Unfortunately, this test lacks context and is artificial in many ways. It tests only recognition of stress and is of limited use for ear-training purposes.

Type 2[7] The testee hears a brief conversation, which is spoken three times: the first utterance remains the same, but each time the response is spoken in a different way. Two of these responses are appropriate and natural, but a third response is inappropriate and unnatural. Testees have to indicate the exchange which is inappropriate.

    (Spoken)   You can't smoke yet: Bill's father won't let him smoke.
            A. But *I'm* older than Bill.
            B. But I'm *older* than Bill.
            C. But I'm older than Bill?

(Spoken)   Are you going out tonight, too?
A. Yes, *I'm* going to the cinema at seven.
B. Yes, I'm going to the *cinema* at seven.
C. Yes, I'm *going* to the cinema at seven.

Understanding intonation patterns in context is an important skill. Attitudes and intonation features, however, are very personal, and, indeed, there seems to be a real danger of encouraging students to interpret what are essentially personal and idiosyncratic speech characteristics as the stress and intonation patterns employed by the members of a large speech community. Moreover, the range of possible intonation patterns is extremely wide and varies from person to person.

Sometimes ambiguities may occur. All three responses are correct in the following test item:

Does anyone know whether it'll rain tomorrow?
A. *Mary* thinks it'll be a nice day.
B. Mary *thinks* it'll be a nice day.
C. Mary thinks it'll be a *nice* day.

Type 3 The previous comments apply also to the following test of intonation.[8] The examiner makes an utterance and the testee has to select the appropriate description to indicate whether he has understood the original utterance. The utterance is spoken once only, but the test is based on the principle that the same utterance may be spoken in several different tone-patterns indicating a plain statement, a question, sarcasm, surprise, annoyance, etc.

(Spoken)   *Tom's a fine goalkeeper.*
(Written)   Tom's a fine goalkeeper.
             The speaker is
A.   making a straightforward statement
B.   being very sarcastic
C.   asking a question

(Spoken)   *You will send me a couple of tickets.*
(Written)   You will send me a couple of tickets.
             This is probably
A.   a request
B.   a command
C.   an expression of disbelief

(Spoken)   *I'll help Ann.*
(Written)   I'll help Ann.
             The speaker is
A.   reluctant to help Ann
B.   eager to help Ann
C.   making a plain statement

This type of test item is sometimes difficult to construct. Since the context must be neutral it is often hard to avoid ambiguity. There is also a danger of inventing odd interpretations or of concentrating on the rarer meanings: e.g. sarcasm, irony, incredulity. Moreover, it can be argued that the item tests vocabulary and reading comprehension in addition to sensitivity to stress and intonation.

5.4 Testing comprehension through visual materials

Most of the item types in this section are more appropriate for the elementary stages of learning English. They are, however, preferable to the discrimination items previously discussed in so far as they involve the testing of grammar and lexis through phonology. Pictures, maps and diagrams can be used effectively for testing such skills, thereby making the testee's performance less dependent on other skills (e.g. speaking, vocabulary and reading).

Type 1 In this item type a picture is used in conjunction with spoken statements. The statements are about the picture but some are correct and others incorrect. The testee has to pick out the true (i.e. correct) statements and write T (or put a tick √) at the side of the appropriate numbers. He writes F (or puts a cross X) at the side of the numbers of the false (i.e. incorrect) statements.

(Spoken)
1. The lorry's passing the man on the motorbike.
2. The car's travelling in the same direction.
3. A dog's running in front of the car.
4. A little girl's running after her mother.
5. There are two dolls in the pram.
6. A girl's pushing the pram.
7. The two boys are looking in a shop window.
8. A very small boy's helping the old woman.
9. The old woman's going into a shop.
10. A tall man's posting some letters.
11. There are a lot of cars in the street.
12. The two boys are on the same side of the street as the girl with the pram.

(Written)

1.   2.   3.   4.   5.   6.
7.   8.   9.   10.   11.   12.

Type 2 In the following auditory test the student has 5 pictures in front of him. He listens to 4 sentences, at the end of which he is required to select the appropriate picture being described.

The student hears:
(1) Both car doors are open.
(2) It's daylight but both headlamps are on.
(3) The man who's repairing the car is lying underneath it.
(4) Although the boy sees the man working hard, he doesn't help him.

Thus the student is able to narrow down the choice available to him as follows:

(1) B C D E   (Only A shows one door open)
(2) B D E   (Only C shows the headlamps off)
(3) B D   (Only E shows the man standing up)
(4) D   (Only B shows the boy helping the man)

Type 3 The following type of test item [9] is used in a number of auditory comprehension tests. The testee sees a set of 3 or 4 pictures and hears a statement (or a short series of statements), on the basis of which he has to select the most appropriate picture. In the test the testee often sees a total of 10 or 12 such sets of pictures.

The testee hears:
1. The car's going to crash into a tree.
2. Bill can't run as fast as Mary.
3. Tom wishes his sister could play tennis with him.
4. The switch is so high that Ann can't reach it.

Type 4 Simple diagrams (consisting of lines, squares, rectangles, circles and triangles) can be drawn to function as options in a test of elementary comprehension.[10] Illustrations of this nature lend themselves in particular to testing such grammatical features as comparison, prepositions and determiners.

Look carefully at each of the four diagrams. You will hear a series of statements about each of the diagrams. Write down the appropriate letter for each statement.

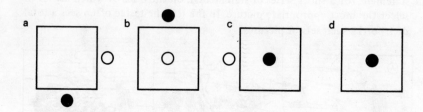

(Spoken)

1. A white circle is inside a square.
2. A black circle is above a square.
3. A circle is on the left of a square.
4. Neither a white nor a black circle is in a square.
5. A black circle is under a square.
6. A square is under a black circle.
7. A square is on the left of a circle.
8. A black circle is in a square but a white circle is outside the square.

All kinds of shapes and forms can be used to test auditory comprehension. The following example illustrates how an understanding of complex structures can be tested in this way. However, there is often a temptation for the test writer to be too "clever" and set an item testing intelligence (or mental agility) rather than language acquisition.

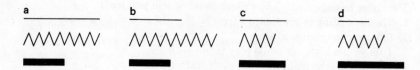

(Spoken)   If the thick line had been only a millimetre longer, it would have been the longest of the three lines.

Type 5. This test is designed to assess the testee's ability to understand simple instructions. Any street map can be used or adapted for this purpose.

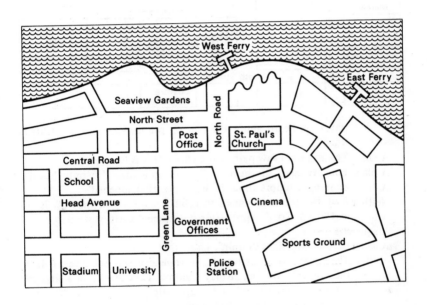

(Spoken) You come out of school into Central Road and walk in the direction of Green Lane. However, you take the left turning just before you reach Green Lane. At the end of the street you turn right and continue until you come to the second turning right. You cross this road and you will see on your right .... (Which building will you see?)

The following listening comprehension test is in the form of a dialogue. The idea on which it is based was suggested by an actual robbery and a police chase. In this way, the listener is given a greater sense of realism and an added interest in the dialogue.

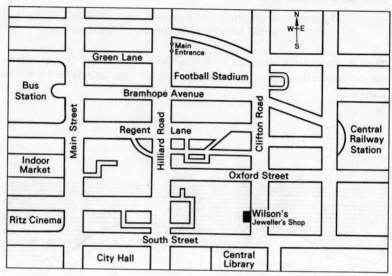

A: Have you heard about the raid on the jewellery shop in Clifton Road?

B: Yes, in fact, I saw part of the chase. It was terrible.

A: You saw part of the chase? Good gracious. I've only heard a very vague report about it. What exactly happened?

B: Well, the thieves planned to rob the shop – you know, Wilson's in Clifton Road – just after it'd opened early yesterday morning.

A: In broad daylight? I didn't know that.

B: They planned to arrive as the jewellery was being taken from the safe into the big display window. They arrived in a large red car which they parked on the opposite side of the road. Can you see the place on this map I've got?

(1) X: Write the letter A on your map at the place where the thieves parked the car.

A: How many robbers were there?

B: Three. One waited inside the car and the other two walked over to the shop, carrying large briefcases. Once inside the shop, they made the manager of the shop and his assistant lie down on the floor while they filled the briefcases with jewellery. What they didn't know, however, was that another assistant was in the room at the back of the shop. He had caught sight of the two thieves and had pressed a small alarm bell. At that precise moment, a police patrol car was at ... what's it called? ... I forget now, but it's the junction between the Ritz and the road that runs past the library.

(2) X: Write the letter B at the junction referred to by the speaker.

    A: So things went wrong for the robbers from the start?

    B: Yes, by the time the two robbers were leaving the jeweller's, the police car was already turning into Clifton Road. The two men hadn't even time to close one of the car doors properly, and a frightened passer-by heard one of the men tell the driver to take the first turning off Clifton Road. A moment later, one of the briefcases fell out as their car swung left.

(3) X: Where did the thieves lose one of the briefcases? Write the letter C on the spot.

    B: But that wasn't the end of their misfortunes. When they glanced back, they saw the police car gaining on them.

    A; Didn't they realise that it was all over?

    B: No, they accelerated. They turned left and then they turned right. Then they swung into a narrow street and stopped a few yards down it at the side of a second car — most likely their get-away car.

(4) X: Where was the get-away car parked? Write D on your map.

    A: Had they managed to throw off the police car?

    B: No. As they were about to change cars, they heard it coming up behind them. So they changed their minds and started off again in the red car. At the end of the narrow street, they turned left into Hilliard Road again and sped off in the direction of the stadium. At the next but one junction before the stadium — you know, on the south side of it — a second police car suddenly cut across their path and forced them to stop.

(5) X: Write E at the place where the robbers were forced to stop.

    A: What on earth did they do then?

    B: Well, by this time, they were really desperate. The driver of the red car got out and fired a pistol at the police car. But this didn't stop the police. One of them scrambled over the bonnet of the police car and chased the man with the pistol down Hilliard Road. The man ran in the direction of the City Hall and then took the first turning left after Regent Lane. Then he made as if to turn right, but just at that moment, he tripped and fell. In a matter of seconds, two policemen were on him.

(6) X: Where was the man caught? Write the letter F to show the place.

    A: Where were the other two robbers while all this was happening?

    B: Well, by this time one was half-way down Regent Lane with two passers-by chasing him. He slipped through the narrow alley at the end of the lane and turned right before dashing across the road. He got most of the way down the road to the station before one of the passers-by finally caught up with him and overpowered him.

(7) X: Where was this robber caught? Write the letter G to show the place.

A: What excitement! I suppose the police soon caught the third man.

B: No, they didn't. The third robber had a shotgun and he'd sprinted along Regent Lane and into Main Street. He was about to set off running in the direction of the Market. Then he caught sight of a butcher's van travelling towards him. He stood quite still in the middle of the road, pointed his gun at the bewildered driver and shouted to him to stop and get out.

(8) X: Write the letter H to show where the robber stopped the van.

B: Then he got into the van, started off down Main Street and turned left only to find himself in the middle of the bus station! He quickly turned round and headed up Main Street. Next he took the road leading to the main entrance of the Football Stadium. Halfway down this road, however, he saw two policemen on motorcycles in front of him at the end of the road.

(9) X: Write the letter I where the two police motor-cyclists were.

A: Well, he must have been well and truly cornered by now.

B: Yes, but he still fired several shots at the motorcyclists. Then he reversed and jumped out of the van at the end of the road. He turned in the direction of the City Hall. He hadn't got more than a yard or two when he found himself surrounded by a dozen policemen.

(10) X: Write the letter J to show where the third robber was caught.

A: And so at last he was caught!

B: Yes, and so was the manager of the jewellery shop.

A: What on earth do you mean?

B: Well, the police have just found that it wasn't real jewellery at all. It was imitation stuff. So the jeweller's been arrested for fraud!

Type 6 There are many other ways of exploiting visual materials for testing simple auditory comprehension. The following kind of item may be useful in the testing of the listening ability of students of science.

1. Draw a straight line AB three centimetres long.
2. Continue the line AB to point C so that AC is twice as long as AB.
3. Draw a perpendicular from point B.
4. Measure an angle 45° to be called DAC.
5. Now draw the line AD until it meets the perpendicular at point D.

Question 1: How long is AD?
6. Now join DC.
   Question 2: What does angle ADC measure?
7. Draw a line from point B parallel to AD and mark the point X where it bisects CD.
 · *Question 3:* How long is BX?
8. Now draw a line from X parallel to AC so that it bisects AD at Y.
   Question 4: How long is AY?
   Question 5: How many figures have you drawn?
                 What are they?

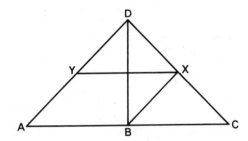

Type 7 Another useful test item (and exercise) which is independent of the speaking, reading and writing skills is that in which the student is presented with an incomplete picture (usually a simple line-drawing) and is required to add to it pieces of visual information according to certain oral instructions he is given. The following is an example of such an item:

(The testee looks at the picture)

(The testee hears):

1. Draw a table and two chairs in front of the café.
2. Draw two traffic lights on the opposite side of the road.
3. Draw a zebra-crossing between Oxford School and the cinema.
4. Draw a lorry travelling in the opposite direction to the car.
5. A policeman directing traffic is standing in the middle of the junction. Draw him.
6. Although there's only one tree at the side of the block of flats, there are four trees on the opposite side of the road. Draw them.
7. Some people have complained about the danger of crossing the road between the café and the cinema. A pedestrian footbridge has now been built at this point. Draw it.
8. A man who has been cleaning the windows of a flat on the second floor of the building opposite the school has forgotten to take his ladder away. It's still leaning against the window on the extreme left of the front of the building. Draw it.

It is clearly important to keep any such drawing simple so that too much is not required from the testee. Basic practice in matchstick drawings would be a useful preparation for such listening comprehension tasks in class progress tests. A simple country scene involving the drawing of cows, trees, tents, pots and pans, rivers, bridges, fish, birds or an indoor scene involving the positions of furniture and simple objects might form a useful basis for such a listening test.

Type 8 Simple paper-folding and drawing can also be used to measure ability to understand instructions. E.g.

(Spoken) Print your name in the top left-hand corner of your paper: draw a one-inch line six inches under it. Draw a small circle on the line and on the right of it draw a square roughly the same size as the circle. Now take the top right-hand corner and the bottom left-hand corner and fold your paper so that the drawing appears on the outside.

Practical considerations, however, should not be ignored in the administration of this type of test. Although useful for ordinary classroom purposes, such tests are difficult to administer in public examinations. Copying is a simple matter and test reliability may thus be greatly affected. Moreover, there is a tendency for such tests to become tests of intelligence rather than of language proficiency. The item writer must be careful to test only the student's ability to understand a spoken message – not his ability to interpret it and see hidden relationships.

Many children under the age of 12 have difficulty in seeing relationships in pictures (without prompting from the teacher) and in recognising familiar objects drawn from an unfamiliar angle (e.g. an aerial view of a school). Students from rural areas, moreover, often lack the degree of sophistication necessary to understand many visual conventions. Although many "westernised" teachers and students understand the conventions used in the following illustrations, countless others find them singularly meaningless.

("The alarm-clock is ringing.")

("John was very frightened.")

The pictorial conventions used in many textbooks, though readily understood by students using those books, have little meaning for other students. Consequently, it is dangerous to adopt such conventions when constructing a listening comprehension test for a number of schools, some of which may not be using the textbook containing the conventions adopted. The following are just two examples of some pictorial conventions used in a textbook.

("He threw the ball over the house.")

("The church can't be seen from here.")

For teaching purposes, such conventions are extremely useful. They can be used for testing purposes, however, only if *every* testee is familiar with them.

5.5   Statements and dialogues

These tests are designed to measure how well students can understand short samples of speech and deal with a variety of signals on the lexical and grammatical levels of phonology.

Type 1 This test item[11] may be included in a test of grammar, a test of reading comprehension, or a test of auditory comprehension, depending on whether the item stem is written or spoken. It tests the ability to understand both the grammatical and lexical features of a short utterance. The testee hears a statement (usually on tape) and then chooses the best option from four written paraphrases.

> (Spoken) I wish you'd done it when I told you.
> (Written) A. I told you and you did it then.
>   B. I didn't tell you but you did it then.
>   C. I told you but you didn't do it then.
>   D. I didn't tell you and you didn't do it then.

> (Spoken) It took Alan a long time to find he couldn't mend my bicycle.
> (Written) A. After a long time, Alan realised he was unable to mend my bicycle.
>   B. Alan spent a long time mending my bicycle but he was at last successful.
>   C. Alan was a long time before he found my bicycle.
>   D. In spite of searching for a long time, Alan couldn't find my bicycle and, therefore, couldn't mend it.

When constructing these items, it is advisable to keep the grammatical, lexical and phonological difficulties in the stem, leaving the written options free of such problems and at a lower level of grammatical and lexical difficulty than the spoken stimulus.

Type 2 These items[12] are more satisfactory than Type 1 in so far as they are an attempt to simulate speech situations. The testee listens to a short question and has to select the correct response from a choice of four printed ones.

(Spoken) Why are you going home?
(Written) A.   At six o'clock.
                   B.   Yes, I am.
                   C.   To help my mother.
                   D.   By bus.

Each option should be so constructed as to appear correct in some way to the testee who has not recognised the correct signals in the question. Thus, in the previous item, option A would appear correct if the testee had confused *Why* with *When*, and option D if he had "heard" *How* signal the question. If, on the other hand, a testee had failed completely to pick up the WH-question signal, he would be tempted to select option B, considering it the answer to a Yes/No question.

The question types should be varied as much as possible and Yes/No questions included as well as WH-questions.

(Spoken) Does Mary mind you playing the piano?
(Written) A. Yes, she's always thinking about it.
           B. No, she rather likes it.
           C. No, she doesn't play the piano.
           D. Yes, she must be careful.

In this item two of the distractors (A and D) are based on confusion relating to *mind* in order to tempt any testee who has failed to understand the question accurately. Distractor C has been included to attract any testee who has generally misunderstood the question and thinks it is about Mary playing the piano.

Type 3 Brief dialogues are used in this type of test. Consequently, the testee has the opportunity of hearing something approximating to a natural dialogue between two speakers. A third voice may then ask the testee a question concerning the dialogue. The question may test straightforward comprehension of the dialogue or the testee's ability to make deductions or draw inferences from the dialogue.

(Testee hears):

"Would you like to watch TV tonight, Tina?"
"No, John. I'm looking forward to a game of chess. What about you?"
"I'm not worried as long as we do something. Let's do what you want."

(Testee reads):

1. John doesn't really mind what he does.
2. Tina wants to look at TV.
3. John doesn't want to play chess.
4. John won't be worried for long if he is with Tina.

(Testee hears):

Man: "You're never ready on time, Mary.
              I'm sure we've missed the bus to town."
Woman: Let's not argue here, Bill. Look. That's Mr Green's car. He's stopping to give us a lift. And there's the bus. We can take our pick now!"

(Testee reads:)

    A.   Mary and Bill have missed the bus to town.

    B.   Mary and Bill are arguing about Mr Green's car.

    C.   Bill is always late because he likes to pick flowers for Mary.

    D.   Mary and Bill can go to town either by bus or in Mr Green's car.

In a few tests the options are spoken instead of being written on the student's test sheet. This method, however, makes it extremely difficult for the testee to make his selection and weigh one option against another since it throws far too heavy a load on memory.

5.6   Understanding talks and lectures

The ability to understand both informal talks and formal lectures is an important skill for students studying subjects in the medium of English at intermediate and advanced levels.

Type 1 Testees listen to a short talk and select the correct answer about the talk.

(Spoken) There's a marked tendency for most developed countries to grow steadily noisier each year. This continually increasing amount of noise is uncomfortable and, what is more important, can affect our health. The noise of machines, heavy traffic and aeroplanes constitutes perhaps the most serious threat to public health. Such noise can interfere with our ability to converse, it can disturb our sleep, and it can quickly make us become nervous wrecks. A loud blast or an explosion may even cause damage to our hearing. But there's another danger – just as great. This is the gradual damage which may be caused if we're continually exposed to noise over several years. Such exposure to noise can undermine our health – as well as our performance and efficiency. Fortunately, technology is progressing at a very rapid rate. Some manufacturers are now designing new silencing mechanisms in their products, and planning experts are even beginning to plan cities according to sound zones.

(Written) Only one of the following statements about the talk you have just heard is correct. Put a circle round the letter opposite the correct statement.

A. Modern technology is now making towns in developing countries free of loud noise.

B. The increase in noise is a problem which cannot yet be solved by modern technology.

C. Gradual noise over a long period may have just as harmful an effect as loud or sudden noise.

D. There is no real solution to the problem of increasing noise in modern life.

Type 2 Like Type 1, this test combines auditory comprehension with reading comprehension. The testees hear a short talk and then read a summary containing blanks. They must then complete the blanks from the talk they have heard. The danger here, however, is that testees could successfully answer the written summary of the talk if only a few of the clues had been heard.

(Spoken) Would you like a robot in your house? It's now generally accepted that in the future robots will take over many of our tasks, especially jobs of a repetitive nature. But it's highly doubtful if robots will ever be able to do any of the more creative types of work – or indeed if people would want them to. In the home, robots would probably be used to do the cleaning, table-laying, scrubbing and washing-up, but it's considered unlikely so far that they'll be used to do the cooking – at least, not in the near future. According to engineers, robots will do nothing more original or sophisticated than they have been programmed to do by human beings. And so robots in the home might not be creative enough to do the cooking, plan the meals, and so on. They would be used as slaves, thereby freeing people to do more of the things they wanted.

In factories, mobile robots would carry out all the distribution and assembly tasks while human beings carried out research and drew up plans for new products. Human beings would still be responsible for diagnosing faults and for repairing and maintaining machinery. On the farm, robots would probably drive tractors; they'd be programmed to keep their eyes on the ground in front to guide the tractor along a straight line or between rows of vegetables.

The robots themselves would probably not look at all like human beings because their design would be chiefly functional. For instance, it would not be at all surprising to find a robot with an eye in the palm of its hand and a brain in one of its feet!

(Written) The following passage is a written summary of the short talk you have just heard. Give the correct word which can be used in place of each number in the following passage.

In future (1) will do many jobs, particularly those which are (2) by nature. It is generally doubted if they could do (3) work and in the home they would probably not do things like (4). Robots will do nothing more (5) than they have been (6) to do by human beings. A robot would be a kind of (7), freeing human beings so that they could do whatever they wanted. Although robots would be used in factories, human beings would probably (8) the machinery. On farms, robots would probably drive (9). The robots would look (10) human beings because they would be (11) in design. It would even be possible for a robot to have an eye in its hand or a (12) in one of its feet.

Type 3 The student hears a short talk or lecture and is required to answer questions on it. Unless the student is allowed to take notes on the talk, the test may put too heavy a load on the memory factor. In certain instances, in fact, it may be desirable to give the testee some guidance for note-taking. The provision of a list of points on which questions will be asked may improve the test.

The following is an example of a test based on a (fictitious) novelist; the questions that follow relate to the novelist's place of birth, early influences on his childhood, the books he read at school, his first publications, his travels, etc. The sheet given to each testee a few minutes *before* the lecture reads as follows:

NOTE PAPER

You are going to hear a talk about Charles Edward Blackwell, a writer of children's books. You are being tested on your ability to listen and understand. After the talk you will be asked 25 questions about Charles Edward Blackwell.

This sheet of paper is for any notes which you wish to take while you are listening to the talk. The notes will not be marked in any way by the examiner.

The questions you will be asked after the talk will be about the points listed below. A space has been left to enable you to write notes for each point.

1. What Blackwell
   enjoys doing.

2. Blackwell's birth.

3. His age at the time
   of the economic
   depression.

4. The books Blackwell
   read

Etc.

The testees may take notes during the lecture. They will later receive the following answer sheet.

INSTRUCTIONS

You have just heard a talk about Charles Edward Blackwell, a writer of children's books. You are being tested on your ability to listen and understand. You now have 15 minutes to answer the questions which follow. The 25 questions follow the order of the talk and you should complete each statement with the best answer. Write 'A', 'B', 'C', or 'D' on the line provided at the side of each question. *DO NOT WRITE OUT THE FULL ANSWER.* Here is an example:

This talk is about   Ex.   C ....
  A. writers of children's books.
  B. children's reading.
  C. Charles Edward Blackwell.
  D. Leeds University.

1.   Blackwell enjoys   1.   ....
  A. writing books for children.
  B. giving lectures for writers.
  C. reading books to children.
  D. talking about himself.

2.   When Blackwell was born, his father was   2.   ....
  A. a cricketer.
  B. an inn-keeper.
  C. a writer.
  D. a factory-worker.

3.   At the time of the great economic   3.   ....
     depression Blackwell was
  A. three years old.
  B. five years old.
  C. twenty-five years old.
  D. thirty years old.

4.   When Blackwell was a boy, he read   4.   ....
  A. books about child geniuses.
  B. Tolstoy's "War and Peace".
  C. stories written for boys of his age.
  D. advice about writing for children.

Etc.

This type of test is generally administered in one of the following ways:
  (i) The testees receive note paper and take notes while they listen to
     the lecture. They are then given the question paper (usually con-
     sisting of multiple-choice items).
or (ii) The testees receive the question paper first and are given a few
     minutes to glance through it. They then hear the lecture and work
     through the questions. The questions are generally in the form of
     (a) m/c items, or (b) T/F items, or (c) incomplete sentences.
     Completion, however, is not usually to be recommended as the
     testees are faced with the tasks of listening, reading and writing
     simultaneously – an extremely difficult operation for native
     speakers. Even m/c items may cause confusion (especially if not
     carefully spaced out throughout the lecture), since the testee has to
     listen while reading carefully through all the options and making
     his selection. Indeed, if this particular procedure is to be adopted
     at all, it is perhaps best to use T/F type items since this reduces the
     amount of reading and the selection to be made.

or (iii) The testees listen to the lecture and then receive the question paper. They read it through and then listen to the lecture given a second time. Although testees will be listening with a purpose during the second "reading" of the lecture, the criticisms made previously still apply. Moreover, this test does not approximate as closely to a normal lecturing situation as does method (i).

In all cases, it is important that the talks and lectures are read out by the examiner in as spontaneous and natural a manner as possible. This can only be achieved if the examiner prepares adequately beforehand by practising reading aloud. If necessary, full use should be made of the blackboard and any visual aids which would normally be required in the lecture situation. Students will then be tested in handling a wide variety of features of a lexical, structural, rhetorical and conceptual nature.

Such tests unfortunately involve extra-linguistic factors — memory, interest in the topic, etc. Since interest in the information content of the lecture or previous knowledge of the topic may favour a particular group of testees, the talk should be kept as "neutral" as possible in both content and language. The taking of notes minimises the memory factor, but the test itself may then become more a test of note-taking skills.

NOTES
1 Wilga M. Rivers, *Teaching Foreign-Language Skills*, University of Chicago Press, Chapter 6. (Rivers also quotes Lado as indicating, in an article called *Memory Span as a Factor in Second Language Learning*, IRAL III/2, 1965, 154–157, that auditory memory span for foreign language material is less than for native language material, probably on a ratio of nine words to fifteen.)
2 This type of test item has been devised and used in the Davies *English Proficiency Test Battery* (EPTB) (1964).
3 This type of test previously formed part of the Northern Universities Joint Matriculation Board *Test in English (Overseas)*.
4 Such item types have been used in the Cambridge Lower Certificate Examination.
5 Elisabeth Ingram reports that native Americans made up to 10% errors in the ELBA phoneme sub-test as compared with an average of 2% errors made by native British speakers. (*Language Testing Symposium*, O.U.P., 1968, 85.)
6 This item type was devised by Elisabeth Ingram for use in the ELBA test (English Language Battery).
7 This type of item was used by the Northern Universities Joint Matriculation Board *Test in English (Overseas)*, 1968.
8 Elisabeth Ingram constructed this type of item to test intonation in the ELBA Test (English Language Battery).
9 Robert Lado has made use of this technique in his Test of Aural Comprehension.
10 This technique is used in the 'Graded Achievement Tests of English' (GATE) of the American Language Institute, Georgetown University.
11 Used in several tests: e.g. the Ingram ELBA Test (English Language Battery), TOEFL (Test of English as a Foreign Language) and the Michigan Proficiency Test.
12 Used in the Ingram ELBA Test and TOEFL.

6 Oral production tests

6.1 Some difficulties in testing the speaking skills

Testing the ability to speak is a most important aspect of language testing. However, at all stages beyond the elementary levels of mimicry and repetition it is an extremely difficult skill to test, as it is far too complex a skill to permit any reliable analysis to be made for the purpose of objective testing. Questions relating to the criteria for measuring the speaking skills and to the weighting given to such components as correct pronunciation remain largely unanswered. It is possible for a person to produce practically all the correct sounds but still be unable to communicate his ideas appropriately and effectively. On the other hand, a person can make numerous errors in both phonology and syntax and yet succeed in expressing himself fairly clearly. Furthermore, success in communication often depends as much on the listener as on the speaker; a particular listener may have a better ability to decode the foreign speaker's message or may share a common nexus of ideas with him, thereby making communication simpler. Two native speakers will not always, therefore, experience the same degree of difficulty in understanding the foreign speaker.

In many tests of oral production it is neither possible nor desirable to separate the speaking skills from the listening skills. Clearly, in normal speech situations the two skills are interdependent. It is impossible to hold any meaningful conversation without understanding what is being said and without making oneself understood at the same time. However, this very interdependence of the speaking and listening skills increases the difficulty of any serious attempt to analyse precisely what is being tested at any one time. Moreover, since the spoken language is transient, it is impossible without a tape-recorder to apply such procedures as in the marking of compositions, where examiners are able to check back and make an assessment at leisure. The examiner of an oral production test is working under great pressure all the time, making subjective judgements as quickly as he can. Even though samples of speech can be recorded during a test, the tape-recording, by itself, is inadequate to provide an accurate means of reassessing or checking a score, since it cannot recapture the full context of the actual situation, all of which is so essential to any assessment of the communication that takes place.

Yet another (though not insuperable) difficulty in oral testing is that of administration. It is frequently impossible to test large numbers of students because of the limited time involved. It is not difficult to appreciate the huge problems relating to a test situation in which thousands of students have to be examined by a handful of examiners, each student being tested for a period of, say, 10 or 15 minutes. Although the use of language laboratories, for such tests, has made it possible in some cases to administer more reliable oral production tests to large numbers of students, the actual scoring of the tests has not been so easily solved.

Excluding tests of reading aloud and one or two other similar tests, oral tests can have an excellent backwash effect on the teaching that takes place prior to the tests. For example, in one country the oral test was retained as part of a school leaving examination simply to ensure that at least some English would be spoken in the last two years of the secondary school – even though the test itself was considered an unreliable measuring instrument as a result of the large number of unqualified examiners who had to administer it. For this reason, and indeed, because oral communication is generally rated so highly in language learning, the testing of oral production usually forms an important part of many language testing programmes.

The following sections in this chapter will give an idea of the range of possible types of oral tests. Some of the exercises (e.g. picture description) have proved very useful in many tests while others (e.g. pencil-and-paper tests) have met with varying degrees of success. In spite of its high subjectivity, an extremely good test is the oral interview. In many cases, one or two sub-tests (or oral exercises) are used together with the oral interview to form a comprehensive test of oral production skills.

6.2 Reading aloud

Many present-day oral tests include a test of reading aloud in which the student is given a short time to glance through an extract before being required to read it aloud. The ability to read aloud belongs to formal speech situations,[1] differing greatly from the ability to converse with another person in a flexible, informal way. Although reading aloud may have a certain usefulness, only a few newsreaders and teachers may ever require training and testing in this particular skill. The majority of students will never be called on to read aloud when they have left school. It is a pity, therefore, that students are required to sacrifice their enjoyment of silent reading in order to practise reading aloud. We read primarily for information or enjoyment and the silent reading skills so necessary for this purpose differ greatly from those of reading aloud. The backwash effects of this kind of test may be very harmful, especially in areas where the reading skills are misguidedly practised through reading aloud. Finally, how many native speakers can read aloud without making any errors?

People read and converse in different ways, using different intonation patterns. Certain hesitation features and occurrences of grammatical re-patterning are peculiar to impromptu speech.

Tests involving reading aloud are generally used when it is desired to assess pronunciation as distinct from the total speaking skills.[2] A suitable passage from one of the set literary texts, a simplified reader or any other appropriate book is given to the testee to read. The testee usually has a few minutes in which to study the text before being required to read it aloud in front of the examiner(s). The reading text should not be given as an unseen passage to the testees; nor should the examiner attempt to assess the whole reading. It is much better if the assessment is limited to a few specific points so that the examiner knows exactly what he is assessing. In addition to the marks allotted to specific features, a mark is frequently given for ease and fluency.

The examiner's copy of a reading test might appear as follows:

A me*r*chant and a farmer were	/ə:/
*wa*lking one day along a country *r*oad	/ɔ:/ and /r/
toge*th*er. The merchant thought the farmer	/ð/
was a fool, so he planned to *pl*ay	weak form and /pl/
a *tr*ick on him.	/k/ and tonic
"Le*t's* play a *game*," he said.	/ts/ and tonic
"*I'll* tell you a strange story.	contracted form /ail/
If you don't believe it, you must	intonation
give me ten pie*ces* of silver. Then	/siz/
you tell a story. If I don't	stress
bel*ie*ve it, I'll give *you* ten pieces	/i:/ and stress
of silver."	
"*V*ery well," the farmer said. "But	v
it's rather a silly game, *isn't it?*"	falling intonation
"Do you remember the *cow* you *sold me?*"	tonic and rising
the merchant began.	intonation
"Yes," said the farme*r*. "*A fine* animal."	/ə/ and stress
"It *died* before I got home," the merchant	main stress
sai*d*.	final consonant

In order to construct suitable tests of reading aloud, it is helpful to imagine actual situations in real life in which the testees may be required to read aloud. Perhaps one of the most common tasks is that of reading aloud directions or instructions to a friend, colleague or fellow-worker: e.g. how to wire a plug, how to trace faults in a car engine, how to cook certain dishes. For example, the following instructions relate to a situation in which a teacher or class monitor may be asked to read aloud:

> First put the headset on. Make sure it is in its most comfortable position with the headband over the centre of the head. The microphone should be about 1½ inches from the mouth.

> To record, put the white switch to the position marked *Work*. Put the red switch to *Speak* and press the red recording button, which will now light up.
> Etc.

Another situation which might occur in real life is that in which the student is asked to read aloud (part of) a letter he has received. For all the different extracts, however, it is advisable to draw up certain features which must be included in each passage: e.g. one Yes/No question, one WH-question, two sentences each containing a subordinate clause, one question tag, the phoneme contrasts i:-i, p-b, ɔ-ɔ: etc. In this way, some degree of consistency can be achieved.

A test more useful in many ways than reading aloud is the re-telling of a short story or incident. In this type of examination, the student is required to re-tell a story he has just read. If carefully constructed, such a method can assess most of the phonological elements which are otherwise tested by reading aloud. Unfortunately, it often measures other skills such as reading comprehension, memory and organisation, too.

6.3   Oral drills

The kinds of drills that can be used to help measure oral production range widely from purely repetitive drills to sentence transformation and construction drills. Repetition is useful for testing phoneme discrimination, stress and intonation, while structure and situation drills are obviously of more use for assessing how well a student can use a certain structure.

(A) Repetition

The student is simply required to repeat words, phrases and sentences which he hears (usually on tape).

Type 1 (Pronunciation)
(a) rag, rug; play, pray; lake, like; wiper, viper; medal, metal; wonder, wander; lock, log; burst, first; here, hair; leaf, leave.

or

rag, play, lake, wonder, rug, first, leave, medal, wiper, lock, pray, viper, metal, hair, leaf, burst, log, like, wander, here.

(b) R*u*b the r*e*d p*a*n with this s*a*ndpaper.
*P*lease *p*ass the *b*oy some *b*read and *b*utter.
The *c*ustomer *p*arked his *f*ast *c*ar in fr*o*nt of the h*u*t.

Type 2 Stress and intonation
(a) When did Tom arrive?
Please switch the television off.
What time was it when I saw you?
If there are going to be a lot of people at the party, I won't go.
What do you think he'll say when I tell him that I can't help him?
(The sentences gradually increase in length but a few shorter sentences are interspersed at various points. The testee is advised to concentrate on the total meaning conveyed by the sentence rather than on individual words and phrases.)

This type of test differs from tests of reading aloud in so far as the material is spoken – not written. To this extent, it is a test of auditory discrimination as well as of oral production: the testee must be able both to hear and to produce the correct sounds.

(B) Structure drills

Structure drills are useful devices for inclusion in class progress tests, ensuring some revision of the various structures learnt. Structure drills fall into two main divisions: mechanical and natural drills. The tester gives the student two or three examples of the patterns he wishes to elicit and then gives several stimuli. In the following drills only the examples are given, the student's responses being denoted by the use of brackets.

Mechanical drills

Type 1 Transformation of sentences: positive to negative, statements to questions, present tense to past tense, adjectives to adverbs, etc.

(a) positive to negative
 I went to the cinema last night.
 (I didn't go to the cinema last night.)
 I fell asleep at the party last night.
 (I didn't fall asleep at the party last night.)

(b) adjectives to adverbs
 He's a very careless driver.
 (He drives very carelessly.)
 He's a very good worker.
 (He works very well.)

Type 2 Addition
 Mr White didn't let Paul go to the cinema.
 —play football
 (Mr White didn't let Paul go to the cinema
 but he let him play football.)

 She wouldn't allow Peggy to turn on the radio.
 —watch television
 (She wouldn't allow Peggy to turn on the radio
 but she allowed her to watch television.)

Type 3 Combination
 We played chess. Then we went out.
 (After we'd played chess, we went out.)

 Tom began to read a book. Then he fell asleep.
 (After Tom had begun to read a book, he fell asleep.)

Type 4 Substitution drills
 It is often possible to construct substitution drills which make several changes in the sentence necessary.

 We're going to read a book tomorrow.

−next week
(We're going to read a book next week.)
−I
(I'm going to read a book next week.)
−buy
(I'm going to buy a book next week.)

All the possible changes which the student may be required to make should be shown in the examples. Thus, in Type 2, if the use of the infinitive (with or without *to*) after verbs like *let, make, allow, cause* is being tested, models of both *let/make* + infinitive and *allow/cause* + *to* + infinitive should be given to the student before he begins the test.

Natural drills

Natural drills are to be preferred to mechanical ones because they approximate far more closely to a brief but natural conversational exchange and thus provide a minimum context which acts as a guide to the intonation and stress patterns to be used. Because the previous types of drills are so artificial and mechanical, there is little guide to the intonation and stress patterns that may be required.

Such tags as *What about you?*, *And you?*, *Do you?* often offer a simple way of transforming a mechanical drill into a more natural one. (Note that the student's responses are shown in brackets.)

He's a very careless driver. What about you?
(I drive very carelessly, too.)

Natural drills may take any of the following forms:

Type 1 Question followed by a statement
Will it be necessary to explain everything to the police?
(Yes, you'll have to explain everything.)
Will it be necessary to arrive very early at the concert?
(Yes, you'll have to arrive very early.)

Type 2 Statement followed by a question
John's going to Japan in August.
(Didn't he go there last month?)
Tom's having a week's holiday in June.
(Didn't he have one last month?)

Type 3 Statement followed by a statement
Your hair's very thin.
(Yes, I wish it was thick.)
Dick'll be very late.
(Yes, I wish he'd be early.)

For purposes of sentence combination drills, the stimulus can be given by two voices.

A. Is there a shelf?
B. Yes, you can put your books there.
   (Is this the shelf where I can put my books?)

A. Is there a cupboard?
B. Yes, you can put your music there.
   (Is this the cupboard where I can put my music?)

Earlier in this section, it was pointed out that natural drills usually provide a good guide for the intonation patterns to be used. Here is an example of a drill where stress and intonation play a very important part.

Don't worry. It won't get lost.
(But I *am* worried about it getting lost.)

Don't worry. I shan't be late.
(But I *am* worried about you being late.)

(C) Situational drills

Type 1 The testees are given a series of situations and are required to construct sentences on the lines of a certain pattern or group of patterns.[3] Again, it is essential that two or three models be given to the student so that he knows exactly what is required. (The student reads or hears the situation and then makes the appropriate responses, shown in the brackets.)

Examples: Mrs Green lives in a flat. She doesn't like living in a flat and would like to live in a small house with a garden. (She wishes she lived in a small house with a garden.)

It's raining heavily. Tom and Ann are waiting impatiently at home to set off on their picnic. (They wish it would stop raining.)

1. Mr Black has a small car but his neighbours all have large cars. He would like a large car, too.
2. Ann hasn't learnt how to swim yet but most of her friends can swim.
3. Tom is waiting for Bill outside the cinema. The show is just about to start but Bill has not arrived yet.
4. Mrs Robinson doesn't like living in towns; she wants to live in the country.

Etc.

Type 2 This type of test item is similar to the previous type but not as strictly controlled.[4] No model responses are given by the examiner and the student is free to use whatever patterns he wishes.

A friend of yours has forgotten where he has put his glasses. He cannot see too well without them. What will you say to him?
(Let me help you to look for them. Etc.)

You are on your way to school when it starts to rain heavily.

Unfortunately, you and your friend have no raincoats. There is nowhere to shelter but your school is only a hundred yards away. What do you say to your friend?
(Shall we make a dash for it?/Let's run the rest of the way.)

1. You are trying to get to the public library but you are lost. Ask a policeman the way.
2. Your friend has just returned from a holiday abroad. What do you say to him?
3. A waitress has just brought you the bill but has totalled it up incorrectly. What do you say to her?
4. A friend of yours wants to see a film about a murder. You have already arranged to see it another evening, but you know he would be hurt if he knew. Make up an excuse.

Type 3 The student hears a stimulus to which he must respond in any appropriate way.[4] (This test often relies on conventional greetings, apologies, acceptable ways of expressing polite disagreement, etc.)

Do you mind if I use your pencil for a moment?
(Not at all/Certainly/Please do/Go ahead, etc.)

What about a game of tennis?
(Yes, I'd love a game/All right. I don't mind/
Don't you think it's a bit too hot?, etc.)

1. Please don't go to a lot of trouble on my behalf.
2. Oh dear, it's raining again. I hope it stops soon.
3. We shan't be late, shall we?
4. Betty asked me to say she's sorry she can't come tonight.

6.4   Using pictures for assessing oral production

Pictures, maps and diagrams can be used in oral production tests in similar ways to those described in the previous chapter on testing the auditory skills. Pictures of single objects can be used for testing the production of significant phoneme contrasts while a picture of a scene or an incident can be used for examining the total oral skills. This section will concentrate on the use of pictures for description and narration after dealing briefly with the use of pictures to elicit certain structures.

By serving as stimuli for oral responses, pictures provide a realistic context for the structural pattern being tested. A real situation is simulated by relating a brief conversational exchange to a picture: two people (the tester and the testee) simply comment on scenes or actions depicted in a series of pictures.[5] Each picture provides the student with the necessary clue or stimulus either to respond to the examiner or to initiate the conversational exchange. E.g.

After providing a few examples, the examiner asks: *How long did Mr Binns stay?* to which the testee should respond: *He stayed until he'd mended the car.*

    2. How long did Mr Green stay?
       (He stayed until he'd marked the books.)
    3. How long did I stay?
       (You stayed until you'd written a letter.)
    4. How long did Ann stay?
       (She stayed until she'd watered the flowers.)

More common in school and public examinations, however, is the use of pictures for descriptive and narrative purposes. The student is given a picture to study for a few minutes; he is then required to describe the picture in a given time (e.g. often two or three minutes). Generally, the number of words he speaks is counted by one examiner in the room, while the other examiner counts the number of errors made. The score is thus obtained on the basis of the number of words spoken and the errors made (though this procedure is very unreliable). Separate scores for general fluency, grammar, vocabulary, phonology, and accuracy of description/ narration are more reliable. Advertisements, posters and strip cartoons may be used in this way for class tests, provided that there are enough available to prevent the students from preparing one or two set pieces. It is this problem of test security which, in fact, prevents a number of testing organisations from using pictures in tests of oral production.

Careful selection of the pictures used for the examination will help in controlling the basic vocabulary required and may, to some extent, determine the type of sentence structure that predominates. Different styles and registers can be tested by including maps and diagrams as well as pictures for comparison, pictures for instructions and pictures for description and narration. If the pictures depict a story or sequence of events, it is useful to give the testee one or two sentences as a "starter", thereby familiarising him with the tense sequencing he should employ.

Examiner: Last summer Tony spent a few days at his uncle's house in the country. When it was time for him to return home, his uncle took him to the station. Tony had made a lot of friends and he felt sad on leaving them. He got on the train and waved goodbye to them. . . . Now you continue to tell this story.

The most effective type of oral examination using pictures consists not only of narration or picture description on the part of the testee but also of a discussion about the picture(s) concerned. If the examiner asks questions and discusses the picture(s) with the student, the formal speech situation is combined with the reciprocal speech situation and two

different types of oral production skills can thus be measured. Even if no discussion is included in the examination, the examiner would be well advised to prompt the testee whenever he appears to need encouragement. It is always important to find out what the student knows — not what he doesn't know: long periods of silence will tell the examiner very little.

A similar technique[6] to that described in the previous chapter can be used to test oral production. The student and the examiner have five pictures in front of them, each picture differing in only one respect from the other four pictures. The student is given a card bearing a letter (A, B, C, D, or E); the examiner cannot see the letter. The student is required to describe the appropriate picture (according to the letter). The examiner then selects a picture according to the descriptions, assessing the student not only on the correctness and fluency of his speech but also on the length of time taken before the student's description results in the identification of the appropriate picture. He then checks the card.

6.5   The oral interview

Like many other examinations of oral production, the scoring of the oral
interview is highly subjective and thus sometimes has only low reliability.
In addition, the performance of a student in a particular interview may not
accurately reflect his true ability.

Supporters of the oral interview claim that the examination at least
appears to offer a realistic means of assessing the total oral skill in a
"natural" speech situation. Opponents of the oral interview, however,
argue that the examination nevertheless is artificial and unrealistic:
students are placed not in natural, real-life speech situations but in examination situations. They are thus susceptible to psychological tensions and
also to constraints of style and register necessary in such a situation. For
example, many students adopt a quiet and colourless tone in interviews;
some even develop a guarded attitude, while others become over-friendly.

One solution to this problem is to have the class teacher as the interviewer; if an external examiner is required, he may sit at the back of the
room or in any other obscure place. The interviewer (whether teacher or
examiner) should endeavour to put the student at his ease at the beginning
of the interview, adopting a sympathetic attitude and trying to hold a
genuine conversation (constantly making his own contribution without, at
the same time, talking too much). He should *never* attempt to note down
marks or comments while the student himself is still engaged in the interview. The dual role (i.e. of both language partner and assessor) which the
examiner is required to assume in the oral interview is always a most
difficult one.

The oral interview, then, should be scored only after the student has
left the room (unless two or more examiners are present — in which case
one of them can sit behind the testee and score). Although this settles the
problem of *when* the interview should be scored, the question of *how* it
should be scored still remains. For example, how should the replies to this
question be scored?

> (Tester)   "What are you going to do this weekend?"
> (Testee A)   "I'm quite well, thank you."
> (Testee B)   "I go to fish. I fish in river near the St. John's
>   Church."

A's reply is perfectly correct but it is nevertheless quite meaningless: the
testee simply hasn't heard the question correctly. On the other hand, B's
reply shows a real attempt to answer the question but unfortunately contains several errors.[7]

The scoring of the interview can range from an impression mark to a
mark arrived at on the basis of a fairly detailed marking scheme (showing
accuracy of pronunciation, stress and intonation, grammar, vocabulary,
and fluency and ease of speech). The following marking scheme[8] (using a
6-point scale) is given as just one example of a number of such schemes in
present-day use.

Rating	Ability to Communicate Orally
6.	Excellent: on a par with an educated native speaker. Completely at ease in his use of English on all topics discussed.
5.	Very good: although he cannot be mistaken for a native speaker, he expresses himself quite clearly. He experiences little difficulty in understanding English, and there is no strain at all in communicating with him.
4.	Satisfactory verbal communication causing little difficulty for native speakers. He makes a limited number of errors of grammar, lexis and pronunciation but he is still at ease in communicating on everyday subjects. He may have to correct himself and re-pattern his utterance on occasions, but there is little difficulty in understanding him.
3.	Although verbal communication is usually fairly satisfactory, the native speaker may occasionally experience some difficulty in communicating with him. Repetition, re-phrasing and re-patterning is sometimes necessary; ordinary native speakers might find it difficult to communicate.
2.	Much difficulty experienced by native speakers unaccustomed to "foreign" English. His own understanding is severely limited, but communication on everyday topics is possible. Large number of errors of phonology, grammar and lexis.
1.	Extreme difficulty in communication on any subject. Failure to understand adequately and to make himself understood.

Many examining bodies prefer fairly short descriptions of grades in order to enable the examiner to glance quickly through the marking scheme. When an examiner is faced with a lot of reading in his assessment, he will be tempted to rely solely on the numerical grade itself (e.g. 5) — which makes his scoring extremely subjective and liable to fluctuation. Wherever possible, it is useful in public examinations to have two or more examiners listening for particular areas or features before later pooling their assessments. The importance of examiners' meetings and "practice" interviews (using tape-recorders and marking guides) cannot be too greatly emphasised, Such sessions, when conducted with a large number of examiners, are of considerable help in increasing the marker reliability of oral interviews. Sample recordings and scores are discussed and some degree of standardisation of marking is thus achieved.

Finally, oral interviews do not simply happen spontaneously. Although each oral interview should simulate as natural and realistic a speech situation as possible, it is essential that a certain amount of material be prepared beforehand. The interview may be carefully structured or may be structured quite loosely: in both cases, the examiner should have plenty of material on which to fall back if necessary. He may lead in to the interview by asking a Yes/No question, followed at some stage or other by certain WH-questions and question tags.

There are dangers, however, in adhering to a very rigid structure or plan. For example, a student may develop a certain topic and be proceeding happily in one direction when the examiner interrupts and stops the whole flow of the interview in order to include a *How-often* question. Again, the demand for certain set responses may reach an absurd stage: in a certain oral examination, for example, it was agreed that *Whereabouts...?* ought to signal a different response to *Where...?* Consequently, the more helpful students, who anticipated the interviewer, "failed" on this item:
e.g.

Interviewer:	Whereabouts do you live?
	(Requiring the name of the *district* where the testee lived.)
Student:	341 King's Road, North Point.

Had the testee replied *North Point* in a natural speech situation, the other person would probably have asked: *Where(abouts) in North Point?* In the interview the student merely anticipated such a reaction (consciously or subconsciously) and gave a full answer initially.

Provided that flexibility can be retained, it is useful to prepare a series of questions on a wide range of topics. The following list of 20 topics is given here to help the examiner − not to inhibit him:

family, home, school, sports, hobbies, books, films, transport, weekends, holidays, radio, health, teeth, shopping, traffic, crime, friends, money, fines, careers, etc.

At least ten or twelve questions can be asked on each topic, but the tester should never attempt to "work through" lists of questions. Indeed, he should contribute to the interview from time to time by mentioning his favourite sport or discussing his own experience of dentists, etc. Examples of the types of questions which can be asked on two topics are:

Sports and Games
Do you play any games?
What's your favourite sport?
How often do you play?
Are you in your school team?
Do you like watching sport?
Which do you think is the most interesting sport to watch?
Can you swim?
How did you learn to swim?
Whereabouts do you go swimming?
Which game would you advise me to take up? Why?

Which is the most difficult game to play?
Which is better as an exercise: basketball or football?

Teeth
Are your teeth good?
When did you last visit a dentist?
Do you wait until you get toothache before going?
How often do you clean your teeth?
Why is it necessary to clean them often?
What kinds of food are good for your teeth?
How many teeth have you had extracted?
Do you prefer having your teeth filled or pulled out?
Tell me about your worst visit to the dentist.
Has either of your parents got false teeth?

Where considered necessary, current affairs and highly controversial issues may be introduced in an interview to stimulate or provoke a student, provided that some allowance is made for the emotive content of the discussion. It is even more important here that the examiner should remain flexible and vary his range of questions for discussion.

If the oral interview is recorded on tape, the tester can score the interview at leisure, playing and re-playing whichever sections he wishes. Extensive notes can be taken from the recordings, comparisons made and confirmation sought where there is doubt concerning a particular mark. If interviews are recorded, the tester must of course take care to identify each student at the beginning of the interview, especially when comparisons involving re-winding and re-playing are to be made.

6.6 Some other techniques for oral examining

The short talk
In certain examinations students are required to prepare a short talk on a given topic. They may be allowed several days or only a few minutes in which to prepare the talk and, in some cases, they may be provided with notes or reference material. This is clearly a realistic test of sustained speech but it constitutes an extremely difficult examination for second-language learners at all but the most advanced stages. Indeed, this particular type of examination is generally very difficult for first-language speakers. The examination can be improved slightly by reducing the time allotted for the talk and asking the student questions based on his talk, thus introducing a reciprocal speech situation. The questions might be asked either by the examiner or by a group of students (if the talk is given in front of an audience). In whatever situation the talk is given, however, the examiner must make every attempt to put the student at ease.

Care must be taken to prevent students from learning whole sections of their talk. Subjects about which an individual student knows very little should be avoided. Experience of such examinations has shown that candidates talk better when they have something worthwhile to say and can bring into the talk a genuine interest in the subject coupled with experience and imagination.[9] A co-operative audience also helps greatly.

Vague subjects are best avoided; many topics are best presented as questions:

Should countries spend huge sums of money on space exploration?
Do demonstrations serve any really useful purpose?
Do people ever really learn anything from the mistakes they make?

Group discussion and role playing

Other techniques for examining oral production include group discussion and role playing. Reciprocal speech (i.e. conversational skills as opposed to lecturing skills) is tested in each situation, but the examinations themselves are more appropriate for native speakers than for foreign learners. The little work which has been done on examining oral skills through group discussions has pointed to the importance of having a leader and also of having something to do. The group may be given a simple problem to solve, or plans to make, or even a meal to eat; whatever the task, it will probably be less inhibiting to discussion than the situation in which a group of students simply sit in a circle.

Directed conversation examinations involve role-playing and thus include many extra-linguistic factors. Two or three students are given a situation and then assigned roles: for example, one may be told to act as a policeman, another as a bus-conductor, and the third as a passenger. The passenger is hurrying to catch a bus but the bus is full. He has got on the bus but the conductor tells him to get off. He can see an empty seat and he begins to argue. The students then enact the roles they have been given, using appropriate registers of language, etc.

General conclusions

Generally speaking, a reliable method of obtaining measurements of oral production skills is that which involves the student's class teacher. The tensions and artificialities that inhibit the student in an oral examination conducted by an external examiner will now be avoided since the teacher is a familiar figure and the classroom a realistic part of the student's life. Continuous assessment by the teacher, with all his classroom experience behind him, is generally (but not always) a reliable method of measuring the oral skills. Yet the oral interview (conducted by a sympathetic examiner) is still a useful examination to retain, particularly for its beneficial backwash effects on teaching. A comprehensive and balanced examination of oral production might thus consist of:

(i) an oral interview (accounting for roughly 60% of the total score);
(ii) a short passage for reading aloud (20%); and
(iii) a picture, or series of pictures, for description or narration (20%).

The examiner must frequently consider the effects of his examination on teaching and learning, however, and if, for instance, the reading aloud section is considered harmful in its effect on teaching, then it should be omitted from the examination.

6.7   Pencil-and-paper techniques

The tests listed in this section should be regarded as tests of an awareness of sound/symbol correspondence rather than as tests of pronunciation. Some of these tests are interesting for students and have a limited usefulness for the classroom. They also serve to focus attention on problem areas and may have a good backwash effect on the teaching in the classroom.

Sound identification

Type 1   (a)   In each of the following groups of words, one of the underlined letters (or groups of letters) represents a sound that is different to the sounds in the other words. Put a circle round the letter at the side of the word that contains the different sound.

Example: A. f<u>a</u>ther B. c<u>a</u>lm Ⓒ w<u>a</u>lk D. p<u>a</u>rk E. l<u>au</u>gh

1. A. w<u>ai</u>t B. l<u>a</u>te C. p<u>ai</u>d D. s<u>ai</u>d E. r<u>a</u>dio
2. A. <u>th</u>is B. <u>th</u>em C. <u>th</u>ose D. <u>th</u>ese E. <u>th</u>ink
3. A. b<u>ou</u>ght B. <u>au</u>tumn C. h<u>o</u>ld D. w<u>a</u>ter E. <u>a</u>lways
4. A. m<u>a</u>t B. f<u>a</u>st C. p<u>a</u>tch D. f<u>a</u>t E. m<u>a</u>tter

(b)   One of the words in List B contains the same sound as that shown by the underlined letter(s) in the word given in List A. Write the word containing the same sound in each space on the right.

(A)	(B)				
1. h<u>air</u>	d<u>ear</u>	w<u>ear</u>	h<u>ere</u>	oth<u>er</u>	. . . .
2. <u>ou</u>r	l<u>ow</u>er	col<u>ou</u>r	fl<u>ow</u>er	p<u>our</u>	. . . .
3. fe<u>rry</u>	ma<u>rry</u>	Ma<u>ry</u>	fai<u>ry</u>	me<u>rry</u>	. . . .
4. <u>o</u>we	g<u>o</u>t	h<u>o</u>ld	b<u>oy</u>	p<u>oi</u>nt	. . . .

Type 2   (a)   If the word in capital letters rhymes with one of the words that follow it, write that word in the space on the right. If none of the words rhymes with the word in capital letters, put a cross (X) in the space.

Examples: PEAR clear we're fair   . . fair . .
           BITE weight fit seat   . . . X . . .

1. NECK	leg	rake	beak	. . . .
2. PAIN	lane	when	van	. . . .
3. RICE	flies	wise	nice	. . . .
4. BIRD	heard	red	bid	. . . .

(b)   In most of the following groups, one word does not rhyme with the other 3 words. Write the letter of the word in the space; if all 4 words rhyme, write X.

Examples: A. harm B. warm C. calm D. farm   B . . . . .
           A. freeze B. he's C. teas D. fees   X . . . . .

1. A. eight B. late C. wait D. gate   . . . .
2. A. measure B. leisure C. fresher D. pleasure   . . . .
3. A. bird B. heard C. word D. stared   . . . .
4. A. buys B. ice C. flies D. prize   . . . .

Type 3 If the word ends in a D sound, write D. E.g. opened D
If the word ends in a T sound, write T. E.g. washed T
If the word ends in an ID sound, write ID. E.g. painted ID

1. packed   . . . .   4. asked   . . . .
2. finished . . . .   5. listened   . . . .
3. shouted . . . .   6. collected . . . .

Stress[10]

Put a circle round the letter which is under the syllable carrying the main stress.
Example: ad mi ra tion
         A B Ⓒ D

(a) At word level

1. com par i son   3. in vis i ble
   A   B C D   A B C D

2. rev o lu tion   4. e lec tri cal
   A B C D   A B   C D

(b) At phrase level

1. Look out for it
   A   B C D

2. the sit ting room
   A   B   C   D

3. nine teen eight y four
   A   B   C   D E

(c) At sentence level

1. I said you'd help us, but Ann said you wouldn't
                          A   B   C
   help.
   D

2. It isn't your umbrella – I believe it's my
                            A   B   C
   umbrella.
   D

3. I simply love strawberries — don't you?
   A   B   C   D

4. I thought he was the murderer — somehow I had a
   A   B   C   D

suspicion all along.

It is difficult to test intonation features accurately using such techniques, however, since intonation patterns vary so greatly according to contexts, attitudes, emotions, etc. A slightly improved version of the previous test can be seen in the following item, in which the testee reads an utterance followed by a brief description of the situation in which it occurs. This in turn is followed by three possible responses spoken by another person. The testee has to indicate which of the three responses is the most appropriate.

"My leg hurts. What shall I do, sir?"
The speaker has come out of school and was about to walk home. However, he has just hurt his ankle.
The teacher says:

A. "You'd *better* get a bus home."
B. "You'd better get a *bus* home."
C. "You'd better get a bus *home*."

NOTES

1 Andrew Wilkinson makes this distinction between the formal speech situation (FSS) and the reciprocal speech situation (RSS) in his paper "The Testing of Oracy" in *Language Testing Symposium*, ed. Davies, O.U.P., 1968, p. 117–119.

2 The item type illustrated on page 85 has been used in the McCallien Tests of Oral English, devised by Mrs C. McCallien for the West African Schools Examinations Council to examine spoken English for the School Certificate. The tests are described by Peter Strevens in his article 'The Development of an Oral English Test for West Africa', in *English Language Teaching*, Vol XV, No. 1., 1960.

3 Some excellent drills of this type are contained in Robert O'Neill's *English in Situations*, O.U.P., 1970.

4 This type of question has been used effectively in the ARELS Oral Examination (Association of Recognised English Language Schools).

5 For further examples of this type of drill, see *Practice through Pictures: Drills in English Sentence Patterns*, (J. B. Heaton) Longman, 1971.

6 This technique is derived from a similar one used by A. S. Palmer and described in the article "Testing Communication" in *IRAL* (*International Review of Applied Linguistics in Language Teaching*), Issue X/1, February 1972.

7 George Perren made this point in his article 'Testing Spoken Language: Some Unsolved Problems' in *Language Testing Symposium* (ed. Alan Davies), O.U.P., 112.

8 Based on the marking scheme devised by Dr Frank Chaplen for use in assessing the oral skills of overseas students at British universities. (The scheme is, itself, derived from the American Foreign Service Institute rating scale.)

9 C.S.E. Trial Examinations – Oral English (Examinations Bulletin No. 11, Secondary School Examinations Council, H.M.S.O. London, 1966.)

10 Robert Lado first described such testing techniques in *Language Testing*, 113–116.

7 Testing reading comprehension

7.1 The nature of the reading skills

By emphasising the oral/aural skills, the modern audio-lingual approaches in general tended initially to neglect the reading skills. Furthermore, it is true to say that since so many language courses are limited to the elementary and early intermediate stages of language learning, efficient reading skills have been pushed into the background. Attempts at dealing with the many complex reading skills frequently come too late at the tertiary level (i.e. at university, technical college, college of education) when the student suddenly finds himself confronted with professional and technical literature in the foreign language.

In spite of the wide range of reading material specially written or adapted for English language learning purposes, there is as yet no comprehensive systematic programme which has been constructed from a detailed analysis of the skills required for efficient reading.[1] Most exercise material is still limited to short reading extracts on which are based general "comprehension" questions. Since one of the chief concerns of the constructor of any test must always be to define the precise nature of what he is measuring, it would seem that here is a positive contribution which testing can make to the development of the reading skills. As with listening comprehension, reading comprehension test material is very closely related to the type of practice material used by the teacher to develop the reading skills. Few language teachers would argue against the importance of reading: what is so urgently required is a knowledge of the actual processes involved in reading and the production of appropriate exercise material to assist in the mastery of these processes.

Before reading tests in the second or foreign language can be successfully constructed, the first language reading skills of the testees must be ascertained. Clearly there is often little purpose in testing in the second language those basic reading skills which the student has not yet developed in his own language. However, the mere fact that a student has mastered some of the required reading skills in the first language is no guarantee at all that he will be able to transfer those skills to reading another language.

At this stage in our examination of reading difficulties, it would be helpful to attempt to identify some of the specific skills involved in reading. Broadly speaking, these can be defined as the ability to:

(i)   distinguish between letters and recognise letter-sound relation-
      ships (rather than letter-name relationships) e.g. pan/fan/man/
      pen/fat/map;

(ii) recognise words and word groups, requiring an ability to associate
      sounds with their corresponding graphic symbols and understand
      meanings: e.g. /kau/cow, /kɔf/cough, /θru:/through, /'θʌrə/
      thorough, /kɑ:nt/can't

(iii) understand the meaning of words and word groups in the context
      in which they appear. (This also includes an ability to use context
      clues to determine the meaning of a particular word.) E.g. *One of
      the members of the group* exposed *the plot and it did not take
      long for the police to arrest the leaders;*

(iv) recognise structural clues and comprehend structural patterns:
      e.g. *I wish Ann had come. (= Ann did not come – hence my
      wish*);

(v)   comprehend the plain meaning of a sentence or any complete
      sequence of words: e.g. *The man ate the fish/The fish was eaten
      by the man/The fish ate the man*;

(vi) perceive relationships (temporal and spatial) and sequences of
      ideas (as denoted by linkage and reference features): e.g. *Al-
      though it was raining heavily, everyone in Class 5B went on the
      picnic and they enjoyed themselves tremendously. On the other
      hand, few out of 5A went and those who did were miserable
      without their companions*;

(vii) comprehend paragraphs and longer units of prose and select the
      main idea and other salient features;

(viii) draw conclusions, make inferences and "read between the lines"

(ix) scan and read for specific information;

(x)   read critically, quickly and with ease, adopting a flexible
      approach and varying the reading strategies being applied accord-
      ing to the type of reading material used.

No mention has been made here of reading aloud, since this particular skill
is unique in that it involves different skills from silent reading.

Two different kinds of complementary reading activities to which
students are usually exposed are generally classified as *intensive* and *extensive* reading. Short reading extracts of a moderate degree of difficulty and
containing features which merit detailed study form a basis for intensive
reading practice. Whole articles, chapters and books (usually simplified
readers) are used for extensive reading practice; in this case, however, the
material selected is generally slightly below the language attainment level of
the students using it. Unfortunately, most reading tests concentrate on intensive reading to the exclusion of extensive reading, probably because it is
more economical to have a large number of items based on a short reading
extract than a few items based on a much longer one. However, these are
insufficient grounds for neglecting to test extensive reading at certain
levels.

7.2   Initial stages of reading: matching tests

The tests described in the first half of this section are concerned purely with word and sentence recognition. They test the student's ability to discriminate visually between words which are spelt in fairly similar ways. If used in exercise material and progress tests, these test items will develop word recognition speed. Though not administered as speed tests in the strict sense in the very early stages, word and sentence matching items should be covered by the student as quickly as possible. Once a student has gained familiarity and confidence with this type of test, his performance should be timed so that he is forced to read under some pressure. At first, it is advisable to confine the words used in the items to those already encountered orally; later a number of words not encountered orally should be introduced.

1. Word matching

The student is required to draw a line under the word which is the same as the word on the left.

now	bow/not/how/<u>now</u>/mow
sheep	shop/shape/sleep/heap/<u>sheep</u>
ever	never/over/<u>ever</u>/fewer/even
top	top/stop/tap/pot/ton
wonder	wander/wonder/window/fonder/won
has gone	is gone/has won/has gone/his game/had gone
clothes	cloth/clothing/cloths/clots/clothes
most pleasant	most pleasant/more pleasant/most present/not pleasant/most peasants

2. Sentence matching

This item is similar to the word-matching item. The testee is required to recognise as quickly as possible sentences which consist of the same words in the same order. He reads a sentence, followed by four similar sentences, only one of which is exactly the same as the previous one.

(1) Tom is not going to your school.
   A. Tom is not going to your pool.
   B. Tom is going to your school.
   C. Tom is not coming to your school.
   D. Tom is not going to your school.

(2) The thief can hide in the jungle.
   A. The thief can die in the jungle.
   B. The thieves can hide in the jungle.
   C. The thief can be hidden in the jungle.
   D. The thief can hide in the jungle.

3. Pictures and sentence matching

In the remainder of this section the items will concentrate on word and sentence comprehension, using pictures to test this skill.

Type (a) This type of item is similar to that used to test listening comprehension and described on Page 67. The testee looks at four pictures and then reads a sentence about one of the pictures. He is required to identify the correct picture.

They are cycling to work.

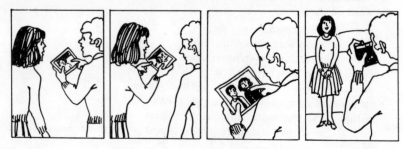

He is showing her the photograph.

Type (b) This type is similar to the previous one but is much more economical in that only one picture is required for each item (instead of four). The testee looks at a picture and reads four sentences, only one of which is about the picture. He then has to select the correct sentence.

A. Ann is throwing the ball to Peter.
B. Peter is kicking the ball to Ann.
C. Peter is throwing the ball to Ann.
D. Ann is kicking the ball to Peter.

A. The boy under the tree is reading his book.
B. The boy resting under the tree is looking at his book.
C. The boy with the book is sleeping under the tree.
D. The boy carrying the book is going to sit down under the tree.

Type (c) Although this item type is referred to here as a matching item, it could equally well take the form of a true/false item (in which the student writes T or F at the side of each sentence according to whether or not the sentence agrees with the contents of the picture). In this particular instance, the testee has to select the (four) sentences which match the picture.

Four of the following sentences agree with the picture. Put a circle round the letter of each of the four sentences.

A. The dog on the floor is asleep.
B. The baby is playing with the dog.
C. The baby has just broken a toy car.
D. The television set is on fire.
E. The dog is in front of the baby.
F. The woman has taken the flowers out of the bowl.
G. One of the two boys is helping the woman.
H. The woman is going to pick up a book.
I. The two boys are listening to the radio.
J. The radio is on the table but the book is on the floor under the table.

7.3   True/False reading tests

The true/false test is one of the most widely used tests of reading comprehension. Not only is the scoring of such a test straightforward and quick,
but the scores obtained by the testees can be very reliable indices of
reading comprehension provided that the items, themselves, are well-
constructed and that there are enough of them. True/false tests are of
considerable use for inclusion in class progress tests chiefly because, unlike
multiple-choice test items, they can be constructed easily and quickly,
allowing the teacher more time for his many other tasks.

The true/false test, however, has two main disadvantages: firstly, it can
encourage guessing, since testees have a 50% chance of giving a correct
answer for each item. Secondly, as the base score is 50% (and thus the
average test difficulty generally in the region of 75%) the test may fail to
discriminate widely enough among the testees unless there are a lot of
items.

It is, of course, possible to penalise the testee for guessing, and instructions on the lines of the following may be included in the rubric:

> "Each correct answer will be awarded two marks. However, for each
> wrong answer, one mark will be deducted from your score. It is better,
> therefore, not to guess blindly and to leave a blank if you do not know
> the correct answer."

Such penalties, however, are of dubious value and the whole subject of
guessing is treated in greater detail in Chapter 10.

In addition to the ease and speed with which the items can be constructed, the great merit of the true/false reading test lies in the ease with which
suitable test passages can be selected: a short reading extract, for example,
can provide a basis for numerous items. Moreover, the true/false test can
be used as a valuable teaching device with which the students' attention is
directed to the salient points in the extract by means of the true/false
items.

If the student's comprehension of the true/false reading extract (and
not the true/false items) is being tested, each of the true/false items should
be as clear and concise as possible. In such cases, it is essential that the
problem posed by each item is fully understood. In many true/false reading tests some indication of the number of correct and incorrect statements is given to the testees. Although this may make the test slightly
easier for the student, it does at least present him with a clear statement of
the problem.

True/false reading tests fall into two general categories: (a) those which
are independent of a reading text and (b) those which depend on a text.

Type (a) It is possible to construct true/false items which are complete in
themselves: the testee's comprehension of each true/false item is tested by
means of a series of general truths.

E.g. Put a circle round the letter T if the statement is true. If it is not true, put a circle round the letter F.

1. The sun rises in the west.	T	F
2. Fish can't fly, but birds can.	T	F
3. Lagos is as large as London.	T	F
4. When ice melts, it turns into water.	T	F

Type (b) The construction of true/false items based on a reading extract forms one of the most widely used types of reading tests. It is often used at elementary levels of reading comprehension, but it can be used equally effectively at more advanced levels. The following example illustrates its use at a fairly advanced level:[2]

Eye-gazing and eye-avoidance have meanings and patterns of profound significance. Gazing at others' eyes generally signals a request for information and perhaps affection, but embarrassment can result from too long a mutual gaze. In fact, in intimate situations, there seems to be an equilibrium involving proximity, eye contact, intimacy of topic, and smiling. If one component is changed, the others tend to change in the opposite direction.

But the extended gaze seems to have a function much deeper than that of maintaining a balance or ensuring a smooth flow of conversation. It signals, not surprisingly, an intensification of relationship, not necessarily along amorous lines. It may be a threat, or a challenge for dominance.

A definite pecking order of dominance and submission emerges from the very first eye contact of strangers. Curiously, when conversation is possible, it turns out that the one who looks away first tends to be dominant. The averted eye is a signal that its owner is about to take the floor. When conversation is not possible, however, the first to look away will be the submissive one.

Abnormal use of eye contact or aversion may well indicate an abnormal personality. Adult schizophrenics tend to use their eyes at all the wrong points in a conversation, and the bold liar can hold a steady gaze far longer than his truthful colleague when both are caught in the same misdemeanour.

According to the passage, six of the following statements are true and six are false. Put a tick ☑ in the box after each true statement and a cross ☒ in the box after each false statement.

1. Looking at someone else's eyes or looking away from them means a person is thinking very deeply. ☐

2. We generally look towards another person's eyes when we want information from that person or even a sign of affection. ☐

3. If two people look too long at each other's eyes, they will usually become embarrassed. ☐

4. When engaged in very friendly conversation, a couple will probably look less at each other's eyes the more they smile and the closer they sit.   ☐

5. Looking for a long time towards the other person's eyes is only a means of continuing a conversation smoothly.   ☐

6. When two people gaze for a long time at each other's eyes, it is a sign that they are going to argue.   ☐

7. An extended gaze can signal a threat or a bid for authority over the other person.   ☐

8. When two strangers meet, they use their eyes to control or influence the other or to show their surrender to the other's authority.   ☐

9. When it is possible to talk, the first person who looks away is the one who submits to the other person.   ☐

10. A person shows that he wants to talk by looking towards the other person's eyes.   ☐

11. Abnormal people usually turn their eyes away from the other person's eyes more often than normal people do.   ☐

12. It is possible to tell the difference between a liar and an honest man by their eye-gazing patterns when both are trying to tell a lie.   ☐

The reading text in the preceding example contained language at a higher difficulty level than that used in the true/false items. It is possible (though not common practice), however, to construct a relatively simple text followed by more difficult true/false items: in such cases, the comprehension problems will be contained in the true/false items rather than in the text itself.

7.4   Multiple-choice items (1): short texts

Type 1 It can be argued that the type of item in this section is in many ways a test of vocabulary rather than of reading comprehension. These particular items, however, have been included here because it is felt that a comprehension of the text is generally of at least as much importance as an understanding of the meaning of the words for selection. This, of course, is true of any vocabulary item presented in context: however, here the emphasis is more on the correct understanding of the context. The following three examples show the use of this item type at elementary, intermediate and advanced levels respectively.

1. The eyes are wonderful teachers – even musicians, who deal with sound, learn as much by (doing, playing, watching, practising) as by listening.

2. The housewife who could not afford to buy clothes would spend hours at her spinning wheel, spinning her wool into yarn – a job which took little skill but required a lot of (ability, patience, talent, wisdom) and was done by the fireside during the long winter evenings.

3. Two-thirds of the country's (fuel, endeavour, industry, energy) comes from imported oil, while the remaining one-third comes from coal. Moreover, soon the country will have its first nuclear power station.

Type 2 Just as the previous item type is closely related to the testing of vocabulary, so this type is perhaps more accurately described as a test of comprehension of grammatical structure. The testees are required to identify the correct paraphrase of a statement from a choice of four or five. The testees are told in the rubric that the (four) statements may refer to the entire sentence or only part of the sentence. Again, examples are provided for each of the three general levels.

(1) John is not as tall as Miss Green but he's a little taller than Bill.
    A. Miss Green is taller than John and Bill.
    B. John is not as tall as Bill.
    C. Miss Green is taller than John but not as tall as Bill.
    D. Bill is taller than John and Miss Green.

(2) In spite of the loud music, I soon managed to fall asleep.
    A. The loud music soon helped me to fall asleep.
    B. I soon fell asleep as a result of the loud music.
    C. The loud music made me unable to fall asleep soon.
    D. I soon fell asleep even though the music was loud.

(3) If you'd forgotten to put out your hand, you wouldn't have passed your driving test.
    A. You didn't forget to put out your hand and you passed your driving test.
    B. You forgot to put out your hand and you failed your driving test.
    C. You forgot to put out your hand but you passed your driving test.
    D. You didn't forget to put out your hand but you didn't pass your driving test.

Type 3 This item type consists of a very short reading extract of only a few sentences (or sometimes of only one sentence). The testees are required to answer only one comprehension test item on each reading passage. The actual construction of multiple-choice reading comprehension items based on a reading extract will be treated in greater detail in the next section. Meanwhile, here are two examples of the use of multiple-choice items for testing reading comprehension, the first being at a fairly elementary level and the second at a more advanced level.

(1) The president was talking to a young woman in the crowd when Bill suddenly caught sight of a man standing several yards behind her. The man had something in his hand: it was a short stick.

What made Bill notice the man in the crowd?
A.   He was very close to Bill.
B.   The president was talking to him.
C.   He was standing in front of the woman.
D.   He was carrying a stick.

(2) There were only two ways of moving along the narrow ledge: face outwards or face to the wall. I concluded that even the smallest of bottoms would push a person with his back to the wall far enough out to overbalance him and so, with arms outstretched in the shape of a cross and with chin pointed in the direction I was heading, I inched my way along.

The writer managed to cross the narrow ledge by
A.   crawling along on his knees with his arms stretched out in front of him.
B.   moving sideways inch by inch with his back to the wall.
C.   working his way forward on his stomach with his face almost touching the ledge.
D.   walking slowly with his face and stomach close to the wall.

7.5   Multiple-choice items (2): longer texts

The multiple-choice test offers a useful way of testing reading comprehension. However, not all multiple-choice reading tests are necessarily good tests of reading comprehension. As was clearly indicated in the first two chapters, the extent to which a test is successful in measuring what it sets out to measure depends largely on the effectiveness of each of the items used. Indeed, certain general aspects of many reading tests may be suspect. For instance, does the usual brief extract for reading comprehension concentrate too much on developing only those skills required for intensive reading, encouraging frequent regressions and a word-by-word approach to reading?

The sampling of the reading passage is of the utmost importance and must be related to the broader aims of the language teaching situation. Many of the texts in both school and public examinations concentrate too much on a literary kind of English. If certain students are learning English in order to read technical journals, for example, then the sampling of the reading extract should reflect this aim. Ideally, in a test of proficiency the text should contain the type of reading task which will be demanded of the testees in later real-life situations. If the test is a class progress or achievement test, the reading passage should be similar to the type of reading material with which the student has been confronted in his work at school. In other words, if other subjects are being taught in the medium of English (as in many second language situations), the text should frequently (though not *always*) reflect the type of reading the student is required to do in history or chemistry, etc.

In this section, it is assumed that only intensive reading skills are being tested. Thus, the length of the reading extract recommended might vary from 50 to 100 words at the elementary level, 200 to 300 words at the intermediate level, and 400 to 600 words at the advanced level. These figures are, of course, extremely rough guides and may not be appropriate for many reading situations. Moreover, the extract selected should be capable of providing the basis for a sufficient number of multiple-choice comprehension items. It is not an easy task to find an extract which will support a number of multiple-choice items — even though the same extract may form a basis for a large number of true/false items or open-ended questions. Generally speaking, passages dealing with a series of events, a collection of facts, or different opinions and attitudes make the best types of texts for testing purposes; those dealing with a single idea or main theme are rarely suitable.

The length of the extract should also be related to its level of difficulty: a particularly difficult or complex passage would probably be considerably shorter than a more straightforward one. On the whole, the difficulty level of the text, however, should coincide with the level of the students' proficiency in English, but we must remember that the reading matter used outside the test situation (e.g. simplified readers) should be selected for enjoyment and should thus be at a slightly lower level than the actual standard of the reading skills acquired. (The difficulty level of a text depends chiefly on the degree of the structural and lexical complexity of the language used.)

When writing test items based on a reading text, the tester should attempt to construct more items than the number actually required. After the construction of the items, it is useful to secure the services of one or two colleagues so that all the items can be moderated. Invariably this process brings to the attention of the item writer certain flaws in some of the items. Although a number of the flaws will be easily rectified, in certain cases it will be necessary to dispense with entire items. In tests of grammar and vocabulary, new items can always be constructed in place of the discarded items, but this does not follow with reading comprehension items. The text, itself, has to be rewritten, certain sections added and others deleted in order to obtain the required number of items. Such processes are difficult and time-consuming: thus, it is always an advantage to construct in the first instance more items than are actually required. If the text will not allow for more items, another, more suitable text should be chosen to avoid wasting time at a later stage.

How many multiple-choice items should be set on one text? Clearly, the number of items will depend on the length and complexity of the text. However, tests of reading comprehension generally contain fewer items than other skill tests. Furthermore, the testee requires much more time to work through a reading comprehension test since he first has to read the text carefully once or twice before he can begin to answer the items based on it. While as little as ten or fifteen seconds for each item can be allowed in multiple-choice tests of grammar and vocabulary, at least one or two minutes must be allowed for each item in the average reading test (if the time required to read the text is taken into account). Consequently, such tests, though long in terms of time, must of necessity be short in terms of items and, therefore, less reliable.

The construction of items depending simply on a matching of words and phrases should be avoided. Items should test more than a superficial understanding of the text and should require the testee to digest and interpret what he has read. The following examples show how ineffective such items can be if testees are simply required to match the words in the items with the words in the text.

At four o'clock on September 30th two men armed with iron bars attacked a soldier in Green Street.

What happened at four o'clock on September 30th?
A.   Two men armed with iron bars attacked a soldier, etc.

Imagine that the testee did not understand much of the sentence in the text. In order to appreciate this fully, it is necessary to change the situation slightly: the text might appear to us like this:

At four o'clock on September 30th two neminsi deraden with rinot babblers tacklened a derisoldt.

What happened at four o'clock on September 30th?
A.   Two neminsi deraden with rinot babblers tacklened a derisoldt.
Etc.

A slightly better item stem would be:

What happened one afternoon at the end of September?

However, to be completely satisfactory, it would be necessary to re-write both the text and the item, as in the following example:

Tom was surprised when he met Ann at the party. He was under the impression she had gone away from the locality. The last time he saw her was when Bob was teaching her to drive. A few days afterwards she had suddenly become ill.

(first version)

Tom was surprised when
A.   Ann went away.

   B.   he met Ann at the party.
   C.   Bob was teaching Ann to drive.
   D.   Ann suddenly became ill.

(second version)

Tom did not expect to see Ann because
A.   he knew she was at the party.
B.   he thought she had left the district.
C.   he had seen Bob teaching her to drive.
D.   he had heard she was ill.

There is often a temptation to concentrate too much on facts, figures and dates when constructing test items based on a factual text. Generally speaking, figures and dates are included in a text chiefly for the purpose of illustration or to show the application of a general principle. It is useful in such cases to construct items which require the testee to use the figures in the text to state (or re-state) the general principle behind them.

E.g. From January to December last year, 291 people were killed and 6,248 were injured in road accidents on the city's roads. 157 of all the fatal accidents involved motor-cyclists or their pillion passengers, while 95 involved pedestrians and the remaining 39 the drivers and passengers of motor vehicles.

Over half of all the people killed in road accidents last year were
A.   motor-cyclists and pillion passengers.
B.   pedestrians.
C.   drivers of buses, cars and lorries.
D.   both pedestrians and motorists.

Testees can also be encouraged to use the figures they are given in a text and to work out simple arithmetical sums and problems. Clearly, there is a limit to the tasks which the testee may be required to perform: otherwise the test writer will find himself testing something other than language skills. The following is an example of an item which tests the student's ability to handle simple facts and figures in English: the stem presents a useful task *provided that this kind of reading exercise is not overdone.*

Latest reports from the north-east provinces state that at least sixteen people lost their lives in Saturday's floods. A further nine people, mostly children, are reported missing, believed dead. Seven small boys, however, had a miraculous escape when they were swept onto the branches of some tall trees.

The total number of people reported dead or missing as a result of Saturday's floods is
A. 7   B. 9   C. 16   D. 25   E. 32

The choice of the correct option in each multiple-choice item must depend on the testee's comprehension of the reading text rather than on his general knowledge or intelligence. The following item, for example, can be answered without any knowledge of the text on which it has been based.

Memorising is easier when the material to be learnt is
A. in a foreign language.
B. already partly known.
C. unfamiliar but easy.
D. of no special interest.

Care must be taken to avoid setting distractors which may be true, even though they may not have been explicitly stated by the writer. In the following test item based on a reading text about the United Nations Organisation and the dangers of war, C is the required answer; however, all four options are true − even though not stated in so many words by the writer.

What would happen if there was a global war?
A. Nations would train men for war.
B. Lots of terrible weapons would be made.
C. The whole human race would be completely destroyed.
D. People would grow very desperate.

The correct option must be roughly the same length as the distractors. In the following test item the correct option has been modified to such a degree that it appears as the obvious answer without even necessitating any reference to the text.

The curriculum at the new college is a good one in many ways because it
A. includes many science courses.
B. offers a well-balanced programme in both the humanities and the sciences.
C. is realistic.
D. consists of useful technical subjects.

All the options must be grammatically correct: there is a tendency especially in reading comprehension to overlook the grammatical appropriateness of some of the distractors used. Option D in the following item can be ruled out immediately because it is ungrammatical.

The writer says that he had studied engineering for
A. a long time.
B. only a very short period.
C. several years.
D. never.

Double negatives are only confusing and such items as the following (based on the extract on Page 114) are best avoided:

Tom did not expect to see Ann because
A. he did not know she was at the party.

　　B.　no one knew she had left the district.
　　C.　he hadn't seen Bob teaching her to drive.
　　D.　he didn't realise she was well.

A useful device in multiple-choice tests of reading comprehension is the option ALL OF THESE or NONE OF THESE: e.g.

　　According to the passage, what do some people think there should be outside a modern city?
　　A.　Buses
　　B.　Car parks
　　C.　Office buildings
　　D.　Taxis
　　E.　ALL OF THESE

If an option like E is used, it is advisable to have it as the correct answer in at least one of the items. The testee should not be encouraged to think that it has been included simply to make up the required number of options.

The following text and comprehension items[3] illustrate some of the guidelines laid down in this section:

　　Study the following passage and then answer the questions set on it.

　　"The Captive" is a strange but sincere and tender film, as indeed one would expect from a director of the calibre of Marcel Lyme. In addition to his keen sensitivity, Lyme has a strong feeling for historical atmosphere, so apparent in his earlier film "Under the Shadow of the Guillotine", in which the events of the French Revolution are depicted with surprising realism and vitality. In "The Captive" Lyme manages to evoke the atmosphere of an English town in the early part of the nineteenth century, not so much through the more obvious devices of stage-coaches, old inns, and thatched cottages as through minute attention to details of speech, dress, customs, and mannerisms. Similar in theme to "Adam Brown", "The Captive" is distinguished by a sincerity which the former lacks and which helps to transform this film from an ordinary adventure story into a memorable and a very moving tragedy. Especially unforgettable is the farewell scene at Plymouth, when Jonathan Robson sees Catherine Winsome on his way to the grim, squalid ship which is waiting to take him to Australia. Robson breaks loose from his captors for a fleeting moment to bid farewell to Catherine. "I'll prove my innocence," he cries vehemently as he shakes his fist at Catherine's cousin.

　　As the ship sets sail, one enters a grotesque nightmare world in which evil seems triumphant. Our identification with Robson becomes so personal that we feel every stroke of the flogging after he has been caught stealing medicine for his sick companion. We share his sympathy for Joe Biggs as the old sailor is hauled under the ship's keel. Indeed, events might well have become unbearable but for the light relief provided by the comical antics of Bobo, the small cabin boy who skips about uncomplainingly doing whatever task he is given. We know, of course, that ultimately evil will be vanquished, and so we are given strength to endure the adversities which confront the hero. The mutiny and the consequent escape of Jonathan Robson, therefore, come as no surprise.

Questions:
(a) For each of the following statements choose the word or phrase that best completes the statement according to the information contained in the passage. Write the number of the question and the answer you have chosen in your answer book.

(i) "The Captive" was directed by
    Jonathan Brown.
    Adam Brown.
    Marcel Lyme.
    Catherine Winsome.

(ii) In "The Captive" Marcel Lyme conveys the atmosphere of the nineteenth century chiefly through
    close attention to small details.
    the use of conventional scenery.
    stage-coaches, old inns, and thatched cottages.
    depicting dramatic events of the time.

(iii) The passage implies that "Adam Brown" was
    a very moving film.
    a realistic and vital film.
    an ordinary adventure film.
    a sincere film.

(iv) Jonathan Robson is angry as a result of
    having to wait to go to Australia.
    being wrongly convicted.
    meeting Catherine.
    being recaptured.

(v) On the voyage to Australia Robson
    becomes ill.
    begins to have nightmares.
    is hauled under the ship's keel.
    receives a flogging.

(vi) Bobo is introduced into the story to help us to bear the grim events by
    behaving in a strange but interesting way.
    making us laugh.
    doing everything without complaining.
    acting kindly towards the hero.

  (vii) We can endure the hero's sufferings because we know
          things cannot get worse.
          the crew will mutiny.
          good will win in the end.
          the hero is very brave.

 (viii) The writer's attitude to this film is
          appreciative.
          patronising.
          scornful.
          critical.

(b) Each of the following words and phrases can be used to replace one
    word in the passage. Find the words and write them in your answer
    book. Number your answers.

    (i)   dragged
    (ii) conquered
    (iii) troubles and misfortunes
    (iv) very brief
    (v)   finally

7.6 Completion items

Completion items measure recall rather than recognition. Although such
items are supply-type items and thus similar in many ways to open-ended
questions in tests of reading comprehension, they are often regarded as
belonging more to the objective category of test items. There is very little
difference, however, between the following open-ended reading comprehension question:

Why was the author surprised to meet Dr Short?

and the equivalent completion item:

The author was surprised to meet Dr Short because
. . . .

Usually, completion items require the testee to supply a word or a short
phrase. Unless great care is taken to ensure that there is only one correct
answer, the marking will prove very difficult when the tester is confronted
with a variety of answers ranging from acceptable to unacceptable. All
valid interpretations, whether or not these were in the test writer's mind at
the time of the construction of the test, must be regarded as correct.

Types of completion items for testing reading comprehension are
divided into two groups for ease of treatment: type 1 consisting of blanks
for completion in the items following the text, and type 2 consisting of
blanks in the text itself.

Type 1 Unless well constructed, this type of completion test can become merely a matching exercise in which the words and phrases required in the completion are determined after a process of matching the whole item with the appropriate part of the text. However, less emphasis is placed on the writing skills in such a test than in a test consisting of open-ended questions. The following example illustrates how a short informal letter can be used to provide the basis for completion-type items.

> 256 Weeton Road,
> 2nd Floor,
> Hong Kong.
>
> 7th June, 1974.

Dear David,

    I am very sorry that I could not meet you last night. I hope that you did not wait too long outside the New York Theatre. I had to look after my small brother until my mother returned home. She was a long time at the doctor's and she arrived home very late. I ran all the way to the bus-stop, but I had already missed the bus. I decided to get on a tram and I arrived at the New York Theatre at eight o'clock. I did not think that you would still be there because I was three-quarters of an hour late. I do hope that you will forgive me.

> Your friend,
> Peter

Write one word or more in each blank.

(1) Peter lives at . . . .
(2) He wrote the letter on. . . . .
(3) Peter could not leave home because he had to wait for . . . .
. . . . to return.
(4) His mother had been to the . . . .
(5) Peter went to the New York Theatre by . . . .
(6) He thought that David. . . . .
(7) The word . . . . means
excuse.
(8) Peter had arranged to meet David at . . . . seven on June
. . . .

Type 2
(1) In this item type the testee is required to complete the blank spaces in a reading text. The blanks have been substituted for what the test writer considers are the most significant content words. Consequently, a possible weakness of such a test may result from the failure to supply adequate guidelines to the testee; the following is an example of a poor item because the framework is insufficient to guide the testee. The linguistic clues are thus inadequate and the testee is faced with the task of having to guess what was in the examiner's mind.

When we (1) . . . . something along the (2) . . . ., it will cause (3) . . . .

The following text illustrates how blanks should be interspersed; the testee's degree of success in completing the blanks depends almost entirely on his comprehension of the whole text.

When we slide something along the floor, it will cause (1) . . . . If something is very (2) . . . ., there will be a lot of friction between it and the ground. However, friction is (3) . . . . when something rolls instead of (4) . . . . The invention of the (5) . . . . was really an attempt to reduce friction. Unless there is snow or ice, it is much harder to pull something on a (6) . . . . than in a cart. Ball-bearings are used a lot in machinery to (7) . . . . friction. It is friction which causes (8) . . . . to machinery as the various parts (9) . . . . against one another. Friction is reduced if we put oil onto the (10) . . . . It should not be forgotten, however, that (11) . . . . is also useful to us: it is necessary, for instance, for car wheels to grip the (12) . . . .

(2) In some tests certain letters of missing words are given. In these cases, the testee is generally informed that each dash in the blank signifies a letter. e.g.:

The mighty Amazon f———s into the Atlantic near the Equator: its es————y is about 170 miles wide. The w——th—— is often so misty that the b———s of the river cannot be seen from a ship, even if it is p—s———g quite close to them.

In one widely used test of English proficiency[4] only the initial letter of the missing word is given. e.g.

Unlike the Arctic c . . . ., the Antarctic c . . . . no land animals at all. It has also very few p . . . . of any kind. However, there is an infinite n . . . . of f . . . . and b . . . . along the whole c . . . . of the Antarctic.

(3) A variation of this type of reading comprehension may incorporate the multiple-choice technique. e.g.

Astrology is the ancient (1) . . . . of telling what will (2) . . . . in the future by studying the (3) . . . . of the stars and planets. (4) . . . . astrologers thought that the stars and planets influenced the (5) . . . . of men, they claimed they could tell (6) . . . .

(1)	system	business	magic	study	art
(2)	coincide	happen	chance	come	foretell
(3)	places	shapes	times	positions	light
(4)	However	Because	Although	For	While
(5)	affairs	matters	businesses	chances	times
(6)	horoscopes	futures	advice	fortunes	luck

7.7   Cloze procedure

Although similar in appearance to completion items, cloze tests should not be confused with simple blank-filling tests. Whereas in ordinary completion tests the words for deletion are selected subjectively (consisting largely of structural words in certain tests and key content words in other tests), in cloze tests the words are deleted systematically. Thus, once the actual text has been chosen, the construction of a cloze test is quite objective: every *n*th word is deleted by the test writer. Certain test writers argue that the blank substituted for the deleted word should correspond to the length of the missing word but in many cloze tests all the blanks are of uniform length. Unless a photostat copy of the actual printed text is being used (in which case small pieces of white paper are glued over the words for deletion during the photo-copying process), it is simpler to insert blanks of uniform length.

The interval at which words are deleted is usually between every 5th and every 10th word. However, if every 7th word has been deleted in the first few sentences, then every 7th word must be deleted for the rest of the text. The 5th, 6th, and 7th words are the most widely favoured for deletion in cloze tests.

The cloze test, which was originally intended to measure reading difficulty, has been applied to first language testing of reading comprehension for some time now. Only recently, however, have constructors of foreign-language tests started using the cloze procedure. The principle is based on the Gestalt theory of "closure" (closing gaps in patterns subconsciously) and thus cloze tests measure the reader's ability to decode "interrupted" or "mutilated" messages by making the most acceptable substitutions from all the contextual clues available.

The length of the text, itself, is generally about the same as that of texts used for multiple-choice reading items. However, it is important to have a reasonable number of deletions and most cloze tests favour around forty or fifty blanks. The more blanks contained in a text, the more reliable the test will prove.

There are two methods of scoring a cloze test: one mark may be awarded for each *acceptable* answer or else one mark may be awarded for each *exact* answer. Both methods have been found reliable: some argue that the former method is very little better than the latter and does not really justify the additional work entailed in defining what constitutes an acceptable answer for each item. Nevertheless, it appears a fairer test for the student if any reasonable equivalent is accepted. In addition, no student should be penalised for mis-spellings unless a word is so badly spelt that it cannot be understood.

Where possible, the testee should be required to fill in each blank in the text itself, since this procedure approximates more closely to the real-life tasks involved than any method which requires the testee to write the deleted items on a separate answer sheet or list. If the text chosen for a cloze test contains too many facts or if it concerns a particular subject, it may favour a certain part of the test population to such a degree that some students may be able to make the required completions from their background knowledge without understanding much of the text. Consequently, it is essential in cloze tests (as in other types of reading tests) to draw upon a subject which is neutral in both content and language variety used. Finally, it is always advantageous to provide a "lead-in": thus no deletions should be made in the first few sentences so that the testee has a chance to become familiar with the author's style and approach to the subject of the text.

Instructions for students engaged on cloze tests should make certain that they fully understand the problem which is being tested. They should be advised to read quickly through the text in order to become familiar with the general meaning before completing each blank.

The following examples are somewhat shorter than most normal cloze tests: nevertheless, they should suffice to show how the cloze procedure can be applied to the testing of reading comprehension at both the elementary and the more advanced levels.

Example 1 (Elementary)

Once upon a time a farmer had three sons. The farmer was rich and had many fields, but his sons were lazy. When the farmer was dying, he called his three sons to him. "I have left you . . . . which will make you . . . ." he told them. "But . . . . must dig in all . . . . fields to find the . . . . where the treasure is . . . ."

After the old man . . . . died, the three sons . . . . out into the fields . . . . began to dig. "I'll . . . . the first to find . . . . place where the treasure . . . . buried," cried the eldest . . . . "That's the field where . . . . father put the treasure," . . . . another son. The three . . . . dug all the fields . . . . several years, but they . . . . no treasure. However, many . . . . grew in the fields . . . . the sons had dug. . . . . . vegetables made them very . . . .

Example 2 (Advanced)

It is estimated that in the last two thousand years the world has lost more than a hundred species of animals. A similar number of species of birds has also become extinct. The real significance of . . . . figures, however, lies in . . . . fact that almost three-quarters . . . . all the losses occurred . . . . the past hundred years . . . . as a direct result . . . . man's activities on this . . . . It is essential for . . . . whole process of evolution . . . . the extinction of certain . . . . should occur over a . . . . of time. But extinction . . . . occur by nature's design . . . . not as a result . . . . the activities of man . . . . is by no means . . . . to the preservation of . . . . species of animal and . . . . life. Conservation means the . . . . of a healthy environment . . . . a whole. If conservation . . . . . . ignored, then within a . . . . short time our water . . . . will be found inadequate,

.... seas and rivers will .... fewer fish, our land .... produce fewer crops, and ... : ... air we breathe will .... poisonous. It
becomes only .... matter of time before .... health deteriorates
and before ...., together with every other .... thing, disappears
from the .... of the earth.

7.8 Cursory reading

The title of this section serves as a general term to denote the skills
involved in reading quickly, skimming and scanning. The term *skimming* is
used to denote the method of glancing through a text in order to become
familiar with the gist of the content; *scanning* refers to the skills used when
reading in order to locate specific information.

In tests of reading speed the student is generally given a limited time in
which to read the text. Care must be taken to avoid constructing questions
on the less relevant points in the text, but the testee should be expected to
be familiar with the successive stages in which the text is developed. The
actual reading speed considered necessary will be largely determined by
the type of text being read and will vary according to the purpose for
which it is being read. It is sufficient to note here that poor readers (native
speakers) generally read below 200 words per minute; a speed of between
200 and 300 words per minute is considered to be an average speed;[5] and
300 to 500 words is considered fast. On the whole, it is realistic to expect
no more than a reading speed of 300 words from many advanced learners
of a second language. Most people tend moreover to read at a slower rate
under test conditions or in any situation in which they are required to
answer questions on a text.

In tests of skimming, the rubrics generally instruct the student to glance
through the text and to note the broad gist of the contents. The student is
then given a small number of questions concerning only the major points
and general outline of the text. Sometimes at the end of the skimming he
is allowed a few minutes to jot down any notes he wishes to make, but he
is *not* usually allowed to refer back to the text. If the student is allowed to
retain the text, the time for answering the various questions on it will be
limited in order to discourage him from referring back too often to the
text.

In scanning tests, the questions are given to the student before he begins
to read the text, thus directing him to read the text for specific information. In such cases, it is helpful to set simple open-ended questions (e.g.
"What is the writer's view of modern transportation?") rather than
multiple-choice items. The latter type of item tends only to confuse the
student since he then finds it necessary to keep in mind four or five options
for each item while he is reading.

Such tests as those described briefly in this section are few, but more
work should be done on the examination and construction of such tests
for classroom use at advanced levels since the skills being tested here are

important in many fields, particularly in higher education. Tests of speed reading, however, should be administered only when students have been adequately prepared for the tasks involved in such tests. It is grossly unfair to test those reading strategies which have never previously been practised.

NOTES

1   Such simplified reading material as the *New Method Simplified Readers*, (Longman), *Longman Structural Readers, Stories Told and Retold* (O.U.P.), offer excellent practice in wide reading, but do not attempt to break down the reading skills in order to give practice in particular areas. The S.R.A. Reading Laboratories (Science Research Associates, Inc., Chicago) at present come closest to providing a systematic reading development programme.
2   The text is slightly adapted from an article by Anthony Tucker appearing in the Guardian, September 5th, 1969.
3   This comprehension test was constructed by the author for the Hong Kong English School Certificate Examination (Education Department, Hong Kong), 1968.
4   The test referred to is the *Davies English Proficiency Test Battery* (Form A, 1964). In this test, however, the missing words are chiefly structural words.
5   Manya and Eric de Leeuw quote an average initial speed of 230–250 w.p.m. for native speakers of English. (*Read Better, Read Faster*, Penguin, 1965, p. 28–29.)

8 Testing the writing skills

8.1 Testing composition writing

It is useful at the outset to distinguish between the terms *composition* and *essay*. The writing of a composition is a task which involves the student in manipulating words in grammatically correct sentences and in linking those sentences to form a piece of continuous writing which successfully communicates the writer's thoughts and ideas on a certain topic. Moreover, since in real-life situations there is generally a specific purpose for any writing, composition writing frequently takes the form of letters, reports, extracts from diaries, etc. Essay writing, on the other hand, involves far more than the production of grammatically correct sentences: it demands creativity and originality, since it is generally intended not only to inform but also to entertain. Essays on such topics as *Clouds, The Importance of Being Last* and *The Countryside at Night* are written to sparkle and impress, and good essayists are as rare as good poets.

Since no examiner would ever dream of requiring a poet to sit down and compose a poem in half an hour under examination conditions, why should he expect anyone – least of all the learner of English as a foreign language – to sit down and write an original essay in this time? Indeed, few essayists would wish to be assessed on the first draft of their essay: the final product is usually the result of many hours of revision and re-writing. Therefore, while it is reasonable to expect the learner to write accurate English for a meaningful purpose, it is generally neither reasonable nor realistic to demand creativity and originality in the form of an essay.

An attempt should be made to determine the type of writing tasks with which the student is confronted every day. Such tasks will probably be associated with the writing requirements imposed by the other subjects being studied at school if the medium of instruction is English. Short articles, instructions and accounts of experiments will probably form the main body of writing. If the medium of instruction is not English, the student's written work will often take the form of consolidation or extension of the work done in the classroom. In both cases, the student may be required to keep a diary, produce a magazine and to write both formal and informal letters. The concern of students following a profession or in business will be chiefly with report-writing and letter-writing, while at college or university level the student will usually be required to write (technical) reports and papers.

In the construction of class tests, it is important for the test writer to find out how composition is tested in the first language. Although the emphasis in the teaching and testing of the skills in English will of necessity be quite different to the development of the skills in the first language, a comparison of the abilities acquired and methods used is very helpful. It is clearly ludicrous, for instance, to expect in a foreign language those skills which the student does not possess in his own language.

In the past, test writers have been too ambitious and unrealistic in their expectations of testees' performances in composition writing: hence the constant complaint that relatively few foreign learners of English attain a satisfactory level in English composition. Furthermore, the backwash effect of examinations involving composition writing has been unfortunate: teachers have too often anticipated examination requirements by beginning free composition work far too early in the course. They have "progressed" from controlled composition to free composition too early before the basic writing skills have been acquired.

However, once the student is ready to write free compositions on carefully chosen realistic topics, then composition writing can be a useful testing tool. It provides the testee with an opportunity to demonstrate his ability to organise language material, using his own words and ideas, and to *communicate*. In this way, composition tests provide a degree of motivation which many objective-type tests fail to provide.

In the composition test the student should be presented with a clearly defined problem which motivates him to write. The writing task should be such that it ensures he has something to say and a purpose for saying it. He should also have an audience in mind when he writes. How often in real-life situations does a person begin to write when he has nothing to write, no purpose in writing and no audience in mind? Thus, whenever possible, meaningful situations should be given in composition tests. For example, a brief description of a real-life situation might be given when requiring the student to write a letter.

E.g. Your pen-friend is going to visit your country for a few weeks with his two brothers. Your house is big enough for him to stay with you but there is not enough room for his brothers. There are two hotels near your house but they are very expensive. The third hotel is cheaper, but it is at least five miles away. Write a letter to your pen-friend, explaining the situation.

Composition titles which give the testee no guidance as to what is expected of him should be avoided. Examples of poor titles which fail to direct the student's ideas are *A pleasant evening, My best friend, Look before you leap, A good film which I have recently seen*.

Two or more short compositions usually provide more reliable guides to writing ability than a single composition, enabling the testing of different registers and varieties of language (e.g. a brief, formal report). If the composition test is intended primarily for assessment purposes, it is advisable not to allow for any choice of composition items to be answered. Examination scripts written on the same topic give the marker a common basis for comparison and evaluation. Furthermore, no time will be wasted by the testees in deciding which composition items to answer. If, on the other hand, the composition test forms part of a class progress test and actual assessment is thus of secondary importance, a choice of topics will cater for the interests of each student.

8.2 Situational composition

In addition to providing the necessary stimulus and information required for writing, a situational composition determines the register and style to be used in the writing task by presenting the student with a specific situation and context in which to write. Since it is easier to compare different performances when the writing task is determined more exactly, it is possible to obtain a greater degree of reliability in the scoring of situational compositions. Furthermore, tests of situational composition have an excellent backwash effect on the teaching and learning preparatory to the examination.

The difficulty in constructing situational compositions arises in the writing of the rubrics. On the one hand, if the description of the situation on which the composition is to be based is too long, then the text becomes more of a reading comprehension test and there will be no common basis for evaluation. On the other hand, however, sufficient information must be conveyed by the rubric in order to provide a realistic, helpful basis for the composition. It is important, therefore, that exactly the right amount of context be provided in simple language written in a concise and lucid manner. The following rubric, for example, can be simplified considerably:

> You have been directed by your superior to compose a letter to a potential client to ascertain whether he might contemplate entering an undertaking that would conceivably be of mutual benefit . . .

The following are provided as examples of situational compositions intended to be used in tests of writing:

(1) Read the following letter carefully.

176 Wood Lane,
London, N.W.2.

15th May, 1974.

Dear Mr Johnson,
I wish to complain about the noise which has come from your home late every night this week. While I realise that you must practise your

trumpet some time, I feel you ought to do it at a more suitable time. Ten o'clock in the evening is rather late to start playing. Even if you could play well, the noise would still be unbearable at that time.

I hope that in future you will be a little more considerate of the feelings of others.

Yours sincerely,
W. Robinson

Now write a reply to this letter. You do not play the trumpet but on two or three occasions recently you have played some trumpet music on your record-player. You did not play the record very loudly — certainly not as loudly as Mr Robinson's television. You want to tell him this but you do not want to become enemies so you must be reasonably polite in your letter.

Care must be taken in the construction of letter-writing tasks to limit the amount of information to which the student must reply. If this is not done, scoring can become extremely difficult.

(2) A dialogue can be very useful in providing a basis for composition work. In such a writing task, the student must demonstrate his ability to change a written text from one register to another, as in the following example:

Read the following conversation carefully.

Mr Black: What was the weather like while you were camping?
Bill: Not too bad. It rained for a few days towards the end of our holiday, but mostly it was fine. We weren't able to visit the Gorge Waterfalls on the next to the last day, but . . .
Mr Black: What a pity!
Bill: Well, apart from that we did everything we wanted to — walking, climbing and just sitting in the sun. We even managed a visit to Hook Cave.
Mr Black: How on earth did you get that far?
Bill: We cycled. We also went to the beach several times.
Mr Black: Did you take your bikes with you?
Bill: No, we borrowed some from a place in the village.
Mr Black: Whereabouts in fact were you?
Bill: Oh, in a lovely valley — covered with woods and about twenty miles from the sea. Just north of Hilson.
Mr Black: I remember one time when I went camping. We forgot to take a tin-opener!
Bill: That's nothing. A goat came into our tent in the middle of the night — it ate all the food we had with us!
Mr Black: Well, you seem to have had a good time.

Now write an account of Bill's holiday, using the conversation above as a guide. Imagine other things which happened to him during the camping holiday.

(3) Tables containing information are also useful for situational composition since they can generally be read by the testee without much difficulty. Moreover, as only a short written text is used, the student is thus not encouraged to reproduce part of the rubric for use in his composition.

> Imagine that a local newspaper has asked you to write an article of approximately 250 words about the information in the following table. Write down the conclusions you draw from the figures about the various ways in which people spent their holidays in 1970 as compared with 1950. Attempt to explain the reasons for these differences.

	1950	1970
Travelling abroad	4	17
Going to seaside	38	31
Camping	8	31
Visiting friends/relatives in another town	11	10
Going to another town (but *not* to visit friends/relatives)	16	3
Staying at home	23	8
TOTAL	100	100

(4) Information conveyed in the form of a simple graph or histogram may also provide a suitable stimulus for writing. Such writing tasks of this nature, however, are suitable only for the more advanced student.

Use the chart together with the information in the table below it to give a brief survey of the causes of accidents on Link Road between 1962 and 1972.

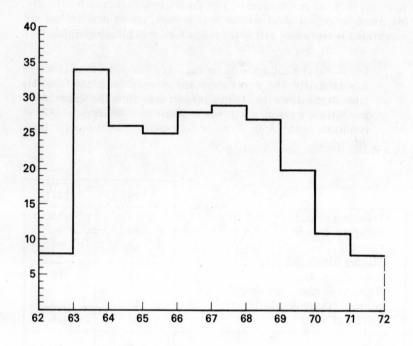

1962–63 Road not in great use
1963–64 Nearby road closed: road now in great use
1964–65 Bus stop moved 100 yards
1965–68 No changes
1968–69 Sign: *Beware animals*
1969–70 No parking signs
1970–71 Sign: No right turn
1971–72 Double white line: *no overtaking*

(5) The stimulus for a situational composition may even take the form of notes.

Use the following notes to write an account of an accident for a newspaper. You should write about 250 words.

Cyclist about to turn right.
Not put hand out.
Lorry behind slows down.

Sports car behind lorry overtakes.
Swerves to avoid boy.
Knocks over old man on pavement.

(6) An excellent device for providing both a purpose and content for writing is the use of pictures. A picture or series of pictures not only provides the testee with the basic material for his composition but stimulates his imaginative powers.

The picture below shows a dangerous junction where accidents often happen. Write a letter to your local newspaper, describing the junction and mentioning some of the dangers and causes of accidents.

Link Road: An Accident "Black Spot"

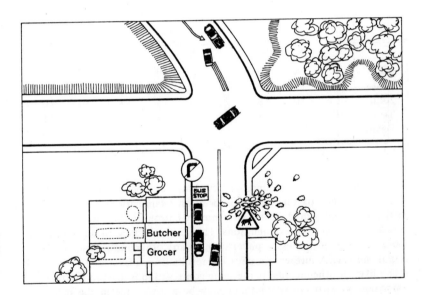

If the stimulus in a situational composition is purely verbal, the testees often tend to reproduce the phrases and sentences contained in it. Pictures and diagrams fortunately avoid this weakness.

8.3 Grading the composition

The chief objection to the inclusion of the composition question as part of any test is generally on grounds of unreliability. Considerable research in the past[1] has shown how extremely unreliable markers are — both in their own inconsistency and in their failure to agree with colleagues on the relative merits of a student's composition.

Markers may award their marks on (i) what the testee has written; (ii) what they believe he meant by what he wrote; (iii) handwriting and general appearance of what the student has written; and (iv) previous knowledge of the student. Moreover, two markers may differ enormously in respect of spread of marks, strictness and rank order. For example, marker A may give a wider range of marks than marker B (i.e. ranging from a low mark to a high mark); marker C may have much higher expectations than marker A and thus mark much more strictly, awarding lower marks to all the compositions he assesses; and finally marker D may place his compositions in a different order of merit. An example of these differences can be seen in the following table. (The total number of possible marks was 20.)

	Spread		Standard		Order	
	A	B	A	C	A	D
Bill	14	10	14	9	14	9
Ann	11	9	11	6	11	12
John	10	8	10	5	10	10
Tina	7	7	7	2	7	11
David	5	6	5	1	5	6

The whole question of unreliability, however, does not stop here. Even if a testee were to take two composition examinations of comparable difficulty, there would be no guarantee whatsoever that he would score similar marks on both examinations. This particular type of unreliability is more common to the essay paper than to any other and is termed *test/retest reliability*. A further complication results from a lack of *mark/re-mark* reliability: in other words, if the same composition is marked by the same examiner on two occasions there may be a difference in the marks he awards.

In spite of all such demonstrations of unreliability, composition is still widely used as a means of measuring the writing skills. Although there appears to be an increasing tendency in many public examinations to replace the composition with more objective-type items, composition still remains popular with constructors of school examinations. The value of practice in continuous writing cannot be stressed too greatly. The student's ability to organise his ideas and express them in his own words is a skill so essential for real-life communication. Thus, composition can be used to provide not only high motivation for writing but also an excellent backwash effect on teaching, provided that the teacher does not anticipate at too early a stage the complex skills required for such a task. Moreover, if a more reliable means of scoring the composition could be used, sampling the student's writing skills in this way would appear a far more valid test than any number of objective tests of grammar.

As is clearly demonstrated at the end of this section, it is impossible to obtain any high degree of reliability by dispensing with the subjective element and attempting to score on an "objective" basis, according to a carefully constructed system of penalties. However, composition marking can be improved considerably once the subjective element is taken into account and once methods of reducing the unreliability inherent in the more traditional methods of assessment are employed. To start with, testees should be required to perform the same writing task. Although there may sometimes be a case for a limited choice of composition topics in the classroom, attempts at accurate assessment of writing ability can only be successful if the choice of topic is severely restricted or abolished completely. A well-defined task in terms of one or two situational compositions, can help enormously to increase the reliability of the examination. The compositions may then be graded according to one of two methods: the *impression method* or the *analytic method*.

The **impression method** of marking entails one or more markers awarding a single mark (= multiple marking), based on the total impression of the composition as a whole. As it is possible for a composition to appeal to a certain reader but not to another, it is largely a matter of luck whether or not a single examiner likes a particular script. As has been demonstrated, the examiner's mark is a highly subjective one based on a fallible judgement, affected by fatigue, carelessness, prejudice, etc. However, if assessment is based on several (fallible) judgements, the net result is far more reliable than a mark based on a single judgement.

Generally, three or four markers score each paper, marks being combined or averaged out to reveal the testee's score. The following table shows how four markers can score three compositions using a five-point scale for impression marking.

	Comp. 1	Comp. 2	Comp. 3
Marker A:	3	5	4
Marker B:	2	4	2
Marker C:	2	4	3
Marker D:	3	4	1
Total:	10	17	10(?)
Average:	2.5	4	2.5(?)

In those cases where there is a wide discrepancy in the marks allocated (e.g. Composition 3 in the previous example), the script is examined once again by all four markers and each mark discussed until some agreement is reached. Fortunately, such discrepancies occur only rarely after the initial stages in multiple-marking.

All the examiners participating in a multiple-marking procedure are required to glance quickly through their scripts and to award a score for each one. The marking scale adopted may be as little as from 0 to 5 or as large as from 0 to 20 (although it has been the author's experience that most markers prefer to use a 5-point scale or any similar scale with only a few categories in order to obtain a wide range of marks). It is most important that all examiners be encouraged to use the whole range of any scale: clearly, marks which bunch around 9 to 12 on a 20-point scale are of little use in discriminating among candidates. It is also important that each examiner read through a certain number of scripts in a given time (usually about 20 per hour) and time himself. If he finds himself slowing down, marking fewer scripts per hour, he is advised to rest and resume work when he feels able to mark at the required rate. Impression marking is generally found more exhausting than mechanical methods of marking; thus, it is essential that the examiner stops work when his attention begins to wander or when he finds himself laboriously reading through the content of each composition. Impression marks must be based on impression *only*, and the whole object is defeated if examiners start to reconsider marks and analyse compositions. Most examiners find it more enjoyable than any other method of scoring compositions. Some argue in favour of marking for one or two hours at a stretch in order to maintain consistency, but little conclusive research has been carried out in this area and there appears to be no evidence that marking for a long period produces more consistent and reliable marks than marking for short periods. Impression marking is generally found to be much faster than analytic or mechanical marking. If compositions are scored by three or four impression markers, the total marks have been found to be far more reliable than the marks awarded by one analytic marker.[2] (The comparison is a fair one, since it takes as long for one analytic marker to score a composition as it does four impression markers.) On the other hand, the marks awarded by one impression marker are less reliable than those awarded by one analytic marker.

Since most teachers have little opportunity to enlist the services of two or three colleagues in marking class compositions, the **analytic method** is recommended for such purposes. This method depends on a marking scheme which has been carefully drawn up by the examiner or body of examiners. It consists of an attempt to separate the various features of a composition for scoring purposes. Such a procedure is ideally suited to the classroom situation: because certain features have been graded separately, each student is able to see how his particular grade has been obtained. The following is reproduced simply as one example of such an analytic scheme: in this particular case duplicate (blank) copies of this scheme were stencilled by the teacher and attached to the end of each composition.

	5	4	3	2	1
Grammar			X		
Vocabulary				X	
Mechanics		X			
Fluency				X	
Relevance			X		

TOTAL = 14

Note that *Mechanics* refers to punctuation and spelling; *Fluency* to style and ease of communication; and *Relevance* to the content in relation to the task demanded of the student. A 5-point scale has been used.

If the analytic method of scoring is employed, it is essential that flexibility is maintained. At the various levels it may become necessary to change either the divisions themselves or the weighting given to them. At the elementary level, for example, the tester may be far more interested in *Grammar* and *Vocabulary* than in fluency, thus deciding to omit *Fluency*. At the intermediate level, he may be particularly interested in *Relevance* and may, therefore, decide to award a maximum of 10 marks for this feature while awarding only 5 marks for each of the others. At the more advanced level, he may wish to include separate divisions for *Organisation* and *Register* and to include *Mechanics* and *Fluency* in one division.

A third method of scoring compositions is the **mechanical accuracy** or **error-count method**. Although this is the most mechanical of all methods of scoring, it is the least valid and is not recommended. The procedure consists of counting the errors made by each testee and deducting the number from a given total: for example, a student may lose up to 10 marks for grammatical errors, 5 marks for mis-use of words, 5 for mis-spellings, etc. Since no decision can be reached about the relative importance of most errors, the whole scheme is actually highly subjective. For example, should errors of tense be regarded as more important than certain mis-spellings or the wrong use of words? Furthermore, as a result of his own intuition and experience, it is fairly common for an examiner to feel that a composition is worth several marks more or less than the score he has awarded and to alter his assessment accordingly. Above all, the mechanical accuracy method unfortunately ignores the real purpose of composition writing — communication; it concentrates only on the negative aspects of the writing task, placing the student in such a position that he cannot write for fear of making mistakes. The consequent effect of such a marking procedure on the learning and teaching of the writing skills can be disastrous.

8.4   The writing skills

The writing skills are complex and difficult to teach, requiring mastery not only of grammatical and rhetorical devices but also of conceptual and judgement elements. The following analysis attempts to group the many and varied skills necessary for writing good prose into four main areas:

- (i) Grammatical skills: the ability to write correct sentences;
- (ii) Stylistic skills: the ability to manipulate sentences and use language *effectively*;
- (iii) Mechanical skills: the ability to use correctly those conventions peculiar to the written language – e.g. punctuation, spelling;
- (iv) Judgement skills: the ability to write in an appropriate manner for a particular purpose with a particular audience in mind, together with an ability to select, organise and order relevant information.

For purposes of testing, grammatical skills can be measured by an objective test of grammar. As shown in Chapter Three, it is possible to construct grammar items of this nature by drawing on the errors made by students in their free written work.

Whereas tests of grammar are concerned with the *correct* use of language, tests of stylistic skills are concerned chiefly with the *effective* use of language. Obviously, there can be no strict division between the two areas and several of the errors which may be grouped under this heading also concern the incorrect use of language. Nevertheless, those stylistic skills related to cohesion and involving the use of reference, linkage and expansion devices for co-ordination and subordination are rarely included in most tests of grammar and usage.

The actual writing conventions which it is necessary for the student to master relate chiefly (at the elementary stages) to punctuation and spelling, and often to the Roman alphabet. However, in punctuation there are many areas in which personal judgements are required, and tests of punctuation must guard against being too rigid by recognising that several answers may be correct. Tests of punctuation and spelling have long occupied a prominent place in elementary tests of English as a first language, the effect of which has often been to inhibit writing and creativity.

Of far greater importance in the teaching and testing of writing are those skills involving the use of judgement. The ability to write for a particular audience using the most appropriate kind of language is essential for both native-speaking and foreign student alike. The use of correct registers becomes an important skill at advanced levels of writing. Failure to use the correct register frequently results in incongruities and embarrassment. Whereas native speakers learn to make distinctions of register intuitively, students of foreign languages usually experience problems in mastering this complex area of language. The various kinds of register include colloquialisms, slang, jargon, archaic words, legal language, standard English, business English, the language used by educated writers of English, etc. The purpose of writing will also help to establish a particular register: for example, is the student writing to entertain, inform, explain, etc?

A piece of continuous writing may take the form of a narrative, description, survey, record, report, discussion, argument, etc. In addition to the subject and the format, the actual audience (e.g. an examiner, a teacher, a student, a friend) will also determine which of the various registers is to be used. Consequently, use of appropriate register in writing implies an awareness not only of a writing goal but also of a particular audience.

After the purpose of writing and the nature of the audience have been established, judgement is again required to determine the selection of the material which is most relevant to the task at hand (bearing in mind the time available). Organisation and ordering skills then follow selection.

8.5 Objective tests of writing: reference, linkage and expansion

Although the total writing skill clearly does not lend itself to objective testing, it is possible to identify certain of its components and to use them for test construction purposes. This section will attempt to show the application of objective procedures to the testing of the stylistic skills. As was emphasised earlier, however, it is neither possible nor desirable to draw a strict division between grammatical and stylistic features.

Type 1: Multiple-choice items: replacement

The construction of multiple-choice items has been treated in detail in Chapter Three; this section is simply intended to show how such testing techniques can be applied to testing the student's ability to handle reference, linkage, and expansion devices. In each of the following examples the testee is required to replace the underlined word(s) with the correct option.

(a) Reference

My book is the new one; your book is the torn one.
A. your
B. the book of you
C. yours
D. the book of your

(b) Linkage

By the time he arrived, everyone was cold and hungry.
A. Since B. After C. When D. Until

(c) Expansion

She smiled innocently and convinced everyone she was telling the truth.

A. She smiling innocently
B. Since smiling innocently, she
C. Upon her having smiled innocently, she
D. Smiling innocently, she

Type 2: Multiple-choice items: completion

The correct option in each of the following examples is used to complete the sentence.

(a) Reference

I'm not certain whether there are any seats left, but Tom seems to think . . . .
A. it B. such C. thus D. so

(b) Linkage

. . . . not having seen each other for fifty years, the two old ladies chatted like the best of friends.
A. Although B. Whereas C. Despite D. However

(c) Expansion

The students quickly found the correct answer, once . . . .
A. having learnt the basic principles
B. learning the basic principles
C. the basic principles being learnt by them
D. the basic principles having been learnt by them

Type 3: Completion items

(a) Reference

Mary went to the dance and so . . . . Jane.

Someone was at the door . . . . was John!

(b) Linkage

The drowned man was given artificial respiration; . . . ., it was too late. He was dead.

. . . . agreeing to a certain extent with you, I must point out that your conclusion is a mistaken one.

(c) Expansion

The driver and his two passengers were lucky to be alive, the car . . . .'. . . . .

You should tell someone about the plans . . . .

The item types included in this section represent only a few of the various methods of testing stylistic skills in writing. Matching items and transformation items (see 3.2 and 3.7) are particularly suited to tests of reference, linkage and expansion. The following is an example of another interesting item type which is suitable for inclusion in a class progress test and which measures to some extent the skills involved in the use of cohesion devices (reference and linkage) and in the ordering of information.

Write three different paragraphs in answer to the following question:

How can we keep our teeth healthy?

Each paragraph should consist of six sentences, and you must use only ONE sentence from each group in the same paragraph. (You must not change the order of the sentences.)

(1) Firstly, we should visit a dentist twice a year
    (a) so that our teeth can be checked regularly.
    (b) but this is of little use unless we clean our teeth daily.
    (c) although this is only one of the things we must do.

(2) (a) We should eat the kind of food that makes our teeth healthy.
    (b) Such daily care of our teeth prevents food from sticking to them.
    (c) He will control any tooth decay by filling the small holes in our teeth.

(3) (a) Moreover, he will examine our teeth to ensure that they are growing in the right way.
    (b) Milk, cheese, fish, brown bread, potatoes, red rice, raw vegetables and fresh fruit are good for them.
    (c) It is advisable to brush our teeth with a toothbrush and toothpaste after breakfast and at bed-time.

(4) (a) However, chocolate, sweets, biscuits and cakes are bad, especially when we eat them between meals.
    (b) Unfortunately, many people never visit a dentist until they have toothache.
    (c) Although many people do this regularly, they do not know how to clean them correctly.

(5) (a) In most cases, they finish up by having their teeth extracted.
    (b) The recommended way is to move the brush from the gum to the tip of the teeth.
    (c) They stick to the teeth and cause decay.

(6) (a) We can also use wooden tooth-picks to clean between the teeth after a meal.
    (b) Consequently, it is good to finish a meal with an apple as it helps to clean the teeth.
    (c) Then they have to wear false teeth while they are still young.

8.6　Objective tests of writing: mechanics

Punctuation

Type 1 The following type of punctuation exercise is very popular and is generally used to cover a wide range of punctuation marks. It is not truly objective, and the scoring of such an exercise would take considerable time since punctuation is to a large degree subjective and one particular use of a punctuation mark may well determine the correctness of the punctuation mark following it.

> In the following passage there is no punctuation.
> Write out the passage, putting in all the punctuation and capital letters.
>
> lend me your pen please peter asked
> i took my pen out of my pocket
> be careful i said
> ill give it back to you in a moment he promised
> dont worry i said you can keep it as long as you want

It is advisable, however, to maintain some degree of control over the task which the testee is expected to perform. One method of doing this is by substituting lines or circles for those punctuation marks which are being tested, thus also facilitating scoring.

Type 2 Put the correct punctuation mark in each circle.

○What do you want,○ I asked Henry○
○May I use your telephone? ○he asked.
○Certainly ○ ○ I said. ○ When you ○ ve finished ○please let me know ○ ○
○I shall only be a moment ○○Henry answered.
○Has John Lee invited you to his party ○○I asked.
○No, he hasn○t yet○○Henry replied.
○He○s invited Paul ○ David ○Tony and Mary○○I continued.
○He○s probably forgotten about me○○Henry laughed.
○How strange ○ ○ I answered. ○ I'm sure he wants you to go to his party.○

Type 3 A greater degree of objectivity can be obtained by using the multiple-choice technique, e.g.:

> Put a circle round the letter (A, B, C, or D) of the correctly punctuated sentence.
>
> A.　Tom asked me if I was going to the meeting?
> B.　Tom asked me, if I was going to the meeting.
> C.　Tom asked me, "If I was going to the meeting?"
> D.　Tom asked me if I was going to the meeting.

Spelling

Type 1: Dictation

As with vocabulary testing, sampling is of primary importance in the construction of spelling tests. Words used in connection with students' free composition work or everyday writing form the most suitable basis for tests of spelling, although items may also be drawn from the students' reading provided that the tester is aware of the implications of testing the more passive items of the students' vocabulary.

Dictation of long prose passages is still regarded as an essential method of testing spelling. However, as will be seen in the appropriate section in the Appendix, dictation measures a complex range of integrated skills and should not be regarded as constituting simply a test of spelling. The dictation of single words, nevertheless, can prove a fairly reliable test of spelling, and dictated word tests are used extensively in the testing of English as a first language. A number of such tests consist of up to 50 words and use similar procedures to the following:

(i) Each word is dictated once by the tester;
(ii) the word is then repeated in a context; and finally,
(iii) the word is repeated on its own.

Type 2: Multiple-choice items

Another fairly widespread method of testing spelling is through the use of multiple-choice items usually containing 5 options, 4 of which are spelt correctly. The testee is required to select the word which is incorrectly spelt, e.g.:

1. A. thief   B. belief   C. seize
   D. ceiling   E. decieve

2. A. happening   B. offering   C. occuring
   D. beginning   E. benefiting

3. A. illegal   B. generally   C. summary
   D. beggar   E. neccessary

4. A. interrupt   B. support   C. answering
   D. ocasional   E. command

In some tests only four words are given as options, the 5th option being _No mistakes_ or _All correct:_ e.g.:

A. exhibition   B. punctually   C. pleasure
        D. obayed   E. _All correct_

Type 3: Completion items

Such items as the following differ from similar ones used in tests of vocabulary because sufficient clues are provided both in the blanks and in the definitions to enable the student to know exactly which word is required.

The blanks, for instance, occur only in that part of the word which gives rise to a spelling difficulty for many students. One advantage of such a test arises from the fact that it does not present the students with incorrect forms. (Many native speakers argue that they frequently fail to recognise correct forms after exposure to mis-spellings.)

Write one or more letters in each of the spaces in the following words. (The definitions will help you to recognise the correct word.)

1. om s n   something left out
2. di uade   persuade someone not to do something
3. o u ing   happening, taking place
4. rec t   a written statement to show that a bill has been paid

It is helpful in tests of this nature to provide a context for the word (in addition to giving a synonym or definition).

1. The horse gal   ed (= ran) to the front of the race.
2. I doubt if anyone ever prof   ed (= gained) from that business deal.
3. The school has an enro   ment (= number on its register) of over 500 students.
4. Don't worry; my dog will go into the water and retr   ve (= bring back) your ball.

Type 4: Error-recognition items

In these items the student is required to identify (according to its letter) the part of the sentence in which a word has been mis-spelt.

                    A   B   C
1. The dissatisfied woman/refused to admit/that there was sufficent/
                                        D
   coffee for everyone.

                    A   B   C
2. Don't be decieved/by the new procedure:/ it hardly differs from/
                                        D
   the old corrupt system.

                        A   B   C
3. The man was equipped/with a double-barrel shotgun/ and his coleague/
                                        D
   with an innocent-looking walking-stick.

                    A   B   C
4. Mr Black's exaggerated/account of the importance/of his new apoint-
                                        D
   ment/ was quite unnecessary.

8.7   Objective tests of writing: judgement skills

For convenience, the judgement skills required in successful writing will be grouped in four divisions: style, register, relevance and organisation.

Style

The following multiple-choice items are concerned chiefly with measuring the student's sensitivity to style. Some of the distractors in the two examples are incorrect on grammatical grounds while others are grammatically correct but not representative of the kind of English used by an educated native speaker in the particular context in which they appear. Indeed, some test writers distinguish tests of writing from tests of grammar and usage in terms of the performance of native speakers: whereas all native speakers of a language would be expected to score high marks in a test of grammar, only certain educated native speakers possessing the required writing skills would score high marks in an objective test of writing.

Some of the reviews were favourable to the new play
- A.   and as many were unfavourable.
- B.   although others of the same amount were unfavourable.
- *C.   while an equal number were unfavourable.
- D.   but the same number were unfavourable.
- E.   in spite of half being unfavourable.

The weather has always been an important factor in men's lives
- *A.   because of its effects on all aspects of farming.
- B.   for it has considerable influence over farming. .
- C.   since farmers concern themselves with it.
- D.   as weather constitutes the dominant worry for farmers.
- E.   on account of its affecting farming affairs.

(* = *Correct answer*)

Register

The use of the correct register denotes the ability to write for a specific purpose with a specific audience in mind. Confusion and embarrassment result from the use of inappropriate registers. Tests of register are still new and quite rare; such tests as the following, however, are not too difficult to construct and present the student with an interesting task, provided that the extract used is written in a fairly distinctive style.

Type 1 The following type of register test requires the student to identify those words which are incongruous, replacing each with a much more suitable word. The student is instructed to replace 16 of the 32 words underlined in the passage.

It has now been <u>made out</u> beyond any doubt whatsoever that the nicotine <u>contained</u> in tobacco smoke is poisonous. One <u>minute</u> drop of pure nicotine <u>plunged</u> into the bloodstream of a rat is <u>sufficient</u> to kill it. It has also been proved that the nicotine <u>contained</u> in tobacco smoke <u>sends up</u> the pulse rate and the blood pressure. There is also strong <u>evidence</u> that the nicotine <u>content</u> in <u>fags</u> is a <u>primary</u> cause of loss of weight and <u>hungriness</u>. It is also likely that a few <u>heavy</u> smokers will lose control of their finer muscles and be unable to <u>play around with</u> objects with ease and precision. Such a loss of muscle activity may <u>widen</u> the eyes and <u>spoil</u> vision. Moreover, smoking <u>puts back</u> growth in adolescents and <u>lowers</u> athletic ability.

However, the most <u>serious</u> disease connected with smoking is cancer of the lung: the direct <u>connection</u> between smoking and cancer has <u>recently</u> been established so <u>assuredly</u> that cancer research <u>folk</u> and public health authorities throughout the world have <u>begun</u> intensive <u>campaigns</u> against smoking. In certain countries not only are cigarette advertisements <u>banished</u> from cinema and television screens but also <u>makers</u> are <u>forced</u> to print on each packet a <u>warning</u> <u>concerning</u> the dangers of smoking.[3]

Type 2 Matching tests are well-suited to tests of register; such tests can be constructed both at word and sentence level.

(a) Word level: The testee is instructed to match each word in List A with a word in List B.[4]

	List A		List B	Answers
1.	cry	a.	boss	(1e)
2.	commence	b.	gee gee	(2c)
3.	kid	c.	expire	(3a)
4.	pussy	d.	hospitalise	(4b)
5.	entrain	e.	draw	(5d)

(b) Sentence level: The testee is instructed to put the letter of the most appropriate sentence in List B with the number of each sentence in List A. The sentences have been taken from instructions, legal documents, scientific English, advertisements, children's comics and newspapers.

List A

1. Build the assembly formers flat on the plan and bend the undercarriage down to the pattern shown.
2. The Tenant shall keep the interior of the premises in good order and condition.
3. A bicycle pump is a device for moving air against a pressure difference.
4. Because the Barcelno has front wheel drive, there's no prop shaft. So you get big car roominess in only 13 feet.
5. But it's too late! The evil plan, cooked up by the monster Balbo, has led Cato to Madame Zena.
6. Ace driver injured in thrilling race of year.

List B

a. There's a new landmark for lovers and others at Waterloo Station. The Drum Bar and Buffet.

b. An object normally becomes hot when it is placed in the sun.

c. The mixture should be taken three times daily after meals.

d. Gang fight death — youth killed when pushed onto electric line.

e. Any amendment of this certificate or failure to complete any part of it may render it invalid.

f. Give over. I'm not a genius. The radio transmits a kind of buzz. A beam that can be picked up for a couple of miles.

Type 3 A similar test of register consists of the writing of three separate paragraphs on the same subject. The test is, in fact, a matching test since the student is required to select the sentences in the appropriate register for each paragraph.

> Write three versions of the same paragraph, each in a different style. Select the most appropriate sentence from each of the following groups (A, B, C, D, and E) for use in each paragraph. Keep to the same order and use each sentence once only.

A. (1) Come to Aberdeen. It's just the place you've been looking for.

   (2) It is not difficult to understand the attraction the picturesque fishing town of Aberdeen has for tourists.

   (3) Aberdeen, the oldest village on Hong Kong island, is one of the chief centres of the fishing population.

B. (1) Although Aberdeen — named after Lord Aberdeen and not its namesake in Scotland — has grown in size over the past few years, it has not lost any of its unique charm.

   (2) Aberdeen has always been an important centre of fishing: a settlement existed long before the commencement of British jurisdiction in 1842.

   (3) Quaint, sunny and full of activity, this rare and picturesque spot is not in Scotland, but — you'll never guess — Hong Kong!

C. (1) The town not only provides a permanent berth for its world-famous floating restaurants but also houses the site of the wholesale fish market operated by the Government.

   (2) There's practically everything in Aberdeen for both young and old, but the two magnificent floating restaurants are a must for everyone.

   (3) Everywhere in Aberdeen one gets the impression of people, but the most fascinating are the water people, who spend all their lives on board their sampans and junks.

D. (1) Once you've managed to stumble on board one of the restaurants, you can choose whatever fish you fancy and treat yourself to an exotic oriental meal.

(2) Across the straits from Aberdeen lies the small island of Aplichau, the centre of a prosperous ship-building industry.

(3) The main attractions of Aberdeen, however, are the floating restaurants which glitter on the water at night like a thousand jewels.

E. (1) The various types of small craft built there range from sampans of traditional design to modern cabin cruisers.

(2) Eat, drink and be merry — it is the closest you'll ever get to paradise this side of heaven.

(3) Built in the rich style of Chinese palaces, these restaurants have long attracted tourists from every corner of the earth.

Relevance

Because assessment of relevance depends so much on a familiarity with the full context of the written material and the audience for which it is intended, this feature is extremely difficult to test objectively. Multiple-choice items allow for the measuring of this skill to some extent, but relevance can only be accurately assessed in the light of a complete letter or composition — not by the relevance or lack of relevance of a particular sentence in a paragraph.

The following is an attempt to measure the advanced student's awareness of relevant information in continuous writing. Testees are instructed to put a circle round the letter marking the beginning of one sentence which they consider irrelevant to the paragraph as a whole.

A. Many African tribes which have recently come into contact with Western civilisation for the first time find that there is a great demand for their own arts and crafts.

B. In Europe and the United States primitive art is growing increasingly popular.

C. Art galleries everywhere also seem to exhibit so-called computer art and other equally hideous art forms.

D. Yet most of the primitive art forms are not expressions of tribal culture in a strict sense.

E. They are really transitional or commercialised aspects of the real primitive art.

Organisation

Although spatial or temporal organisation is required in a number of compositions, much continuous prose need not be organised in this way. Some writers suggest moving from the particular to the general but it is possible also to move from the general to the particular. If a writer is conscious of his purpose and is aware of his audience, organisation should present no real problems. Many tests purporting to test organising and ordering skills, in fact, test sensitivity to reference and linkage.

The following test requires the testee to reassemble the scrambled sentences in order to produce a coherent paragraph.

A. The dogs were separated from their human masters and were put into large fields.

B. For instance, they wagged their tails, they barked and growled, and they fawned on animals which possessed food.

C. Psychologists observing them found that they reacted towards each other in much the same way as they used to respond to people.

D. Recently an experiment was conducted with a group of dogs to find out how much their behaviour was, in fact, simply a result of human environment.

E. Puppies born to these dogs and kept out of contact with people showed the same behaviour patterns: they were extremely wild and afraid of human beings.

Such test items are widely used at elementary levels and have a limited use, provided that the test-writer realises that more features than organisation are being tested.

A. "Yes, there are," I said. "Do you like potatoes more than rice?"

B. "Neither do I," I said. "I like rice very much."

C. "Are there any more potatoes?" Jack Green asked me.

D. "No, I don't," he answered.

A. I borrowed two books from the library.

B. I spent half an hour there and enjoyed looking at all the books.

C. Someone picked it up and handed it to me.

D. After school, I went to the public library.

E. While I was waiting for a bus, I dropped one of them.

8.8 Controlled writing

There are numerous ways of controlling the student's freedom of expression in his written work and, as a consequence, reducing the number of errors he makes. However useful such methods are as teaching devices, they will never prove useful for testing purposes unless each testee is completely familiar with the particular task he is required to perform. Moreover, there is often a danger that certain students will feel inhibited rather than helped by such control. Examples of controlled writing exercises are included in this section.

(1) The student is given a short reading extract and then required to write a similar paragraph, using the notes he has been given. E.g.:

> Although dogs are only animals, they are very useful and help men a lot. For example, certain dogs help farmers to look after their sheep. Some dogs are used for hunting and others help to rescue people. Even now policemen use dogs when they are looking for thieves and

criminals. Men also teach dogs to race, and dog racing is a sport which many people like. All dogs like eating meat very much and like bones best of all.

Although – horses – animals, –useful – a lot. For example, – horses – men – cattle. Some horses – hunting – pull things. In the past – soldiers – horses – fighting against the enemy. Men – horses – horse racing – sport – like. All horses – hay – oats.

(2) Several types of exercises can be based on the following reading extract.[5] Any similar text can also be used for:

    (i) copying with minor alterations: e.g. tense/person changes
    (ii) changing the point of view: e.g. *Write this story as seen by* . . .
    (iii) changing the style and register: e.g. *Write this story in the form of a newspaper report/a humorous account,* etc.
    (iv) adding further information.

A young man who refused to give his name dived into the river yesterday morning to save a 12-year-old boy.

The boy, who ran away after being rescued, had been swimming in the river and had caught his foot between two concrete posts under the bridge. He shouted out for help.

At the time, a young man was riding across the bridge on his bicycle. He quickly dismounted and dived fully clothed into the river. He then freed the boy's foot and helped him to the river bank where a small crowd had collected. The boy thanked his rescuer courteously and sincerely, then ran off down the road. He was last seen climbing over a gate before disappearing over the top of the hill.

The young man, who was about 20 years of age, said "I don't blame the boy for not giving his name. Why should he? If he wants to swim in the river, that's his business. And if I wanted to help him, that's mine. You can't have my name either!"

He then ran back to the bridge, mounted his bicycle and rode away.

Test (i) Rewrite this story but imagine that you are actually watching everything that is happening. Begin: There is a small boy swimming . . .

Test (ii) Rewrite this story as told by (i) the young man who saved the boy and (ii) the boy who was saved.

Test (iii) Write this story as if you were giving evidence at a police station.

Test (iv) It was a sunny day but at the time of the rescue it began to rain heavily. Several people were passing nearby on their way to a football match. When the young man went away, everyone thought that he had got wet in the rain. Write out the story, adding these facts.

(3) There are also several methods of practising or measuring the ability to link sentences, involving subordination and co-ordination features. Some exercises involve writing up notes in the form of sentences (largely determined by the connectives given). The following is an example of a controlled writing exercise practising subordination:

> Join the short sentences in each of the groups below to form one sentence. Then write each of the finished sentences so as to form a paragraph. Use the joining words given, but note that sometimes no joining word is necessary; also *-ing* denotes the verb ending only.

Each Olympic Games opens.	before
An athlete appears.	
He holds a torch.	(-ing)
It has been carried from Mount Olympus in Greece.	which
The ceremony was started in Berlin in 1936.	which
It links the sites of the modern Games with the first Olympic Games.	
However, the actual torch ceremony dates back to Ancient Greece.	where
One of the most spectacular events was the torch race.	which
It was always run at night.	
The athlete enters the stadium.	When
He is holding the torch.	who
He runs to the huge bowl.	
The sacred flame will burn there.	in which

Many such tests do not give the required linkers to the testee but leave him free to join the sentences in whichever way he considers appropriate. Indeed, since such tests are still very subjective and require a lot of time to score, it is often better not to provide the student with linkers but to leave him free to solve each problem in his own way.

(4) In some tests of composition, especially at the elementary and intermediate levels, sentences and clauses are provided at first in order to help the student to start writing. He is then required to complete the composition by writing several sentences of his own.

Read these sentences. Finish each one and then complete the story in your own words.

One morning Peter and Tony got up early to go . . . .
They cycled to a small beach where . . . .
"We want to go . . . .," they told an old fisherman.
"Will you lend us your rowing-boat so that . . . .?"
"Yes, but you must not . . . .,"
the fisherman said. "The sea is very rough over there."
The two boys climbed into the boat and . . . .
They rowed quickly towards the small island which . . . .

NOTES

1 See especially "The Marking of English Essays", *International Institute Examinations Enquiry*, 1941, Chairman – Sir Philip Joseph Hartog.

2 Several studies have shown evidence of such reliability: among those with which the writer is acquainted at first hand are (i) a pilot scheme concerning the multiple marking of English compositions conducted by the Colonial Secretariat Examinations Unit in Hong Kong (January 1968) and (ii) an experiment in multiple marking conducted by Dr. A. E. G. Pilliner in Zagreb, Yugoslavia (May 1970).

3 made out (proved), plunged (injected), sends up (increases), fags (cigarettes), hungriness (appetite), play around with (manipulate), widen (extend), spoil (impair), puts back (retards), lowers (reduces), assuredly (conclusively), folk (organisations), begun (launched), banished (banned), forced (required), makers (manufacturers).

4 In an excellent article, "Style and Register Tests", in *Objektive Tests im Englischunterricht der Schule und Universität*, Athenäum Verlag, Robert Pynsent draws attention to the use of semantic and structural distractors in matching tests of register – i.e. including words with the same meaning (or phrases with identical structures) but in a different register.

5 Extracted from *Understanding Modern English*, Book 1 (K. Methold and J. B. Heaton), Longman.

9 Criteria and types of tests

9.1 Validity

This section attempts to summarise much of what was contained in Chapter One. Briefly, the validity of a test is the extent to which it measures what it is supposed to measure *and nothing else*. Every test, whether it be a short, informal classroom test or a public examination, should be as valid as the constructor can make it. The test must aim to provide a true measure of the particular skill which it is intended to measure: to the extent that it measures external knowledge and other skills at the same time, it will not be a valid test. For example, the following test item, taken from a public matriculation examination several years ago, is invalid if we wish solely to measure writing ability: "Is photography an art or a science? Discuss." It is likely to be invalid simply because it demands some knowledge of photography and will consequently favour certain students.

Face validity

Even a superficial inspection of the above essay item would be sufficient to reveal that it was not valid. This type of validity, in fact, is often referred to as face validity: if a test item looks right to other testers, teachers, moderators, and testees, it can be described as having at least face validity. It is, therefore, often useful to show a test to colleagues and friends. As constructors of the test, we can become so involved in the test that we sometimes fail to stand back and look at the individual test items objectively. Only if the test is examined by other people can some of the absurdities and ambiguities then be discovered.

Language tests which have been designed primarily for one country and are adopted by another country may lack face validity. A vocabulary or reading comprehension test containing such words as "typhoon", "sampan", "abacus", and "chopsticks" will obviously not be valid in East Africa no matter how valid and useful a test it has proved in Hong Kong. The same argument applies to many standardised tests designed for immigrants in the United States and used now in many other parts of the world. Although no substitute for empirical validity, face validity can provide not only a quick, reasonable guide but also a balance to too great a concern with statistical analysis. Motivation is maintained if a test has good face validity, for most testees will try harder if the test looks sound.

Content validity

This kind of validity depends on a careful analysis of the language being tested and of the particular course objectives. The test should be so constructed as to contain a representative sample of the course, the relationship between the test items and the course objectives always being apparent. There is a strong tendency, especially in multiple-choice testing, to test only those areas of the language which lend themselves readily to testing. Many tests of phonology, for instance, concentrate too much on testing phoneme discrimination rather than the more important features of stress and intonation: one cannot help but suspect the reason for this is simply that phoneme tests are often easier to construct than items testing stress and intonation.

Construct validity

If a test has construct validity, it is capable of measuring certain specific characteristics in accordance with a theory of language behaviour and learning. This type of validity assumes the existence of certain learning theories or constructs underlying the acquisition of abilities and skills. For example, it can be argued that a speed reading test based on a short comprehension passage is an inadequate measure of reading ability (and thus has low construct validity) unless it is believed that the speed reading of short passages relates closely to the ability to read a book quickly and efficiently and is a proven factor in reading ability. If the assumption is held that systematic language habits are best acquired by means of the structural grammar approach, then a test which emphasises the lexical or situational meaning of language (rather than the structural meaning) will have low construct validity.

Empirical validity

A fourth type of validity is usually referred to as statistical or empirical validity. This validity is obtained as a result of comparing the results of the test with the results of some criterion measure such as:

    (i) an existing test, known or believed to be valid and *given at the same time*; or

    (ii) the teacher's ratings or any other such form of independent assessment *given at the same time*; or

    (iii) the *subsequent* performance of the testees on a certain task measured by some valid test; or

    (iv) the teacher's ratings or any other such form of independent assessment *given later*.

Results obtained by either of the first two methods above are measures of the test's *concurrent validity* in respect of the particular criterion used. The third and fourth methods estimate the *predictive validity* of a test which is used to predict future success. We could estimate the predictive validity of a language test administered to civil engineers embarking on a civil engineering course given in the medium of English, for instance, if we measured their subsequent performances on their academic courses and compared these results with the results of the language test.

The test situation or the technique used is always an important factor in determining the overall validity of any test. Although an ideal test situation will by no means guarantee validity, a poor test situation will certainly detract from it. Is an auditory comprehension test valid if the testee hears only a disembodied voice on, say, a poor quality tape-recorder?

9.2 Reliability

Reliability is a necessary characteristic of any good test: for it to be valid at all, a test must first be reliable as a measuring instrument. If the test is administered to the same candidates on different occasions (with no language practice work taking place between these occasions), then, to the extent that it produces differing results, it is not reliable. Reliability measured in this way is commonly referred to as *test/re-test reliability* to distinguish it from *mark/re-mark reliability* and the other kinds of reliability described later in this section. This latter kind of reliability denotes the extent to which the same marks or grades are awarded if the same test papers are marked by (i) two or more different examiners or (ii) the same examiner on different occasions. In short, in order to be reliable, a test must be consistent in its measurements.

Reliability is of primary importance in the use of both public achievement and proficiency tests *and* classroom tests. Methods of estimating the reliability of individual items in a test will be indicated in Section 3 of Chapter 10. However, an appreciation of the various factors affecting reliability is important for the teacher at the very outset, since many teachers tend to regard tests as infallible measuring instruments and fail to realise that even the best test is indeed an imprecise instrument with which to measure language skills.

Factors affecting the reliability of a test are:

(1) the extent of the sample of material selected for testing: whereas validity is concerned chiefly with the content of the sample, reliability is concerned with the size. The larger the sample (i.e. the more tasks the testee has to perform), the greater the probability that the test as a whole is reliable – hence the favouring of objective tests, which allow for a wide field to be covered.

(2) the administration of the test: is the same test administered to different groups under different conditions or at different times? Clearly, this is an important factor in deciding reliability, especially in tests of oral production and auditory comprehension. The way in which this factor differs from test situation validity can be

seen from the following example: if a recording for an auditory comprehension test is initially poor in quality, then it is poor in quality for all testees. This will consequently make for invalidity (unless speech has been *deliberately* masked with noise, as a testing device). But if the quality of the recording is good and if certain groups hear it played under good acoustic conditions while other groups hear it under poor acoustic conditions, this will make for unreliability and therefore invalidity.

(3) test instructions: are the various tasks expected from the testee made clear to *all* candidates in the rubrics?

(4) personal factors such as motivation and illness.

(5) scoring the test: one of the most important factors affecting reliability. Objective tests overcome this problem of marker reliability, but subjective tests are still faced with it: hence the importance of the work carried out in the field of the multiple-marking of compositions.

One method of measuring the reliability of a test is to re-administer the same test after a lapse of time. It is assumed that all candidates have been treated in the same way in the interval – that they have either all been taught or that none of them have. Provided that such assumptions (which are frequently hard to justify) can be made, comparison of the two results would then show how reliable the test has proved. Clearly, this method is often impracticable and, in any case, a frequent use of it is not to be recommended, since certain students will benefit more than others by a familiarity with the type and format of the test. Moreover, in addition to changes in performance resulting from the memory factor, personal factors such as motivation and differential maturation will also account for differences in the performances of certain students.

Another means of estimating the reliability of a test is by administering parallel forms of the test to the same group. This assumes that two similar versions of a particular test can be constructed: such tests must be identical in the nature of their sampling, difficulty, length, rubrics, etc. Only after a full statistical analysis of the tests and all the items contained in them can the tests safely be regarded as parallel. If the correlation between the two tests is high (i.e. if the results derived from the two tests correspond closely to each other), then the tests can be termed reliable.

The split-half method is yet another means of measuring test reliability. This method estimates a different kind of reliability from that estimated by test/re-test procedures. The split-half method is based on the principle that, if an accurate measuring instrument were broken into two equal parts, the measurements obtained with one part would correspond exactly to those obtained with the other. The test is divided into two and the corresponding scores obtained, the extent to which they correlate with each other governing the reliability of the test as a whole. One procedure widely used is to ascertain the correlation between the scores on the odd numbered items and those on the even numbered items. However, if the items are graded according to increasing difficulty, division according to odd and even numbers would not be an accurate means of assessing reliability, since item 2 would be slightly more difficult than item 1, item 4 again more difficult than item 3, and so on. A more accurate procedure is to balance the items as follows:

item	1	4	5	8	9	12
against item	2	3	6	7	10	11

However, it would be better, though less convenient, to allow chance to decide which items go into one half and which into the other.

The reliability of the whole test can be estimated by using the formula:

$$r_{11} = \frac{N}{N-1} \left(1 - \frac{m(N-m)}{Nx^2} \right)$$

where N = the number of items in the test;
   m = the mean score on the test for all the testees (see page 169), and
   x = the standard deviation of all the testees' scores (see page 170).

(note that in this formula, x has to be squared.)

In Sections 10.1 and 10.2 the calculation of the mean and standard deviation of scores on a language test containing 40 items is illustrated. The mean is found to be 27 and the standard deviation 4.077. Using these figures with the above formula, we obtain:

$$r_{11} = \frac{40}{39} \left(1 - \frac{27 \times 13}{40 \times 16.662} \right) = 0.484$$

This formula is simple to use since (i) it avoids troublesome correlations and (ii), in addition to the number of items in the test, it involves only the test mean and standard deviation, both of which are normally calculated anyhow as a matter of routine.

Finally, it should be noted that a test can be reliable without necessarily possessing validity. However, reliability is clearly inadequate by itself if a test does not succeed in measuring what it is supposed to measure.

9.3 Discrimination

Sometimes an important feature of a test is its capacity to discriminate among the different candidates and to reflect the differences in the performances of the individuals in the group. For example, 70% means nothing at all unless all the other scores obtained in the test are known. Furthermore, tests on which almost all the candidates score 70% clearly fail to discriminate between the various students. Tests which are designed for a large test population (and which are to be standardised) are first tried out on a representative sample of testees. This small sample mirrors the much larger group for whom the test is intended. The results of the test are then examined to determine the extent to which it discriminates between individuals who are different. When the final version of the test is eventually used, therefore, its discriminatory powers have already been established. Consequently, there will then be little need for concern if, for example, it is found that the scores of individuals in a group cluster around a central point. The test has been proved capable of discriminating; it does not do so in this case because there is nothing to discriminate.

The extent of the need to discriminate will vary depending on the purpose of the test: in many classroom tests, for example, the teacher will be much more concerned with finding out how well his students have mastered the syllabus and will hope for a cluster of marks around the 80% and 90% brackets. Nevertheless, there may be occurrences in which the teacher may require a test to discriminate to some degree so that he can assess relative abilities and locate areas of difficulty.

9.4   Administration

A test must be practicable: in other words, it must be fairly straightforward to administer. It is only too easy to become so absorbed in the actual construction of test items that the most obvious practical considerations concerning the test are overlooked. The length of time available for the administration of the test is frequently misjudged even by experienced test-writers, especially if the complete test consists of a number of subtests. In such cases sufficient time may not be allowed for the administration of the test, the collection of the answer sheets, the reading of the test instructions, etc. In the case of all large-scale tests, the time to be allowed should be decided on as a result of a pilot administration of the test (i.e. a try-out of the test to a small but representative group of testees).

Another practical consideration concerns the answer sheets and the stationery used. Many tests require the testee to enter his answers on the actual question paper (e.g. circling the letter of the correct option), thereby unfortunately reducing the speed of the scoring and preventing the question paper from being used a second time. In some tests, the candidate is presented with a separate answer sheet, but too often insufficient thought has been given to possible errors arising from the (mental) transfer of the answer from the context of the item on the question paper to the answer sheet itself. Confusion may result, for example, if the items are numbered vertically on the question papers and horizontal numbering is adopted for the corresponding answer sheet. E.g.:

1. You'd already left by seven o'clock, ... you?
   A. didn't B. weren't C. hadn't D. haven't

2. If you take swimming lessons, you . . . . soon.
   A. will be able to swim   C. can swim
   B. swim   D. shall have swum

3. Did anyone tell Tom . . . . the careless error he made?
   A. off   B. over   C. on   D. about

Put a cross (X) in the box containing the letter of the correct answer.

1.   A | B | C | D   2.   A | B | C | D   3.   A | B | C | D

4.   A | B | C | D   5.   A | B | C | D   6.   A | B | C | D

The use of separate answer sheets, however, greatly facilitates marking (through the use of a mask or key) and is strongly recommended when large numbers of students are being tested.

It is of paramount importance that examiners are fully conversant with the test situation. If the test is to be administered by several examiners working in different test centres, clear directions specifying exactly what each examiner should say and do should be issued in order to ensure that exactly the same procedure is followed in each centre. Although this principle seems obvious enough, it is extremely difficult in many cases for the test writer to see his test from the point of view of the person conducting the test, simply because he is so closely involved in his test that he is inclined to take too many things for granted. Consequently, wherever possible, all test arrangements should be discussed in detail by the test writer and by those conducting the test, the various steps in the administering of each sub-test being stated in simple language and clearly numbered. This is particularly essential in tests of auditory comprehension and oral production, where the administrator's role in the test is so important. Accompanying these instructions should be a clear statement of aims together with a comprehensive (but simple) marking scheme.

Before beginning to construct a test, the test writer must make certain that the necessary equipment will be available in each centre and that there will be a high degree of standardisation in the test administration. Clearly, it is useless to record talks or dialogues on tape if certain test centres do not have a tape-recorder. What is not so obvious, however, is the potential unreliability of an auditory test resulting from the different sizes of the rooms where the test is administered and the different degrees of interference caused by extraneous noise. The question of practicability, however, is not confined solely to aural/oral tests: such written tests as situational composition and controlled writing tests depend not only on the availability of qualified markers who can make valid judgements concerning the idiomatic use of language, etc., but also on the length of time available for the scoring of the test.

A final point concerns the presentation of the test paper itself. Where possible, it should be printed or type-written and appear neat, tidy and aesthetically pleasing. Nothing is worse and more disconcerting to the testee than an untidy test-paper, full of mis-spellings, omissions and corrections.

9.5 Test instructions to the candidate

Since most students taking any test are working under certain mental pressures, it is essential that all instructions are clearly written and that examples are given. Unless all testees are able to follow the instructions, the test will be neither reliable nor valid. Grammatical terminology should be avoided and such rubrics as the following re-written:

Put the correct pronoun in the blanks.
Choose one of the following verbs to go in each blank space and put it in the correct tense.

A student may be able to perform all the required tasks without having any knowledge of formal grammar. Indeed, since his knowledge of formal grammar is not being tested, all reference to grammatical terms should be avoided. Thus, the first of the rubrics above should be re-written and the phrase "words like the following" (followed by examples) be used to replace "pronouns"; the second rubric should refer to "words" instead of verbs, and examples should be given so that the student is shown the tense changes he is required to make. This principle does not apply only to grammatical terms: if students are instructed to put a tick opposite the correct answer, an example of what is meant by the word "tick" should be given — e.g. (√). The same applies to crosses, circles, underlining, etc.

Sometimes it is difficult to avoid writing clumsy rubrics or rubrics consisting of complex sentences above the difficulty level being tested.

E.g. Answer each of the following questions by selecting the word or group of words which best completes each sentence from the words or groups of words which are lettered A, B, C, and D.

or For each of the blanks in the following sentences choose one of the words or groups of words which best completes the sentence. Write in the space shown by the dotted line the letter corresponding to the word, or group of words, which completes the sentence the best.

One possible solution is to write the rubric in short sentences — clearly and concisely.

E.g. Choose the word or group of words which best completes each sentence. Each is lettered A, B, C, or D. Put a circle round the letter of the correct answer.

The rubrics in too many existing tests assume that the testee already knows what to do. While this can be excused to a certain extent in class tests where the teacher is present to explain, it is very disturbing when it occurs in more widely used achievement and proficiency tests where no such help is available. However, it is often difficult to strike the right balance between short, clear instructions and long, involved rubrics. A rubric should never, in itself, become a test of reading comprehension. The following are further examples of clear instructions:

> Complete each of the following sentences. Write in the blank space the letter of the correct word or words. The first one is an example.

> There are 40 questions in this section. Each question consists of an incomplete sentence. This incomplete sentence is followed by five possible ways of completing it. Each way is labelled A, B, C, D, or E. Choose the answer which you think best completes the sentence. The first one is done for you.

Each word should be carefully considered in the writing of a rubric. For example, the word "best" is used in certain instances instead of "correct" because many test items (especially those in tests of vocabulary) contain several "correct" answers, although only one is really acceptable and clearly the required answer. Finally, all rubrics should be tried out on pilot groups in the same way in which items are tried out.

Because the writing of clear and concise rubrics is so difficult, it is essential that simple examples are provided for the testees. One or two examples of the type of task set are recommended, unless the particular testing technique adopted is one with which the students are extremely familiar. Indeed, if the testees are all unfamiliar with the type of test being given, it is advisable for the test supervisor to work through a few examples with them. In one test of proficiency,[1] the testees are given five "practice" items to work through, their answers being subsequently checked before the test is commenced. This small precaution ensures that each testee is conversant with the type of test in which he is about to participate. In certain other tests,[2] a "practice" test is administered beforehand to the testees. Such a test is specially constructed to include examples of all the types of items in the test paper.

If new testing techniques are being used on a large scale for the first time, it is essential for the test writers and test administrators concerned to construct sample items and rubrics to send to schools well in advance, together with sufficient detailed information about the new procedures. No test can possibly be valid if the techniques adopted are so new and unfamiliar as to bewilder the testees.

Finally, the inclusion of numerous different rubrics interspersed through the test paper should be avoided. For example, some class tests consist of 10 multiple-choice items, 15 transformation items, 5 word-order items, 10 completion items, etc., necessitating several different rubrics and examples. Not only does such a variety of test items and rubrics confuse many testees but such tests may well become tests of reading comprehension.

9.6   Backwash effects

In Chapter One and throughout this book the importance of the backwash effects of testing on teaching has been emphasised. In Chapter One reference was made to oral examining, where it was pointed out that, in spite of possible unreliability, oral tests should be continued as far as possible in certain language learning situations, if for no other reason than the backwash effects they have on the teaching that takes place before the test. The possible consequences of many reading comprehension tests on the development of the reading skills was cited as another example of the backwash effects of testing. Each element and skill has been treated in the book in relation to its potential influence on teaching. Nevertheless, the importance of the influence of testing on teaching is worth emphasising again, since the test constructor can so easily become too deeply involved in test statistics and in other test criteria.

A larger issue at stake is the effect of objective tests on language learning in general. Important questions are raised; many as yet remain unanswered. For example, do objective tests frequently lead to a greater emphasis on accuracy than on fluency? It is highly possible that, in spite of all efforts, many testing techniques still emphasise the negative aspects of language learning, encouraging teachers and students to place more emphasis on correctness than on the communicative aspects of language learning. A number of objective tests also encourage the teaching of language in artificially constructed situations, thereby reducing motivation in language learning.

Other issues are equally important in their implications. How much influence do certain tests exert on the compilation of syllabuses and language teaching programmes? How far is such an influence harmful or actually desirable in certain situations? Again, what part does coaching play in the test situation? Is it possible to teach effectively by relying solely on some of the techniques used for testing? Clearly, the answers to these and other questions remain in some doubt. All that can be done at present is to discourage as actively as possible the use of testing techniques as the chief means of practising certain skills. While coaching undoubtedly plays a part in increasing test scores, good teaching can do far more. Moreover, provided that the students have at least one opportunity to participate in a practice test paper before embarking on a particular test, coaching by itself will produce little improvement in test results.

Consequently, while we may deplore, and must guard against, certain backwash effects of testing on the one hand, it is fair to point out on the other hand that testing has been one of the greatest single beneficial forces in changing the direction of language teaching in many areas and in encouraging the more responsive teachers to examine not only their own teaching methods but also the language they are teaching.

9.7   Types of tests

There is some confusion regarding the terminology used to denote the different types of language tests in use. A number of test specialists, however, agree on the following three broad divisions: achievement/attainment tests, proficiency tests, and aptitude tests.[3]

1. Achievement/Attainment tests

This group can be further subdivided into class progress tests and (standardised) achievement tests.

Class progress tests

This book has been concerned chiefly with class progress tests, since these are the most widely used types of tests. Most teachers are, at some time or other, required to construct such tests. Each progress test situation is unique and can only be evaluated fully by the class teacher in the light of his knowledge of the students, the programme which they have been following, and his own particular aims and goals. It is illogical to expect general purpose tests and books of tests to function as effectively as a test constructed specially for a particular situation: hence the purpose of this book in encouraging the teacher to construct his own tests.

The progress test is designed to measure the extent to which the students have mastered the material taught in the classroom. It is based on the language programme which the class has been following and is just as important as an assessment of the teacher's own work as the student's own learning. Results obtained from the progress test enable the teacher to become more familiar with the work of each of his students and with the progress of the class in general. The class progress test is a teaching device, its backwash effect on teaching and motivation being important features.[4] A good progress test should encourage the student to perform well in the target language in a positive manner and to gain additional confidence. Its aim is to stimulate learning and to reinforce what has been taught. Good performances act as a means of encouraging the student, and although poor performances may act as an incentive to more work, the progress test is chiefly concerned with allowing the student to show what he has mastered. Scores on it should thus be high (provided, of course, that progress has indeed been made). Whereas in standardised achievement and proficiency tests, a wide range of performance should be indicated, the progress test should show a cluster of scores around the top of the scale.

Achievement tests

Achievement (or attainment) tests, though similar in a number of ways to progress tests, are far more formal tests and are intended to measure achievement on a larger scale. Most annual school examinations take the form of achievement tests; all public tests which are intended to show mastery of a particular syllabus are also achievement tests. These tests are based on what the student is presumed to have learnt — not necessarily on what he has actually learnt nor on what has actually been taught. Achievement tests frequently take the form of secondary school entrance tests and school certificate examinations; many are based on a published syllabus and exert a strong influence on its effectiveness in schools. Constructors of such tests rarely teach any of the students being tested (often an advantage *provided that* the test constructors are very familiar with the teaching and learning problems of the testees). Indeed, this is often a pre-requisite before anyone can be appointed to any position of responsibility in connection with this type of test, though this principle obviously cannot always be applied to school examinations.

Several achievement tests are standardised: they are pre-tested, each item is analysed and revised where necessary, norms are established and comparisons made between performances of different students and different schools. Since such tests are administered year after year, it is possible to compare performances of students one year with those of students taking the test another year.

2. Proficiency tests

Whereas an achievement test looks back on what should have been learnt, the proficiency test looks forward, defining a student's language proficiency with reference to a particular task which he will be required to perform. Proficiency tests are in no way related to any syllabus or teaching programme; indeed, many proficiency tests are intended for students from several different schools, countries and even language backgrounds. The proficiency test is concerned simply with measuring the student's control of the language in the light of what he will be expected to do with it in his future performance of a particular task. Does the student know enough English, for example, to follow a certain university or college course given in the medium of English? Does he know enough English in order to function efficiently in a particular type of employment for which he has applied? The proficiency test is thus concerned with measuring not general attainment but specific skills in the light of the language demands made later on the student by his future course of study or job.

3. Aptitude tests

A language aptitude test (or prognostic test)[5] is designed to measure the student's *probable* performance in a foreign language which he has not started to learn: i.e. it assesses his aptitude for learning a language. Language learning aptitude is a complex matter, consisting of such factors as intelligence, age, motivation, memory, phonological sensitivity and sensitivity to grammatical patterning. The relative weighting given to these elements must depend on many factors and thus vary considerably from one individual to another. Some specialists in this field maintain that it is neither possible nor desirable to take an overall measurement of language aptitude; consequently aptitude is sometimes divided into various aspects according to the specific tasks for which a person is being trained: e.g. listening, interpreting, translating. Aptitude tests generally seek to predict the student's probable strengths and weaknesses in learning a foreign language by measuring his performance in an artificial language. The ability to learn new phonemic distinctions and also to use language patterns in an unfamiliar but logical manner is tested by means of the artificial language. Since few teachers are concerned with the complex field of aptitude testing, it is not necessary to go into further detail here.[6]

4. Diagnostic testing

Although the term *diagnostic test* is widely used, few tests are constructed solely as diagnostic tests. Achievement and proficiency tests, however, are frequently used for diagnostic purposes: areas of difficulty are diagnosed in such tests so that appropriate remedial action can be taken later. Sections of tests which lend themselves particularly well to diagnostic purposes are phoneme discrimination tests, grammar and usage tests, and certain controlled writing tests. Clearly, weaknesses indicated in a test of vocabulary are not highly significant in themselves and can only be regarded as indicating general weaknesses. Similarly, many existing tests of reading comprehension are not very suitable for diagnostic purposes. Tests of writing and oral production can be used diagnostically provided that there is an appreciation of the limits to which such tests can be put. Since diagnosing strengths and weaknesses is such an important feature of progress tests and of teaching, the teacher should always be alert to every facet of achievement revealed in a class progress test.

NOTES
1   This is a Proficiency Test designed for use with foreign students at British Universities and constructed by Dr. E. F. Chaplen.
2   The practice referred to is generally adopted in tests constructed and administered by the Godfrey Thomson Unit for Academic Assessment, Edinburgh.
3   Rebecca Valette describes four main categories of tests: (Achievement, Progress, Proficiency, and Prognostic or Aptitude), *Modern Language Testing: A Handbook*, Harcourt, Brace & World, New York, 1967, p. 4–5. Alan Davies distinguishes four uses: (Achievement or Attainment, Proficiency, Aptitude and Diagnosis), *Language Testing Symposium: A Psycholinguistic Approach*, Oxford University Press, 1968, p. 6–7.
4   See Section 1.2
5   The two most widely used aptitude tests are the *Modern Language Aptitude Test*, (J. B. Carroll & S. M. Sapon), The Psychological Corporation, New York, 1959, and the *Language Aptitude Battery* (P. Pimsleur), Harcourt, Brace and World Inc., 1966.
6   An excellent article on the subject by R. B. Sloss appeared in the *R. A. F. Education Bulletin*, Autumn 1965, p. 39–47.

10 Interpreting test scores

10.1 Frequency distribution

Marks awarded by counting the number of correct answers on a test script are known as raw marks. "15 marks out of a total of 20" may appear a high mark to some, but in fact the statement is virtually meaningless on its own. For example, the tasks set in the test may have been extremely simple and 15 may be the lowest mark of a particular group of scores.

TABLE 1			TABLE 2				TABLE 3		
Testee	Mark		Testee	Mark	Rank		Mark	Tally	Frequency
A	20		D	35	1		40		
B	25		M	34	2		39		
C	33		C	33	3.5 (or 3=)		38		
D	35		W	33	3.5 (or 3=)		37		
E	29		L	32	5		36		
F	25		G	30	6.5 (or 6=)		35	/	1
G	30		S	30	6.5 (or 6=)		34	/	1
H	26		E	29	8.5 (or 8=)		33	//	2
I	19		P	29	8.5 (or 8=)		32	/	1
J	27		J	27	11 (or 10=)		31		
K	26		N	27	11 (or 10=)		30	//	2
L	32		O	27	11 (or 10=)		29	//	2
M	34		H	26	15 (or 13=)		28		
N	27		K	26	15 (or 13=)		27	///	3
O	27		T	26	15 (or 13=)		26	////	5
P	29		X	26	15 (or 13=)		25	///	3
Q	25		Z	26	15 (or 13=)		24	/	1
R	23		B	25	19 (or 18=)		23	//	2
S	30		F	25	19 (or 18=)		22	/	1
T	26		Q	25	19 (or 18=)		21		
U	22		Y	24	21		20	/	1
V	23		R	23	22.5 (or 22=)		19	/	1
W	33		V	23	22.5 (or 22=)		18		
X	26		U	22	24		17		
Y	24		A	20	25		16		
Z	26		I	19	26		15	Total	26

Conversely, the test may have been extremely difficult, in which case 15 may well be a very high mark. Numbers still exert a strange and powerful influence on our society, but the shibboleth that 40% should always represent a pass mark is nevertheless both surprising and disturbing.

The tables on page 167 contain the imaginary scores of a group of 26 students on a particular test consisting of 40 items. Table 1 conveys very little, but Table 2, containing the students' scores in order of merit, shows a little more. Table 3 contains a frequency distribution showing the number of students who obtained each mark awarded; the strokes on the left of the numbers (e.g. ////) are called *tallies* and are included simply to illustrate the method of counting the frequency of scores. Note that normally the frequency list would have been compiled without the need for Tables 1 and 2; consequently, as the range of highest and lowest marks would then not be known, all the *possible* scores would be listed and a record made of the number of students obtaining each score in the scale (as shown in the example).

Note that where ties occur in Table 2, two ways of rendering these are shown. The usual classroom practice is that shown in the brackets. Where statistical work is to be done on the ranks, it is essential to record the average rank (e.g. testees J, N and O, each with the same mark, occupy places 10, 11 and 12 in the list, averaging 11.)

The following frequency polygon illustrates the distribution of the scores:

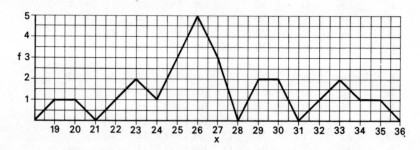

10.2 Measures of central tendency

1. Mode
The mode refers to the score which most candidates obtained: in this case it is *26*, as 5 testees have scored this mark.

2. Median
The median refers to the score gained by the middle candidate in the order of merit: in the case of the 26 students here (as in all cases involving even numbers of testees), there can obviously be no middle person and thus the score half-way between the lowest score in the top half and the highest

score in the bottom half is taken as the median. The median score in this case is also 26.

3. Mean

The mean score of any test is the arithmetical average: i.e. the sum of the separate scores divided by the total number of testees. The mode, median, and mean are all measures of central tendency. The mean is the most efficient measure of central tendency, but it is not always appropriate.

In the following Table 4 and formula, note that the symbol x is used to denote the score, N the number of testees, and m the mean. The symbol f denotes the frequency with which a score occurs. The symbol Σ means *the sum of*.

TABLE 4

x	f	fx
35 X 1		35
34 X 1		34
33 X 2		66
32 X 1		32
30 X 2		60
29 X 2		58
27 X 3		81
26 X 5		130
25 X 3		75
24 X 1		24
23 X 2		46
22 X 1		22
20 X 1		20
19 X 1		19
Total =		702
		= Σfx

$$m = \frac{\Sigma fx}{N}$$

$$= \frac{702}{26}$$

$$= 27$$

Note that x = 702 is the total number of items which the group of 26 students got right between them. Dividing by N = 26 (as the formula states), this obviously gives the average.

It will be observed that in this particular case there is a fairly close correspondence between the mean (27) and the median (26). Such a close correspondence is not always common and has occurred in this case because the scores tend to cluster symmetrically around a central point.

10.3 Measures of dispersion

Whereas the previous section was concerned with measures of central tendency, this section is related to the range or spread of scores. The mean by itself enables us to describe an individual student's score by comparing it with the average set of scores obtained by a group, but it tells us nothing at all about the highest and lowest scores and the spread of marks.

1. Range

One simple way of measuring the spread of marks is based on the difference between the highest and lowest scores. Thus, if the highest score on a 50-item test is 43 and the lowest 21, the range is from 21 to 43: i.e. 22. If the highest score, however, is only 39 and the lowest 29, the range is 10. (Note that in both cases, the mean may be 32.) The range of the 26 scores given in Section 10.1 is: $35 - 19 = 16$.

2. Standard Deviation

The standard deviation (s.d.) is another way of showing the spread of scores. It measures the degree to which the group of scores deviates from the mean; in other words, it shows how *all* the scores are spread out and thus gives a fuller description of test scores than the range, which simply describes the gap between the highest and lowest marks and ignores the information provided by all the remaining scores. Abbreviations used for the Standard Deviation are either s.d. or σ (the Greek letter sigma) or s. One simple method of calculating s.d. is shown below:

$$\text{s.d.} = \sqrt{\frac{\Sigma d^2}{N}}$$

N is the number of scores and d the deviation of each score from the mean. Thus, working from the 26 previous results, we proceed to:

(i) find out the amount by which each score deviates from the mean (d);

(ii) square each result (d^2);

(iii) total all the results (Σd^2);

(iv) divide the total by the number of testees ($\Sigma d^2/N$); and

(v) find the square root of this result ($\sqrt{\Sigma d^2/N}$).

	Score	Mean	Deviation (d)		Squared (d^2)
(Step 1)	35 deviates from 27 by		8	(Step 2)	64
	34		7		49
	33		6		36
	33		6		36
	32		5		25
	30		3		9
	30		3		9

Score	Mean Deviation (d)	Squared (d²)
29	2	4
29	2	4
27	0	0
27	0	0
27	0	0
26	−1	1
26	−1	1
26	−1	1
26	−1	1
26	−1	1
25	−2	4
25	−2	4
25	−2	4
24	−3	9
23	−4	16
23	−4	16
22	−5	25
20	−7	49
19	−8	64
702	(Step 3) Total = 432	

$$\text{(Step 4)} \quad \text{s.d.} = \sqrt{\frac{432}{26}}$$

$$\text{(Step 5)} \quad \text{s.d.} = \sqrt{16.62}$$

$$\text{s.d.} = 4.077$$

$$= 4.08$$

Note: If deviations (d) are taken from the mean, their sum (taking account of the minus sign) is zero. $+ 42 − 42 = 0$ This affords a useful check on the calculations involved here.

A standard deviation of 4.08, for example, shows a smaller spread of scores than, say, a standard deviation of 8.96. If the aim of the test is simply to determine which students have mastered a particular programme of work or are capable of carrying out certain tasks in the target language, a standard deviation of 4.08 or any other denoting a fairly narrow spread will be quite satisfactory provided it is associated with a high average score. However, if the test aims at measuring several levels of attainment and making fine distinctions within the group (as perhaps in a proficiency test), then a broad spread will be required.

Standard deviation is also useful for providing information concerning characteristics of different groups. If, for example, the standard deviation on a certain test is 4.08 for one class, but 8.96 on the same test for another class, then it can be inferred that the latter class is far more heterogeneous than the former.

10.4 Item analysis

Earlier careful consideration of objectives and the compilation of a table
of test specifications were urged before the construction of any test was
attempted. What is required now is a knowledge of how far those objectives have been achieved by a particular test. Unfortunately, too many
teachers think that the test is finished once the raw marks have been
obtained. But this is far from the case, for the results obtained from
objective tests can be used to provide valuable information concerning:

> (i) the performance of the students as a group, thus (in the case of
> class progress tests) informing the teacher about the effectiveness
> of his teaching;
> (ii) the performance of individual students; and
> (iii) the performance of each of the items comprising the test.

Information concerning the performance of the students as a whole and
of individual students is very important for teaching purposes, especially as
many test results can show not only the types of errors most frequently
made but also the actual reasons for the errors being made. As shown in
earlier chapters, the great merit of objective tests arises from the fact that
they can provide an insight into the mental processes of the students by
showing very clearly what choices have been made, thereby indicating
definite lines on which remedial work can be given.

The performance of the test items, themselves, is of obvious importance
in compiling future tests. Since a great deal of time and effort are usually
spent on the construction of good objective items, most teachers and test
constructors will be desirous of either using them again without further
changes or else adapting them for future use. It is thus useful to identify
those items which were answered correctly by the more able students
taking the test and badly by the less able students. The identification of
certain difficult items in the test, together with a knowledge of the performance of the individual distractors in multiple-choice items, can prove just
as valuable in its implications for teaching as for testing.

All items should be examined from the point of view of (1) their
difficulty level and (2) their level of discrimination.

1. Item Difficulty

The index of difficulty (or *the facility value*) of an item simply shows how
easy or difficult the particular item proved in the test. The index of
difficulty (F.V.) is generally expressed as the fraction (or percentage) of
the students who answered the item correctly. It is calculated by using the
formula:

$$F.V. = \frac{R}{N}$$

R represents the number of correct answers and N the number of students
taking the test. Thus, if 21 out of 26 students tested obtained the correct

answer for one of the items, that item would have an index of difficulty (or a facility value) of .77 or 77%:

$$F.V. = \frac{21}{26} = \underline{.77}$$

In this case, the particular item is a fairly easy one since 77% of the students taking the test answered it correctly. Although an average facility value of .5 or 50% may be desirable for many public achievement tests and for a few progress tests (depending on the purpose for which one is testing), the facility value of a large number of individual items will vary considerably. While aiming for test items with facility values falling between .4 and .6, many test constructors may be prepared in practice to accept items with facility values between .3 and .7. Clearly, however, a very easy item, on which 90% of the testees obtain the correct answer, will not distinguish between above-average students and below-average students as well as an item which only 60% of the testees answer correctly. On the other hand, the easy item will discriminate amongst a group of below-average students; in other words, one student with a low standard may show himself to be better than another student with a low standard by being given the opportunity to show his performance on an easy item. Similarly, a very difficult item, though failing to discriminate among most students, will certainly separate the good student from the very good student.

A further argument for including items covering a range of difficulty levels is that provided by motivation. While the inclusion of difficult items may be necessary in order to motivate the good student, the inclusion of very easy items will encourage and motivate the poor student. In any case, a few easy items can provide a "lead-in" for the student — a device which may be necessary if the test is at all new or unfamiliar or if there are certain tensions surrounding the test situation.

Note that it is possible for a test consisting of items each with a facility value of approximately .5 to fail to discriminate at all between the good and the poor students. If, for example, half the items are answered correctly by the good students and incorrectly by the poor students while the remaining items are answered incorrectly by the good students but correctly by the poor students, then the items will work against one another and no discrimination will be possible. The chances of such an extreme situation occurring are very remote indeed; it is highly probable, however, that at least one or two items in a test will work against one another in this way.

2. Item Discrimination
The discrimination index of an item indicates the extent to which the item discriminates between the testees, separating the more able testees from the less able. The index of discrimination (D) tells us whether those students who performed well on the whole test tended to do well or badly

on each item in the test. It is pre-supposed that the total score on the test is a valid measure of the student's ability. (I.e. The good student tends to do well on the test as a whole and the poor student badly.) On this basis, the score on the whole test is accepted as the criterion measure, and it thus becomes possible to separate the "good" students from the "bad" ones in performances on individual items. If the "good" students tend to do well on an item (as shown by many of them doing so — a frequency measure) and the "poor" students badly on the same item, then the item is a good one because it distinguishes the "good" from the "bad" in the same way as the total test score. This is the argument underlying the index of discrimination.

There are various methods of obtaining the index of discrimination: all involve a comparison of those students who performed well on the whole test and those who performed poorly on the whole test. However, while it is statistically most efficient to compare the top 27½% with the bottom 27½%, it is enough for most purposes to divide small samples (e.g. class scores on a progress test) into halves or thirds. For most classroom purposes, the following procedure is recommended.

(1) Arrange the scripts in rank order of total score and divide into two groups of equal size (i.e. the top half and the bottom half). If there is an odd number of scripts, dispense with the script in the middle.

(2) Count the number of those candidates in the upper group answering the first item correctly; then count the number of lower-group candidates answering the item correctly.

(3) Subtract the number of correct answers in the lower group from the number of correct answers in the upper group: i.e. find the difference in the proportion passing in the upper group and the proportion passing in the lower group.

(4) Divide this difference by the total number of candidates in one group:

$$D = \frac{\text{Correct U} - \text{Correct L}}{n}$$

(D = Discrimination Index; n = Number of Candidates in one group*; U = Upper half and L = Lower half. The index D is thus the difference between the proportion passing the item in U and L.)

(5) Proceed in this manner for each item.

The following item, which produced the results shown, was actually used in a test of grammar and usage (administered to 40 students):

I went into the wood . . . . a fine morning.

A. in   (B.) on   C. at   D. by

$$D = \frac{15 - 6}{20} = \frac{9}{20} = \underline{.45}$$

Such an item with a discrimination index of .45 functions fairly effectively, although clearly it does not discriminate as well as an item with an

*The reader should carefully distinguish between n(= the number of candidates in either the U or L group) and N (= the number in the whole group) as used previously. Obvious, n = 1/2N.

index of .6 or .7. Discrimination indices can range from + 1 (= an item which discriminates perfectly — i.e. it shows perfect *correlation* with the testees' results on the whole test) through 0 (= an item which does not discriminate in any way at all) to −1 (= an item which discriminates in entirely the wrong way). Thus, for example, if all 20 students in the upper group answered a certain item correctly and all 20 students in the lower group got the wrong answer, the item would have an index of discrimination of 1.0. If, on the other hand, only 10 students in the upper group answered it correctly and furthermore 10 students in the lower group also got correct answers, the discrimination index would be 0. However, if none of the 20 students in the upper group got a correct answer and all the 20 students in the lower group answered it correctly, the item would have a negative discrimination, shown by −1.0. It is highly inadvisable to use again, or even to attempt to amend, any item showing negative discrimination. Inspection of such an item usually shows something radically wrong with it.

Again, working from actual test results, we shall now look at the performance of three items. The first of the following items has a high index of discrimination; the second is a poor item with a low discrimination index; and the third example is given as an illustration of a poor item with negative discrimination.

(1) High discrimination index:

> NEARLY   When . . . . Jim . . . . crossed . . . . the road, he . .✓. . . ... ran into a car.

$$D = \frac{18 - 3}{20} = \frac{15}{20} = \underline{.75} \qquad F.V. = \frac{21}{40} = \underline{0.52}$$

(The item is at the right level of difficulty and discriminates well.)

(2) Low discrimination index:

> If you . . . . the bell, the door would have been opened.
> A. would ring   C. would have rung
> (B.) had rung   D. were ringing

$$D = \frac{3 - 0}{20} = \underline{.15} \qquad F.V. = \frac{3}{40} = \underline{.08}$$

(In this case, the item discriminates poorly because it is too difficult for everyone, both "good" and "bad".)

(3) Negative discrimination index:

> I don't think anybody has seen him.
> (A.)   Yes, someone has.
> (B.)   Yes, no one has.
> C.   Yes, none has.
> D.   Yes, anyone has.

$$D = \frac{4 - 6}{20} = \frac{-2}{20} = -\underline{.10} \qquad F.V. = \frac{10}{40} = \underline{0.25}$$

(This item is too difficult and discriminates in the wrong direction.)

What has gone wrong with the third item above? Even at this stage and without counting the number of candidates who chose each of the options, it is evident that the item was a trick item: in other words, the item was far too "clever". It is even conceivable that many native speakers would select option B in preference to the correct option A. Items like this all too often escape the attention of the test writer until an item analysis actually focuses attention on them. (This is one excellent reason for conducting an item analysis.)

Note that items with a very high facility value fail to discriminate and thus generally show a low discrimination index. The particular group of students who were given the following item had obviously mastered the use of *for* and *since* following the Present Perfect Continuous tense:

He's been living in Berlin . . . . 1957.

$$D = \frac{19 - 19}{20} = \underline{0} \qquad F.V. = \frac{38}{40} = \underline{0.95}$$

(The item is extremely easy for the testees and has zero discrimination.)

3. Item Difficulty and Discrimination

Facility values and discrimination indices are usually recorded together in tabular form and calculated by similar procedures. Note again the formulae used:

$$F.V. = \frac{\text{Correct U} + \text{Correct L}}{2n} \qquad \left(\text{or } F.V. = \frac{R}{N} \right)$$

$$D = \frac{\text{Correct U} - \text{Correct L}}{n}$$

The following table, compiled from the results of the test referred to in the preceding paragraphs, shows how these measures are recorded.

Item	U	L	U+L	FV	U−L	D
1	19	19	38	.95	0	0
2	13	16	29	.73	−3	−.15
3	20	12	32	.80	8	.40
4	18	3	21	.53	15	.75
5	15	6	21	.53	9	.45
6	16	15	31	.77	1	.05
7	17	8	25	.62	9	.45
8	13	4	17	.42	9	.45

Table continued at top of next page

Item	U	L	U+L	FV	U−L	D
9	4	6	10	.25	−2	−.10
10	10	4	14	.35	6	.30
11	18	13	31	.78	5	.25
12	12	2	14	.35	10	.50
13	14	6	20	.50	8	.40
14	5	1	6	.15	4	.20
15	7	1	8	.20	6	.30
16	3	0	3	.08	3	.15
Etc.						

Items showing a discrimination index of below .30 are of doubtful use since they fail to discriminate effectively. Thus, on the results listed in the table above, only items 3, 4, 5, 7, 8, 10, 12, 13 and 15 could be safely used in future tests without being re-written. However, many test writers would keep item 1 simply as a lead-in to put the students at ease.

4. Extended Answer Analysis

It will often be important to scrutinise items in greater detail, particularly in those cases where items have not performed as expected. We shall want to know not only why these items have not performed according to expectations but also why certain testees have failed to answer a particular item correctly. Such tasks are reasonably simple and straightforward to perform if the multiple-choice technique has been used in the test.

In order to carry out a full item analysis, or an extended answer analysis, a record should be made of the different options chosen by each student in the upper group and then the various options selected by the lower group.

If I were rich, I . . . . work.
A. shan't B. won't C. wouldn't D. didn't

	U	L	U+L
A.	1	4	5
B.	2	5	7
C.	14	4	18
D.	3	7	10
	(20)	(20)	(40)

$$FV = \frac{U+L}{2n} = \frac{18}{40} = .45$$

$$D = \frac{U-L}{n} = \frac{10}{20} = .50$$

The item has a facility value of .45 and a discrimination index of .50 and appears to have functioned efficiently: the distractors pull the poorer students but not the better ones.

The performance of the following item with a low discrimination index is of particular interest:

Mr Watson wants to meet a friend in Singapore this year. He . . . . him for ten years.
A. knew B. had known C. knows (D.) has known

	U	L	U+L
A.	7	3	10
B.	4	3	7	FV = .33
C.	1	9	10	D = .15
D.	8	5	13
	(20)	(20)	(40)

While distractor C appears to be performing well, it is clear that distractors A and B are attracting the wrong candidates (i.e. the better ones). On closer scrutiny, it will be found that both of these options may be correct in certain contexts: for example, a student may envisage a situation in which Mr Watson is going to visit a friend whom he had known for ten years in England but who now lives in Singapore. E.g.

He knew him (well) for ten years (while he lived in England).
The same justification applies for option B.

The next item should have functioned efficiently but failed to do so: an examination of the testees' answers leads us to guess that possibly many had been taught to use the Past Perfect tense to indicate an action in the past taking place before another action in the past. Thus, while the results obtained from the previous item reflected on the item itself, the results here *probably* reflect on the teaching:

John F. Kennedy . . . . born in 1917 and died in 1963.
A. is B. has been (C.) was D. had been

	U	L	U+L
A.	0	2	2
B.	0	3	3	FV = .63
C.	13	12	25	D = .05
D.	7	3	10
	(20)	(20)	(40)

In this case, the item might be used again with another group of students, although distractors A and B do not appear to be pulling much weight.

Distractor D in the following example is ineffective and clearly needs to be replaced by a much stronger distractor:

He complained that he . . . . the same bad film the night before.
A. had seen B. was seeing C. has seen D. would see

	U	L	U+L
A.	14	8	22
B.	4	7	11
C.	2	5	7
D.	0	0	0
	(20)	(20)	(40)

FV = .55
D = .30

Similarly, the level of difficulty of distractors C and D in the following item is far too low: a full item analysis suggests only too strongly that they have been added simply to complete the number of options required.

Wasn't that your father over there?

A. Yes, he was.   C. Yes, was he.
B. Yes, it was.   D. Yes, was it.

	U	L	U+L
A.	7	13	20
B.	13	7	20
C.	0	0	0
D.	0	0	0
	(20)	(20)	(40)

FV = .50
D = .30

The item could be made slightly more difficult and thus improved by replacing distractor C by *Yes, he wasn't* and D by *Yes, it wasn't*. The item is still imperfect, but the difficulty level of the distractors will probably correspond more closely to the level of attainment being tested.

The purpose of obtaining test statistics is to assist interpretation of item and test results in a way which is meaningful and significant. Provided that such statistics lead the teacher or test constructor to focus his attention once again on the *content* of the test, then item analysis is an extremely valuable exercise. Only when test constructors misapply statistics or become uncritically dominated by statistical procedures does item analysis begin to exert a harmful influence on learning and teaching. In the final analysis, the teacher should be prepared to sacrifice both reliability and discrimination to a limited extent in order to include in his test certain items which he regards as having a good "educational" influence on his students if, for example, their exclusion might lead to neglect in teaching what such items test.

10.5 Guessing

Many teachers appear worried by the effect of guessing on the results obtained in an /objective test. Since the testee is generally required to choose one of a number of options, the opportunity of choosing the correct answer solely by chance is always present. There are different opinions, however, on the importance of the effects of guessing. In a multiple-choice test consisting of items with four options, for example, a testee can score 25% simply by chance: this is the *expectation* of his "guessing" score, although, in fact, he might score rather more or rather less.

Guessing can be a serious factor in influencing scores in true/false tests and in multiple-choice items containing only 3 options. Guessing may also exert an undue influence on results when a test is found to be extremely difficult, thereby indirectly encouraging random guessing. Since individual candidates approach guessing in different ways, the reliability of the subsequent scores may be seriously affected. For example, certain students may adopt a cautious approach and feel inhibited if required to guess, thus finding it extremely difficult to select answers which they are not certain about; other students may enjoy "having a go" and may feel wholly uninhibited about guessing.

In the cases referred to in the preceding paragraph a correction factor may be used to compensate for guessing. The formula used is:

$$N = R - \frac{W}{(A - 1)}$$

N = the corrected score; R = the number of correct answers; W = the number of incorrect answers; A = the number of options in each item. For example, a student who has scored 61% in a test comprising multiple-choice items with 4 options will have 61 correct answers and 39 incorrect.

$$N = 61 - \frac{39}{4 - 1} = 61 - \frac{39}{3} = 61 - 13 = \underline{48}$$

A simpler method of putting this (for items with 4 options) would be to describe the corrected score as derived from the number of correct answers minus 1/3 the number incorrect. If each item had had only 3 options, the corrected score would have been the number of correct answers minus 1/2 the number of incorrect answers. More generally:

Options per item	Corrected score
5	R − 1/4 W
4	R − 1/3 W
3	R − 1/2 W
2	R − W

On the whole, however, correction formulae are rarely employed as a means of compensating for guessing. Guessing may indeed be a significant factor but it is rarely detectable, unless it is clear, for instance, that insufficient time has been allowed for the test. The use of a guessing correction factor, moreover, does not affect rank order: the same order of merit exists whether or not any correction factor is applied, provided that all the testees have answered all the questions in the test. However, the most telling argument against the use of a correction factor stems from the fact that guessing is generally based on partial knowledge. Most students very rarely guess at random in objective tests: their guesses are based on some kind of knowledge or understanding, however small. If that knowledge is quite good, the chances of a correct guess will be good; if it is poor, the student will be much more likely to select one of the distractors. The application of the correction factor assumes that the answer is either known or not known and thus takes no account of partial knowledge. Finally, it can be argued that students who do not guess but simply get items wrong are penalised unduly for incorrect answers: in other words, the guessing correction factor, when applied, covers all incorrect answers, whether guessed or not.

The instructions at the beginning of the test should make it perfectly clear if guessing is to be penalised. Indeed, instructions encouraging cautious guessing but discouraging wild guessing will prove helpful to the testee whether or not guessing is penalised.

10.6 Moderating

The importance of moderating classroom tests as well as public examinations cannot be stressed too greatly. No matter how experienced the test writer is, he is usually so deeply involved in his work that he becomes incapable of standing back and viewing his items with any real degree of objectivity. He is bound to display many blind-spots in his test, especially in the field of objective testing, where the items generally contain only the minimum of context.

It is essential, therefore, that the test writer submits his test for moderation to a colleague or, preferably, to a number of colleagues. Achievement and proficiency tests of English administered to a large test population are generally moderated by a board consisting of linguists, language teachers, a psychologist and a psychometrist. The purpose of such a board is to scrutinise as closely as possible not only each item comprising the test but also the test as a whole, so that the most appropriate and efficient measuring instrument is produced for the particular purpose at hand. In these cases, moderation is also frequently concerned with the scoring of the test and with the evaluation of the test results.

The class teacher does not have at his disposal all the facilities which the professional test writer has. Indeed, it is often all too tempting for the teacher to construct a test without showing it to anyone, especially if he has had previous training or experience in constructing examinations of the more traditional type. Unfortunately, few teachers realise the importance of making a systematic analysis of the elements and skills they are trying to test and, instead of compiling a list of test specifications, tend to select testable points at random from course-books and readers. Weaknesses of tests constructed in this manner are brought to light in the process of moderation. Moreover, because there is generally more than one way of looking at something, it is incredibly easy (and common) to construct multiple-choice items containing more than one correct option. In addition, the short contexts of many objective items encourage ambiguity, a feature which can pass by the individual unnoticed. To the moderator, some items in a test may appear far too difficult or else far too easy, containing implausible distractors; others may contain unsuspected clues. Only by moderation can such faults be brought to the attention of the test writer.

In those cases where the teacher of English is working on his own in a school, assistance in moderation from the teacher's wife, a friend, or an older student will prove beneficial. It is simply impossible for any single individual to construct good test items without help from another person.

10.7 Item cards and banks

As must be very clear at this stage, the construction of objective tests necessitates spending a great deal of time and trouble. Although the scoring of such tests is simple and straightforward, further effort is then spent on the evaluation of each item and on improving those items which do not perform satisfactorily. It seems somewhat illogical, therefore, to dispense with test items once they have appeared in a test.

The best way of recording and storing items (together with any relevant information) is by means of small cards. Only one item is entered on each card; on the reverse side of the card information derived from an item analysis is recorded: e.g. the facility value (F.V.), the Index of Discrimination (D), and an extended answers analysis (if carried out). After being arranged according to the element or skill which they are intended to test, the separate cards are grouped according to difficulty level, the particular area tested, etc. It is an easy task to arrange them for quick reference according to whatever system is desired. Furthermore, the cards can be rearranged at any later date.

Although it will obviously take considerable time to build up an item bank consisting of a few hundred items, such an item bank will prove of enormous value and will save the teacher a great deal of time and trouble later. The same items can be used many times again, the order of the items (or options within each item) being changed each time. If there is concern about test security or if there is any other reason indicating the need for new items, many of the existing items can be re-written. In such cases, the same options are generally kept, but the context is changed so that one of the distractors now becomes the correct option. Multiple-choice items testing most areas of the various language elements and skills can be re-written in this way. E.g.

(Grammar) I hope you . . . . us your secret soon.
A. told B. will tell C. have told D. would tell

———➤ I wish you . . . . us your secret soon.
A. told B. will tell C. have told D. would tell

(Vocabulary) Are you going to wear your best . . . . for the party?
A. clothes B. clothing C. cloths D. clothings

———➤ What kind of . . . . is your new suit made of?
A. clothes B. clothing C. cloth D. clothings

(Phoneme beat   bit   beat
discrimination) ———➤ beat   beat   bit

(Auditory Student hears: Why are you going home?
comprehension) Student reads: A.   At six o'clock.
B.   Yes, I am.
C.   To help my mother.
D.   By bus.

———➤ Student hears: How are you going to David's?
Student reads: A.   At six o'clock.
B.   Yes, I am.
C.   To help him.
D.   By bus.

(Reading Two-thirds of the country's (fuel, endeavour, industry,
comprehension/ energy) comes from imported oil, while the remaining
vocabulary) one-third comes from coal. Moreover, soon the country
will have its first nuclear power-station.

———➤ Two-thirds of the country's (fuel, endeavour, industry,
energy) is in the form of imported oil, while the remaining one-third is coal. However, everyone in the country
was made to realise the importance of coal during the
recent miners' strike, when many factories were forced
to close down.

Items rewritten in this way become new items, and thus it will be necessary to collect facility values and discrimination indices again.

Such examples serve to show ways of making maximum use of the various types of test items which have been constructed, administered and evaluated. In any case, however, the effort spent on constructing tests of English as a second or foreign language is never wasted since the insights provided into language behaviour as well as into language learning and teaching will always be invaluable in any situation connected with either teaching or testing.

Appendix

Dictation

Although dictation still remains popular with many teachers and students, it fell into some disrepute as both a testing and teaching device with the advent of the audio-lingual approach. In a way, this reaction has been unfortunate as there are various methods of using dictation effectively as a teaching device. However, dictation has too long been regarded solely as a means of measuring a student's skills of auditory comprehension, the complex elements involved in tests of dictation being completely overlooked.

It is difficult to judge, for example, whether a mistake in a dictation has been made because of the student's inability to

    (i) spell a word
   (ii) "catch" what has been said
  (iii) remember a word by the time he writes it
  (iv) understand the general context.

The integrated skills thus involved in tests of dictation include listening comprehension, the auditory memory span, spelling, the recognition of sound segments, and a familiarity with the grammatical and lexical patterning of the language. Unfortunately, there is no way of assessing the relative importance of the different abilities required and the various levels of difficulty. Each error in a dictation is penalised in exactly the same way without any serious attempt being made to understand the reason for the particular error.

If there is no close relationship between the sounds and the symbols representing them, it may be possible to understand what is being spoken without being able to write it down. However, in the English language, where there is a fairly close relationship between the sounds and the spelling system, it is often possible to recognise the individual sound elements without fully understanding the meaning of what is spoken. Indeed, some linguists and teachers argue that dictation encourages the student to focus his attention too much on the individual sounds rather than on the meaning of the dictation passage as a whole. Such concentration on single sound segments in itself is sufficient to impair the auditory memory span, thus making it difficult for the student to retain everything he hears.

If dictation is included in a class progress test, it is always useful to allow for preparatory work (usually in the form of a brief discussion) so that every testee is at least acquainted with the topic and some of the more specialised vocabulary to be used in the dictation. It is then advisable to read through the whole dictation passage at normal speed before beginning to dictate (either once or twice) in rhythm units and phrases as far as possible. (Some teachers consider that they make the dictation easier by reading out the text word by word: this procedure is extremely harmful and only serves to increase the difficulty of the dictation by obscuring the meaning of each phrase.) Finally, after the dictation, the whole extract is read at *slightly* slower than normal speed.

The following is an example of part of a dictation passage, suitable for use at an intermediate or fairly advanced level. The oblique strokes denote the units which the examiner must observe when dictating.

Before the second half of the nineteenth century/the tallest blocks of offices/were only three or four storeys high.//As business expanded/ and the need for office accommodation/grew more and more acute,/ architects began to plan taller buildings.//Wood and iron,/however,/ were not strong enough materials/from which to construct tall buildings.//Furthermore,/the invention of steel/now made it possible to construct frames/so strong that they would support/the very tallest of buildings.//

To sum up, dictation is a teaching device which merits a much closer examination than has been given to it in the past; the very least of its claims is its capacity to assist in developing sound-symbol relationships. However, as a testing device it measures too many different language features to be effective in providing a means of assessing any one particular skill.

Translation

Translation, as a skill on its own, is not perhaps of the greatest use to many students of English as a foreign language. Where translation is a necessary skill, however, it is generally in the field of technical literature, in which translation from the target language (English) into the mother tongue is demanded. Only on very rare occasions is translation from the mother tongue into English ever required.

Translation is a special skill in its own right and involves language tasks which students are not capable of attempting before a certain level of proficiency in the target language. Unfortunately, when translation is introduced too early in the curriculum, it is often responsible for establishing in the student a mental block between the foreign language and the mother tongue, especially at the elementary and intermediate stages of learning a language.

Many tests of translation tend to be unreliable because of the complex nature of the skills involved and the subjectivity of scoring. In too many instances, the unrealistic expectations of examiners of translation manifest themselves in highly artificial sentences and literary texts set for translation. The testee is expected to display an ability to make fine syntactical judgements and appropriate lexical distinctions – an ability which can only be acquired after achieving a high degree of proficiency not only in English and the mother tongue but also in comparative stylistics and translation methods.

If translation is to be tested at all, the teacher should attempt to identify precisely those features which he wishes to test: e.g. vocabulary, structure, word order. Test items might then be constructed in the form of completion items or multiple-choice items. If, however, the total skills of translation are to be tested, the test writer might at least present a task which is meaningful and relevant to the situation of the testees. Thus, for example, students might be required to write a report in the mother-tongue based on information covered in a series of extracts presented in English. In this case, the test constructor should be aware of the complex range of skills being tested. Above all, word for word translation of difficult literary extracts should be avoided. If translation is taught in the school, a case may be made out for testing it: however, translation should not to be taught at all below the intermediate stages of language learning.

Paraphrase, precis and summary writing

Tests of paraphrase involve both the writing and the reading skills but lack any degree of relevance. Too often literary texts are given to the student to re-write in his own words. It may be asked how the student can possibly express a poem or piece of prose in language which will compete with the original. His own version, written under all the pressures of test conditions, is bound to be a very inferior equivalent. Furthermore, such a test is wholly meaningless in the context of the language tasks demanded of the student in real-life situations. It can be argued that, if the paraphrase test is intended to test comprehension, this skill is much better tested by a reading comprehension test. If intended to test the student's writing ability, again this is better done through a test of writing.

Much the same can be said about precis writing. This test assumes that the various pieces of writing presented to the student can be considerably reduced in length without much real loss. Precis is a traditional classroom "skill", taught to students of English as a mother tongue and extended to foreign-language learners. In both situations, it bears little relation to any real-life task. Why should a particular passage be rewritten in the student's own words in approximately one-third of the length of the original? The student is expected to display a variety of skills which have virtually no connection with those skills involved in learning a language or in using it.

Even the scoring of precis presents a problem because of the variety of features involved. For example, how many marks should be awarded for each point of information included by the student in his precis? How many marks should be deducted for grammatical errors or for a precis which exceeds the required number of words? How many of the words and phrases in the original text should be allowed in a precis before marks are deducted?

Summary, on the other hand, is a useful skill provided that the tasks set are realistic. Generally speaking, the student is required to summarise only a part of the extract or certain aspects of it. Moreover, he is given a specific purpose for writing the summary. E.g.

> Write a brief report of the accident described in the following three eye-witness accounts. The report must be as objective as possible and should not occupy more than one page, as it is to be included in a file for submission to the local inspector of police in order to enable him to decide whether or not to prosecute.

An appropriate number of words for the summary can be given as a guide to the student but no candidate should be penalised unduly for writing more or fewer words than suggested. In the scoring of summaries, the student should be allowed to use as many of the original words and phrases as he wishes, although the test should be so constructed that it is impossible to reproduce lengthy sections of the original passage(s).

Testing literature

Although objective testing does not appear to lend itself to the testing of literature, much more work is still required in this field before valid conclusions can be drawn. It is certainly possible to devise quite sophisticated multiple-choice items testing the different degrees of sensitivity and literary appreciation. Each distractor can take the form of a particular interpretation of a certain section of a poem or prose extract which, though not actually incorrect, is neither the fullest nor the most critical interpretation possible. True/false types of items can be constructed in a similar way.

Testing literary appreciation in this way is an excellent teaching device for developing students' critical faculties. However, it is important that such an approach should be balanced by more subjective, open-ended tests. At such advanced stages when literary appreciation is taught in the school or college curriculum, the students' fluency in the written language should be of such a standard that little difficulty is experienced in the communication skills themselves.

At a lower level, objective tests can be set as a means of ascertaining the degree of a student's familiarity with a reader or text which he is supposed to have read. Such tests can provide a fast and reliable way of checking the student's reading; they are designed to show whether or not a student has read a particular text — and nothing else.

Selected Bibliography

(including books and articles to which reference has been made in this book)

Published tests

Carroll, J. B. and S. M. Sapon,
   Modern Language Aptitude Test (Psychological Corporation, New York, 1959)
Pimsleur, P.,
   Language Aptitude Battery (Harcourt, Brace & World, New York, 1966)

Closed tests and examinations

Davies, Alan:
   English Proficiency Test Battery (EPTB) Forms A and B
Ingram, Elisabeth:
   English Language Battery (ELBA)
Educational Testing Service (Princeton, New Jersey, U.S.A.):
   Test of English as a Foreign Language (TOEFL)
University of Michigan:
   Michigan Test of English Language Proficiency.
University of Cambridge Local Examinations Syndicate:
   First Certificate in English
   Certificate of Proficiency in English
Joint Matriculation Board (Universities of Manchester, Liverpool, Leeds, Sheffield and Birmingham):
   Test in English (Overseas)
Association of Recognised English Language Schools:
   ARELS Oral Examination

Bibliographies

Centre for Information on Language Teaching:
   Foreign Language Testing – Specialised Bibliography 1 (C.I.L.T., 1971)

Books and articles

Anderson, J.,
   "A Technique for Measuring Reading Comprehension and Readability",
   English Language Teaching, 25, 2, 1971, 178–82.
Bright, J. A. and McGregor, G. P.,
   Teaching English as a Second Language, Longman, 1970.

Brodkey, Dean,
   "Dictation as a Measure of Mutual Intelligibility: A Pilot Study", *Language Learning*, 22, 2., 1972, 203–20.
Brooks, Nelson,
   "Tests and Measurements", *Language and Language Learning*, Harcourt, Brace & World, New York, 1960, 119–225.
Cairns, Peterside and Scott,
   Objective Questions in English Language, African Universities Press, Lagos, 1966.
Crocker, A. C.,
   Statistics for the Teacher (or How to Put Figures in their Place), Penguin Books, 1969.
Darnell, Donald K.,
   "Clozentropy: a procedure for testing English language proficiency of foreign students", *Speech Monographs*, 37, 1, 1970, 36–46.
Davies, Alan, (ed.),
   Language Testing Symposium: A Psycholinguistic Approach, Oxford University Press, 1968.
Finocchiaro, Mary,
   Teaching English as a Second Language, Harper and Row, 1969.
Forbes, Duncan,
   "Selling English Short", *English Language Teaching*, 27, 2., 1973, 132–7.
George, H. V.,
   "Testing – Another Point of View", *English Language Teaching*, 16, 1962, 72–8.
Godshalk, Swineford and Coffman,
   The Measurement of Writing Ability, New York College Entrance Examination Board, 1966.
Grayshon, M. C.,
   The Examination of Spoken English, Institute of Education, University of Nottingham, 1968.
Grieve, D. W.,
   English Language Examining: Report of an Inquiry into English Language Examining, African Universities Press, Lagos, 1964.
Harris, David P.,
   Testing English as a Second Language, McGraw-Hill, New York, 1969.
Hartog, Sir Philip Joseph,
   "The Marking of English Essays", International Institute Examinations Enquiry, 1941.
Heaton, J. B.,
   Practice through Pictures, Longman, 1971.
Heaton, J. B. and Methold, K.,
   Reading with Understanding, Intermediate Book 3, Longman, 1969.
Hutchings, Geoffrey,
   "Colourless Green Ideas: Multiple-Choice Vocabulary Tests", *English Language Teaching*, 25, 1970, 68–71.

Ingram, Elisabeth,
"Attainment and Diagnostic Testing", *Language Testing Symposium*, Oxford University Press, 1968.

Lado, Robert,
Language Testing: the Construction and Use of Foreign Language Tests, Longman, 1961.

de Leeuw, Manya and Eric,
Read Better, Read Faster: A New Approach to Efficient Reading, Penguin Books, 1965.

Mackey, W. F.,
"The Measurement of Language Learning", *Language Teaching Analysis*, Longman, 1965, 403−16.

Macmillan, M.,
"Comprehension Testing in Quicker Reading Courses", *English Language Teaching*, **18**, 1964, 109−16.

Marshall, J. C. and L. W. Hales,
Classroom Test Construction, Addison-Wesley Publishing Co., U.S.A., 1971.

Oller, John W. and Christine A. Conrad,
"The Cloze Technique and ESL Proficiency", *Language Learning*, **21**, 2., 1971, 183−95.

Oller, John,
"Dictation as a Device for Testing Foreign-Language Proficiency", *English Language Teaching*, **25**, 3., 1971, 254−9.

O'Neill, Robert,
English in Situations, Oxford University Press, 1970.

Otter, H. S.,
A Functional Language Examination, Oxford University Press, 1968.

Palmer, A. S.,
"Testing Communication", *International Review of Applied Linguistics (IRAL)*, **X/1.**, 1972.

Perren, G. E.,
"Testing Ability in English as a Second Language, (i) Problems (ii) Techniques (iii) Spoken language", *English Language Teaching*, 1967, **21**, 2., 99−106; **21**, 3., 197−202; **22**, 1., 22−9.

Pickett, G. D.,
"A Comparison of Translation and Blank-Filling as Testing Techniques", *English Language Teaching*, **23**, 1., 1968, 21−6.

Pilliner, A. E. G., ed. Alan Davies,
"Subjective and Objective Testing", *Language Testing Symposium*, Oxford University Press, 1968.

Pynsent, Robert,
"Style and Register Tests", *Objektive Tests im Englischunterricht der Schule und Universität*, Athenäum Verlag.

Rivers, Wilga M.,
Teaching Foreign-Language Skills, University of Chicago Press, 1968.

Robinson, Peter,
> "The Composition, Adaptation and Choice of Second-Language Tests", *English Language Teaching*, 25, 1., 1970, 60—8.

Robinson, Peter,
> "Testing the Second Language Competence of Children and Adults", *English Language Teaching*, 27, 2., 1973, 190—9.

Roemmele, J. A.,
> "The language laboratory as an aid in oral tests overseas", *English Language Teaching*, 21, 1966, 50—5.

Sako, Sydney,
> "Writing proficiency and achievement tests", *TESOL Quarterly*, 3, 1969, 237—49.

Secondary Schools Examinations Council,
> *Examinations Bulletin No. 1: The Certificate of Secondary Education: Some Suggestions for Teachers and Examiners*, H.M.S.O., London, 1963.
> *Examinations Bulletin No. 3: The Certificate of Secondary Education: An Introduction to Some Techniques of Examining*, H.M.S.O., London, 1964.
> *Examinations Bulletin No. 4: The Certificate of Secondary Education: An Introduction to Objective-Type Examinations*, H.M.S.O., London, 1964.
> *Examinations Bulletin No. 11: The Certificate of Secondary Education: Trial Examinations − Oral English*, H.M.S.O., London, 1966.
> *Examinations Bulletin No. 12: Multiple-Marking of English Compositions*, H.M.S.O., London, 1966.
> *Examinations Bulletin No. 16: The Certificate of Secondary Education Trial Examinations: Written English*, H.M.S.O., London, 1967.
> *Examinations Bulletin No. 22: Question Banks: Their Use in School Examinations*, Evans/Methuen Educational, 1971.

Sloss, R. P.,
> "Language Aptitude Testing", *R.A.F. Education Bulletin*, Autumn 1965, 39—47.

Spolsky, Bernard,
> "Language Testing: the Problem of Validation", *TESOL Quarterly*, 2, 1968, 88—94.

Spolsky, Bernard with Penny Murphy, Wayne Holm and Allen Ferrel,
> "Three Functional Tests of Oral Proficiency", *TESOL Quarterly*, 6, 3., 1972, 221—35.

Stein, Oswald,
> "Was Prüfen Wir Eigentlich?", *Verlag Lambert Lensing GmbH*, Dortmund, 1972, 357—65.

Strevens, Peter,
> "The Development of an Oral English Test for West Africa", *English Language Teaching*, 15, 1960, 172—224.

Strevens, Peter,
 "Objective Testing" *Papers in Language and Language Teaching,*
 Oxford University Press, 1965, 87−102.

Townson, Michael,
 "Testing Oral Skills at University Level", *English Language Teaching*,
 27, 2., 1973, 199−205.

Upshur, J. A. and J. F. (eds.),
 "Problems in Foreign Language Testing", *Language Learning: Special
 Issue*, **No. 3**, August, 1968.

Valette, Rebecca M.,
 Modern Language Testing: A Handbook, Harcourt, Brace & World, New
 York, 1967.

Wilkinson, Andrew, ed. Davies,
 "The Testing of Oracy", *Language Testing Symposium*, Oxford University Press, 1968.

Wingard, P. G.,
 The Test in English (Overseas), Universities of Manchester, Liverpool,
 Leeds, Sheffield and Birmingham Joint Matriculation Board, 1966.

Practical work

Sections 1.1/1.3/1.9

The following types of test items should be avoided:

    (i) items which test knowledge of grammatical rules;

   (ii) items in which one of the "incorrect" answers is not really incorrect in so far as it forms part of the current usage of native speakers of English; and

  (iii) items which have been constructed with a view to misleading the testee.

    Each of the grammar test items below conforms to one of the types referred to above. Identify the faults and rewrite the items.

(1) I think someone in this class will help me, ...?
    A. do I   C. won't they
    B. don't I   D. isn't it

(2) The house <u>where he lived</u> has now been destroyed.
    The underlined clause in this sentence is a subordinate
    A.   adjectival clause
    B.   adverbial clause of place
    C.   noun clause in apposition
    D.   adverbial clause of time

(3) What part of speech is *down* in the following sentence?

    The car broke *down* so we had to walk home.

(4) Is there . . . . rice in the pan?
    A. some B. any C. a D. those

(5) "Is that Tom Green over there?"
    "No, it's the boy . . . . we met at Ann's place."
    A. him B. which C. whom D. who

(6) Someone's lost . . . . fountain pen.
    A. his B. one's C. their D. its

Section 1.3

Which two of the following essay items do you consider far too difficult and inappropriate for foreign students taking an English examination at the end of their secondary school?

1. Wisdom.

2. A pen-friend of yours is coming to your country to spend a short holiday with you and your family. Your friend is very modern in his outlook, but your parents are very traditional. Unfortunately, you have to attend a school camp and you will not be at home during the first three days of your friend's visit. Your friend is honest but he is not very tactful. Write a letter to him, telling him about some of the customs of your parents and advising him how to behave while at your home.

3. "The mind is in its own place, and in itself
   Can make a Heaven of Hell, a Hell of Heaven." (Milton) Discuss.

4. The people who live next door to me.

Section 1.4

(1) Which two skills does the following test measure?

   Read the letter carefully and answer the questions which follow.

   Sir,
       For the past six weeks the people of my village have had no water.
       We knew several months ago that our well was drying up and wrote to the district engineer about it. He promised to send drilling equipment to dig another well. We waited a month but nothing came.
       We decided to write to the district engineer again. He replied that he had decided not to dig another well in the village but to put in piped water. We were very pleased to hear this . . .

   1. When did the well dry up?
   2. What was the district engineer's reply to the first letter?
   3. Why did the villagers write a second letter?
   4. What news made them very happy?

(2) Which three skills are involved in this test of auditory comprehension? Suggest one or two ways of improving this test by separating as far as possible the skill which it is primarily intended to test.

(The testee hears):

Listen carefully to the short talk you are about to hear and complete each of the following sentences. (The sentences follow the order of the talk.)
   You may be surprised to hear this talk given in a series of talks about the Government, for a large number of people believe that the Redhill-

Weston Railway is a private concern. One person I met recently never knew that a railway existed at all. Let me hasten to assure you that a railway does exist — indeed, not only exists but thrives — playing an important role in the economy of the island by carrying nearly 600,000 passengers a month . . .

(The testee reads):

1. The talk will surprise many people because . . . .
. . . .

2. The railway helps the island's economy as it . . . .
. . . .

Section 1.5

Each of the following test items is designed to test a certain area of phonology, vocabulary or grammar. Identify the language element being tested and the particular area of the language it is designed to test.

E.g. Put a circle round the letter that shows the best answer to the following question.

"Who's just arrived?"
A. "Bill is."
B. "Bill did."
C. "Bill was."
D. "Bill has."
E. "Bill just."

Answer: This item tests grammar and syntax: it is intended to test ability to use the short answer forms in response to a question with the Present Perfect tense. In my particular teaching situation it would be useful at Secondary 3 level.

1. Rewrite the following sentence in another way, using the words given for the beginning of the new sentence.

It isn't necessary for you to go so early.
You needn't . . . .

2. Write the correct word in each space.

His mother divided the cake . . . . six parts.
They live . . . . 23, King's Road.

3. Which word or group of words best explains the meaning of the word in capital letters?

INCREDIBLE
A. strange
B. wonderful

C. unbelievable

D. untrue

E. imaginary

4. In each item 3 words are given on tape, A, B and C. The testee must then decide which words are the same. Sometimes 2 words are the same; sometimes 3 are the same; and sometimes all 3 words are different.

A. leap   B. leap   C. lip

A. glass   B. glass   C. glass

A. cot   B. cut   C. caught

5. Write in each space the correct form of the word in capitals on the left.

DANGER   Joe Black drove the car . . . .

OBEY   Your dog is very . . . ., isn't it?

Section 1.6

Read the passage and the three test questions immediately following it. They test · recall rather than recognition. (Note that they also test two separate skills: the testee's reading ability *and* his writing ability.)

An accident occurred on the Japanese super tanker *m.v. Hoshibo* in the Suez Canal last night.

It is expected that the Canal will be closed to shipping for at least a week until the *Hoshibo*, which is out of control and preventing other ships from using the Canal, can be towed away. The bows of the ship have, in fact, swung round and are resting against one bank of the Canal, its stern almost touching the other bank.

The *Hoshibo*, one of the world's largest and newest tankers, was carrying a cargo of oil from Abadan to Southampton, England. The ship had passed halfway through the Canal when there was a violent explosion in the engine room. Fire broke out but was fortunately extinguished before it could spread to the cargo. However, the explosion blew a large hole in the stern of the ship and the engine room was soon flooded. Even the bridge was slightly damaged by fire.

Two engineers were killed by the explosion and five other crew members were injured. The owners of the tanker, Trans-Oceanic Oil Carriers Ltd., have ordered an immediate enquiry into the cause of the accident.

1. Why will the *m.v. Hoshibo* have to be towed away?

2. What did the cargo consist of?

3. Where was its destination?

(1) Now write 3 more questions to cover comprehension of the remainder of the reading passage.

(2) Write 12 statements based on this reading passage: 6 of them must be true and 6 must be false. (The testee will be required to say which statements are true and which are false, and the test will now be one of recognition.)

Section 1.7

(1) Because of first language interference, certain learners of English as a second or foreign language frequently make such errors as "Do you like some more tea?" or even "Are you liking some more tea?" What should they say? Now write a multiple-choice test item with 4 alternatives based on this particular problem of interference.

The stem has been written for you:

. . . . some more tea?

(2) There is a tendency for certain speakers to confuse *too* and *very*. Provide 4 alternatives for the following multiple-choice item.

This tea is . . . . . . hot for me to drink.

(3) The following is an error taken from the written work of a Chinese learner of English: "I miss my home very much even though I have left it many years." Use this error to construct a test item.

(4) Learners from certain language backgrounds tend to confuse the /p/ and /b/ sounds because there is no /p/ sound in their first language, thus causing them to associate /p/ with the nearest sound – /b/. Learners from certain other language backgrounds frequently confuse /l/ and /r/, usually substituting /l/ for /r/. Construct a test item for each of the two difficulties.

SECTION 2

Sections 2.1/2.3/2.4

The following grammar test items are subjective. Candidates taking the test in which they appear are required to complete each sentence using not fewer than three words.

Read the sentences but do not attempt to complete them.

1. I shan't come unless . . . .
2. Although the first horse fell, ...
3. The sofa is too heavy . . . .
4. I don't agree to . . . .

5. I haven't been to the cinema since . . . .
6. Is that the lady whose . . . . ?
7. You can't go out until . . . .
8. He insisted on . . . .
9. Was it difficult for you. . . . . ?
10. I don't like the place where . . . .
11. Who made you. . . . . ?
12. Tom was punished for . . . .

Now say which area of grammar you think is being tested in each item and construct a multiple-choice test item to replace each. If you have any difficulty in identifying any area of grammar being tested, rewrite the sentence so that you can construct a multiple-choice item.

E.g. 1 (a) The linker *unless* followed by the Present Simple tense.

(b) I shan't come unless it . . . . raining.
A. will stop B. is stopping C. stops

Sections 2.2/2.3

The following example demonstrates how an area of grammar may be tested by a number of item types. Obviously, only one item type would be used in a test and this would be decided upon in accordance with the general purpose of the test and the type of item used in the other parts of the test. After studying the example carefully, write as many different types of objective test items as you can to test each of the following:

(1) while (2) since (3) any

Example: although

Transformation   I had an umbrella but I didn't go out in the rain.
Although . . . . '. ..

Completion   . . . . I had an umbrella, I didn't go out in the rain.

Combination   I had an umbrella. I didn't go out in the rain.
(although)

Matching   Although I had an umbrella,   when it rained.
I usually stayed indoors   it began to rain.
David went on the picnic   it's rained every day.

Since you arrived here,   but it rained all the time.

While we were talking,   I didn't go out in the rain.

Multiple-choice . . . . I had an umbrella, I didn't go out in the rain.
A. But
B. Nevertheless
C. Although
D. However
E. Unless

Sections 2.3/2.4

The following 20 multiple-choice test items form part of a class test.

Imagine that each item has been designed to test a particular area of the language which has recently been practised or revised by all the students taking the test. Draw up a list of the grammatical or structural items being tested. (Note that a few items test the same, or similar, grammatical features.) State also the attainment (or age) level for which each item is suitable according to your syllabus or the general ELT situation in your country.

1. The poor man . . . . if no one tries to save him.
   A. drowns
   B. will drown
   C. would drown
   D. has drowned

2. Who made you . . . .?
   A. cry
   B. crying
   C. to cry
   D. cried

3. Several boys . . . . leave school early yesterday.
   A. ought to
   B. must
   C. should
   D. had to

4. "Does Bill know the answer?"
   "I'm not sure, but I think . . . ."
   A. it
   B. so
   C. yes
   D. that

5. Does that shop stay open . . . . Saturdays?
   A. at
   B. on
   C. in
   D. during

6. My sister enjoys . . . . a lot.
   A. sewing
   B. to sew
   C. sew
   D. to sewing

7. "Do you still go to the club meetings?"
   "Yes, I . . . . them every week for the past six months."
   A. attend
   B. have attended
   C. am attending
   D. attended

8. The man . . . . the pipe is called Harold.
   A. smokes
   B. he smokes
   C. smoke
   D. smoking

9. "You . . . . have seen a doctor. Why didn't you?"
   "I wish I had."
   A. must
   B. ought
   C. should
   D. need

10. I wish you . . . . me the truth.
    A. would tell
    B. will tell
    C. tell
    D. are telling

11. Did you ever meet the person . . . . was knocked down by a bus?
    A. who
    B. whom
    C. which
    D. he

12. I'll visit you . . . . Christmas.
    A. at
    B. in
    C. on
    D. by

13. "Are you . . . . to reach this shelf?"
    "No, I will need to grow another six inches at least!"
    A. so tall
    B. tall as
    C. tall enough
    D. too tall

14. These cases are . . . . heavy for me to carry. I can't even lift them.
    A. much
    B. more
    C. too
    D. so

15. Was he the man . . . .?
    A. you saw him last night
    B. you saw last night
    C. him you saw last night
    D. whom you saw him last night

16. I do hope you . . . . much better in a few days.
    A. would be
    B. would have been
    C. will have been
    D. will be

17. The man . . . . car you bought is at the door.
    A. whom
    B. his
    C. whose
    D. which

18. Just take a look at . . . .
    A. all those new beautiful stamps
    B. all those beautiful new stamps
    C. those all beautiful new stamps
    D. those all new beautiful stamps

19. The stool is . . . . that no one can sit on it.
    A. so small
    B. too small
    C. small enough
    D. very small

20. Stay here until someone . . . . you to go.
    A. will tell
    B. is telling
    C. tells
    D. has been telling

Sections 2.3/2.4

The following are examples of badly-constructed multiple-choice items. Identify the incorrect features and then rewrite each item.

1. The old woman enjoys . . . . television every night.
   A. looking B. looking at C. seeing D. looking for

2. You've already got . . . .
   A. a car of your own, don't you?
   B. a car of your own, haven't you?
   C. an own car, don't you?
   D. an own car, haven't you?

3. Ann's parents have . . . . a small cottage near the sea for a month.
   A. rented B. hired C. loaned D. borrowed

4. Did John travel there by . . . .?
   A. bus B. car C. plane D. foot

5. I'll wait here until David . . . .
   A. comes B. will come C. came D. has come

6. According to the last paragraph of the passage, the early scientists'
   discoveries have helped astronauts . . . .
   A. very little B. quite a lot C. moderately D. not at all

7. Tom . . . . the children playing.
   A. enjoys looking   C. is enjoying looking
   B. enjoys to look at   D. enjoys looking at

8. I'll tell you all the news . . . . Wednesday.
   A. on B. by C. for D. in

9. What was the sphere made of?
   A. It was made of steel.
   B. It was made of aluminium.
   C. It was made of cotton and rope.
   D. It was made of light wood.

10. John is a *dutiful* son.
    A. stern   C. very respectful and obedient
    B. kind   D. lawful

11. According to the writer, ski-ing is probably . . . . . .
    A. more dangerous than skating
    B. less dangerous than skating
    C. as dangerous as skating
    D. neither more nor less dangerous than skating

12. Dick and Paul at last managed to escape by
    A. the tunnel they had made
    B. creating a diversion
    C. their friends in the camp
    D. a piece of unexpected luck

13. Surfing
    A. is a major sport in California
    B. used to be popular with many people
    C. can be dangerous because of sharks
    D. is impossible in the winter months

14. "Are you . . . . for election on the committee?"
    "Yes, will you vote for me?"
    A. embellished B. eligible C. elucidated D. embroiled

Section 2.5

A: Write rubrics suitable for each of the following two item types.

   (i) Did you hurt yourself while you . . . . football?
      A. had played   B. have played
      C. play   D. were playing

  (ii) "Has David passed his examination?"
      A. "I think so."
      B. "I know it."
      C. "So know I."
      D. "I think yes."

B: The following six items have been taken from a test of auditory comprehension. The options are given below in the form of notes; in each case the first option is the correct one. Write out the six test items in their proper form, arranging the correct options at random or in alphabetical order (but bearing in mind what was said about dates and figures).

1. When were steam locomotives withdrawn from service on the Redhill-Weston Railway?
   1962/1966/1967/1963/1960

2. Why may some people be surprised to hear that this talk is included in a series of talks about the Government?
   may think it private business concern/a very controversial subject for talk/importance of railway has diminished/few people really interested in subject/may embarrass Government

3. What happened to No. 26 steam locomotive?
   caught fire/licence expired/presented to fire service/converted into diesel

4. How many people travel by the Redhill-Weston Railway every year?
   almost 600,000/nearly 6,000,000/over 7,000,000/350,000/about 1,500

5. How many tunnels are there between the second and fourth stations?
   three/six/seven/four/one

6. What is there near the workshop at Ashfield?
   a deep cutting/earthworks/reclaimed land/heavy traffic/rolling stock

SECTION 3

Section 3.1

The following six multiple-choice items have been constructed in the same way as Type (e) in Section 3.1. The problem is not presented clearly and, in addition, the testee's time is wasted through a lot of unnecessary repetition. Rewrite each item like Type (b).

1. A. Mrs Robson made Bill return home early.
   B. Mrs Robson made Bill returned home early.
   C. Mrs Robson made Bill to return home early.
   D. Mrs Robson made Bill returning home early.

2. A. Although hard he tried, he couldn't open the door.
   B. Even if hard he tried, he couldn't open the door.
   C. No matter how hard he tried, he couldn't open the door.
   D. Except that hard he tried, he couldn't open the door.

3. A. I shall travel to London with train.
   B. I shall travel to London by train.
   C. I shall travel to London in train.
   D. I shall travel to London on train.

4. A. You haven't seen this film before, haven't you?
   B. You haven't seen this film before, isn't it?
   C. You haven't seen this film before, have you?
   D. You haven't seen this film before, is it?

5. A. When he heard the bad news, he had almost cried.
   B. When he heard the bad news, he almost cries.
   C. When he heard the bad news, he has almost cried.
   D. When he heard the bad news, he almost cried.

6. A. If you had worked harder, you have finished by now.
   B. If you had worked harder, you would have finished by now.
   C. If you had worked harder, you finished by now.
   D. If you had worked harder, you would finish by now.

7. A. He is not strong to lift this heavy table.
   B. He is too strong to lift this heavy table.
   C. He is not strong enough to lift this heavy table.
   D. He is not too strong to lift this heavy table.

8. A. Don't wait until it begins to rain or you'll get wet.
   B. Don't wait until it will begin to rain or you'll get wet.
   C. Don't wait until it would begin to rain or you'll get wet.
   D. Don't wait until it had begun to rain or you'll get wet.

Section 3.2

Construct one multiple-choice item containing four options for each of the following areas of grammar. (You may use the example given to form the stem *if you wish.*)

1. The Present Perfect tense: Let's get off now. The bus has already stopped.

2. *Used to* (past habit):   I used to play chess a lot but I don't now.

3. Question tags: John never arrived early at school, did he?

4. WH-question words: How often do you visit your uncle?

5. Relative pronouns: That's the house where my father was born.

6. Prepositions: Does anyone live on that island?

7. Prepositions following adjectives: Helen's interested in classical music.

8. Modals: We needn't go to school today: we have a holiday.

9. Linkers: It's been a long time since I last saw you.

10. Determiners: "He says he likes the people but not the language."
"I like the French, too."

11. Order of Adjectives: I've seen two interesting new Japanese films recently.

12. Reported Speech: Ann told Bill not to use her new pen.

Sections 3.3/3.4

The following extract is the second paragraph of the student's letter in Section 3.3.

I wonder did you grow more fatter since summer. I will be happy if you sent me one of your photographs. In last letter of your you write that your father is ill. I hope that he would soon be better. You are happy because you have such a nice father. You also mention that he will soon have birthday. I wish him the best to his birthday.

(1) Select any four errors from the paragraph and construct a multiple-choice grammar item for each of the four errors.

(2) Construct suitable error-recognition Type 1 items to test four errors which appear in the extract.

(3) Construct error-recognition Type 2 items to test the student's recognition of the following common errors:

1. The use of the Present Simple for the Present Perfect tense.
2. The passive: "The house was been painted when I arrived."
3. Misuse of articles: "It took the primitive man thousands of years to learn how to make and use tools."
4. The use of the infinitive for the gerund: "enjoyed to fish."
5. The wrong position of the adverb.
6. The wrong order of adjectives.
7. Omission of the preposition.
8. The wrong sequence of tenses.
9. Incorrect subordination: "It is too dark that he cannot study."
10. Errors in the use of relative clauses.

Section 3.5

The following ten sentences contain errors in word order. Identify the problem areas and then construct suitable word-order m/c items.

1. I have never met your little pretty sister.
2. Please help me to pick up the pieces of the blue broken vase.
3. Don't you know when are you leaving?
4. Wherever may you go, I'll always think of you.
5. I have no idea how much will it cost you.
6. You shouldn't behave like that no matter what has Bill done.
7. Let's look through this old interesting photograph album.
8. Mr Short asked me if I already had seen the film.
9. You must never be too proud however you are rich.
10. No matter how he tries hard, he'll never be successful.

Section 3.6

(1) Construct six sentences with blanks to test verb tenses. Write in brackets after each blank the infinitive form of a required verb. Each item should be so constructed that it can only be completed in one way.

(2) Write a short passage of about 100 words suitable for use as a completion item testing the use of the determiners *a/an/the/some*. Try to construct the passage so that there is only one correct answer for each blank. Here are some notes to help you to write the passage:

> swimming in sea with friend – saw clothes on beach but no one there – after hour left beach and took clothes – cycled to nearby police station and gave clothes to police – on leaving police station saw angry man in swimming-trunks getting on a bus

Section 3.7

Transformation items can be based on the following twelve sentences. Write the beginning of each new sentence; then write out and underline the required answer.

1. The two cars crashed into each other, but no one was hurt.
2. The food for the wedding is being prepared by Mrs Atkinson.
3. You've been very kind to invite Sarah and Ann.
4. Surely Tom is much heavier than David.
5. The students cannot leave school until the money has been found.
6. Someone brought a glass of water and then the speaker rose to his feet.
7. "I have enjoyed this evening very much," Tony said.
8. I'll be able to finish painting today unless it rains.
9. It's impossible for anyone to survive such a crash.
10. I last went to the cinema at Easter.
11. Mr Lee told his wife that he would not arrive home until late that night.
12. People drink a lot of tea in England.

SECTION 4

Section 4.1

A. Which of the words in the following list would you select for inclusion in a vocabulary test designed to test the reading proficiency of students about to follow advanced courses in civil engineering? Select thirty words which might form the core of an imaginary fifty-item test.

arch, archaic, artifice, bacteria, beam, block, brutality, cable, catalyst, collapse, compatriot, component, concrete, console, contract, convalesce, crack, cross-section, culture, disguise, distaste, divine, efficiency, epidemic, evaporation, expansion, extend, fertility, firm, forces, gratitude, hygienic, inherit, immune, inoffensive, load, lunacy, obsession, oscillate, purge, psychological, proportion, prosaic, rapture, relatively, resistant, sacrilege, solitary, span, stability, stimulate, stream-lining, stress, structure, sublime, support, surface, suspend, sustain, symbolic, tension, trust, vaccination

B. Each of the following sentences contains an error of lexis. Identify the error and then write (a) the correct option suitable for inclusion in a multiple-choice vocabulary test and (b) a distractor (i.e. the original error). Do *NOT* construct test items as such.

1. Do you pay a high fee every month for your flat?
2. I'll book two places for us at the cinema.
3. Ann can't endure her new teacher.

4. My brother is making research in London.
5. Breaking the window charged me five dollars.
6. The ambulance has arrived to carry you to hospital.
7. Swimming is my favourable sport in summer.
8. You shouldn't make such a custom of getting up at seven every morning.

Section 4.2

A. Write four options for six of the following stems:

1. easily seen and understood
2. something that happens
3. warm and comfortable
4. can be seen or observed
5. move on one's hands and knees
6. rule in a cruel and unjust way
7. not interested in
8. belonging to all parts of the world
9. make up one's mind
10. refuse to obey

B. Select twelve words from the following list and construct six multiple-choice vocabulary items like Type 3, and six like Type 4 (i.e. in a context).

absurd, abundant, agreeable, antique, assault, barely, blend, break in, casual, chaos, collapse, come to, consign, customary, dense, device, endure, enforce, erect, exterminate, festive, foremost, frail, gauge, on hand, hesitation, homely, illusive, immune, indispensable, lethal, look up to, loyal, mystify, obscure, offensive, partition, permit, pluck, portion, presently, purchase, pursue, rare, recompense, redundant, resolute, rotate, savage, seldom, signify, stable, stir, superfluous, talent, tender, timid, turn up, unite, view

Section 4.3

A. Provide four options (one correct option and three distractors) for each of the following stems.

1. I'm sure you'll pass if you keep your . . . .
2. He tricked us all because he was so . . . .
3. Mr Smith's got a very . . . . business and makes several thousand pounds a year in profit.
4. The island was . . . . populated; I hardly saw one house.
5. Let's . . . . the plan in detail before we reject it.
6. Please . . . . me: I know I have hurt you very much.

 7. His behaviour was anything but . . . .: he shouted and screamed.
 8. People no longer. . . . . . . Tom because he is always drunk.
 9. He spoke in a voice that was almost . . . ., so most people didn't hear him.
10. I'm sure he won't lie: he's very . . . .
11. The photograph is . . . .: everything is out of focus.
12. The patient's condition rapidly . . . . and he died the next day.

B. For each of the following groups of options construct a multiple-choice item. You must determine which option you wish to be the correct one and then construct a suitable stem.

1. cosy, tidy, small, neat
2. current, modern, present, up-to-date
3. defiant, bold, angry, violent
4. abandon, depart, separate, ignore
5. go without, lack, need, want
6. intention, purpose, meaning, ambition
7. glance, look, stare, wink
8. murmur, grumble, complain, object

Section 4.4

Construct sets for the following words. Each set should consist of four words. Write the first five items at a fairly elementary level and the second five at an intermediate or advanced level.

 1. flat
 2. book
 3. kitchen
 4. aeroplane
 5. tree
 6. newspaper
 7. radio
 8. basketball
 9. guitar
10. typewriter

Section 4.5

Construct eight matching items from this reading comprehension test. The original passage may be altered or rewritten in any way at all. (See Type 6 on Page 52.)

The appearance of an athlete holding a torch now marks the commencement of every Olympic Games. This particular ceremony, in which a lighted torch is carried by athletes from Mount Olympus in Greece, is still an important feature of every modern Olympic Games.

In 1968, for example, a torch was carried half-way round the world to Mexico City. Three times the torch exploded on the way, but the flame was never actually extinguished.

This ceremony, linking the different places where the modern Games are held every four years with the site of the ancient Olympics, was started in Berlin in 1936. But the actual torch ceremony itself dates back to Ancient Greece, where one of the most spectacular events was the torch race, always run at night. In the race athletes with torches ran across the stadium to the bowl in which the sacred flame was kept burning. They then lit their torches and raced back.

Section 4.6

A. Rewrite the following twelve sentences as vocabulary items testing word formation. Also write a suitable rubric for this test.

Example: The concert was very enjoyable, wasn't it?
        ENJOY   The concert was very . . . . . ., wasn't it?

1. The president's popularity increased after he had promised to reduce taxes.
2. Saving the drowning man was a very courageous act.
3. I can't understand the reason for this sudden gaiety.
4. Bill is very energetic, isn't he?
5. I'm sure you've invented this story and the person you've described is a fictitious character.
6. We're travelling in a circular direction, aren't we?
7. You must be a little more attentive in lectures and take notes.
8. The explosion was followed by a huge flame.
9. It's rained continuously since last Thursday.
10. You must try to control your curiosity: this matter is no concern of yours.
11. Mr Brown is building an extension to his house.
12. Many complaints were made about the student's expulsion from the college.

B. Construct vocabulary test items like Type 2(a) in this section. The answers appear in List 1 below; in List 2 synonyms, etc. are given for each of the answers in List 1 (but the order has been altered). Find the correct synonym for each word in List 1; next use the synonymous word or phrase in a sentence. Write out all the sentences as a test.

List 1	*List 2*
(1) punctually	turn to ice
(2) here	from time to time
(3) fast	put off
(4) recover	at hand

(5)	beside	on the cards
(6)	freeze	at great speed
(7)	besides	on time
(8)	occasionally	get better
(9)	permanently	at the side of
(10)	postpone	with pleasure
(11)	gladly	in addition to
(12)	likely	for good

Example: (1) Bill is always late: I've never known him arrive *on time*.

. . . .

Section 4.7

Use the reading text on Page 109 (Section 7.3) as the basis for constructing a completion item like either Type 2(a), or Type 2(b) in Section 4.7.
You may make as many changes as you wish to the original passage. You
may also wish to simplify the passage so that it is suitable for students at a
lower level.

SECTION 5

Section 5.1

Read the following passage two or three times. Then either make notes on
it *or* use the notes given at the end of the passage. Give a short talk from
the notes, if possible recording it on tape. Remember that your listeners
will understand the talk a little more easily if you repeat or rephrase
certain pieces of information.

It has been found in a recent survey that most people have roughly
the same ideas about the ideal place for a holiday. The availability of
public transport appeared to play little part in the choice of a locality,
even for those people who did not own a car. Congested roads and
financial considerations, however, were the two chief factors in deterr-
ing people from taking holidays in certain localities. Forty per cent of
the people interviewed in the survey gave scenery as the most important
factor in determining where to go. Visiting friends was the reason why
twenty-two per cent chose a particular destination. Thirty-six per cent
were primarily affected in their choice by the facilities provided at the
holiday resort. Climate was an important factor amongst the minority
group who regularly spent their holidays abroad.

Recent survey — most people have same ideas about ideal holiday place.
Public transport — little influence on choice.
But congested roads and money — influence.

40% — scenery = most important.
22% — visiting friends.
36% — facilities at holiday resort.
A few went abroad because of climate.

Section 5.2

(1) The following pictures for a phoneme discrimination test appear on the student's own test sheet. For each picture, write two appropriate words (i.e. phoneme contrasts) for the teacher to read out in a test of phoneme discrimination.

(2) Construct a phoneme discrimination test, consisting of the sound contrasts listed after the examples. Note that in a few cases (as in Example 3) only one phoneme is given and, therefore, no contrast will be possible.

Example: (1) /æ/ /ʌ/
            A. sack   B. sack   C. suck

      (2) /ə:/ , /æ/ and /ɛ/
            A. bird   B. bad   C. bed

      (3) /i:/
            A. heel   B. heel   C. heel

1. /i/ and /i:/	13. /k/ and /g/
2. /v/ and /w/	14. /tʃ/ and /tr/
3. /ɔ/	15. /u:/ and /ou/
4. /r/	16. /ʌ/ and /ɔ/
5. /t/ and /d/	17. /a:/ and /ʌ/
6. /u/	18. /j/ and /tʃ/
7. /e/ and /i/	19. /i/, /e/ and /æ/
8. /ʌ/ and /ə:/	20. /v/, /f/ and /w/
9. /ʃ/ and /dz/	21. /ʌ/
10. /æ/ and /e/	22. /a:/, /ɔ/ and /ɔ:/
11. /ɛə/	23. /p/ and /b/
12. /n/, /l/ and /r/	24. /e/ and /ʌ/

(3) Write six sentences for inclusion in a test similar *either* to Type 2(b) *or* 3(b). Each sentence must contain one of the following words and test the student's ability to discriminate between the appropriate phoneme contrasts.

1. /æ/ b*a*nd   2. /i/ p*i*n   3. /f/ *f*ew

4. /tʃ/ *ch*oke   5. /ʌ/ c*u*t   6. /k/ *c*oat

Section 5.3

Use the following short conversational exchanges to construct test items similar to Type 2 in this section.

1. "Mr Lee wants his class to have more homework."
   "But I've just given them a lot of homework."

2. "Bring me a ladder, please."
   "Will this one be high enough for you?"

3. "No one will help Mary."
   "Couldn't you try to help her?"

4. "I met Mr Robinson again yesterday."
   "I hope he was more polite to you this time."

Section 5.4

(1) Choose a suitable picture (preferably a poster) and write twelve sentences about it for a listening comprehension test. Six of the sentences must be true and six must be false. Write a suitable rubric (i.e. instructions) for the test.

(2)

Use these pictures to write a test item similar to that given in Type 2. Make Picture E the correct answer. (Remember that each picture differs in only one respect from the other four pictures.)

(3) Use each of the groups of pictures on Page 217 to write items similar to the Type 3 items on Page 67. Write one sentence for each picture and write in brackets at the side the grammatical/structural area you are testing.

(4) Choose either a map of the district where your students live or a street plan of the city/town/village in which your school is situated. Use the map or plan to test ability to understand simple directions. (Try to avoid using the names of streets in your directions.)

(3)

(5) The following geometrical figure is the correct "answer" you require the testee to produce. Write instructions similar to those given in the test item listed under Type 6 in this section.

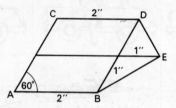

Section 5.5

(1) Construct test items similar to the ones in Type 1(a) from the following sentences by writing four options (written paraphrases) for each sentence.

1. We shan't be able to play tennis unless it stops raining.
2. Do you prefer music to art?
3. We're going to have our house painted next week.
4. I wish you'd offered to help before you left the party.
5. You should have cut the lawn this morning instead of going swimming.
6. If only you'd entered the competition, you'd certainly have won.
7. You ought to practise a lot more: then you wouldn't come last.
8. Half of the ship's thirty passengers were picked up by life-boats while another eight were rescued by helicopter. The other passengers are still missing.

(2) Construct test items similar to the ones in Type 2 from these sentences. Write four responses for each question, three of which must be distractors.

1. Why was Tom late for school yesterday?
2. When are you going to play football?
3. Must we wear suits for the meeting?
4. Is Alan having his hair cut as well as a shampoo?
5. Where have you put my white shorts?
6. Has anyone here been to both England and America?
7. Need Tina stay until everyone's finished?
8. Do you ever feel as if you want to leave your present job?
9. How did you get to Tim's place last night?
10. Do athletes have to spend a long time training every day?

(3) Write four brief dialogues, similar to Type 3 test items, each followed by four options.

Section 5.6

(1) Write four options (one correct option and three distractors) for the following talk. Then practise giving the talk as naturally as possible.

Remember to lengthen the pauses slightly if you are reading the talk. (The talk is intended for teenagers or adults who have been learning English for at least three or four years.)

The history of medicine is one of a long fight against disease – the oldest and most terrible enemy man has ever known. During the past twenty or thirty years or so, however, there's been a tremendous advance in medical research. Nowadays most of our diseases and illnesses – as well as many of our injuries – can be successfully treated by doctors. Being ill now is vastly different from being ill not so long ago, thank goodness. Unfortunately, however, very little research has been done on ageing – that is, the causes and processes of ageing. But strangely, many doctors now believe that no one ever dies simply because he's old: death is actually caused by diseases or illnesses, many of which can be cured in younger people.

(2) Construct a listening test similar to the one described in Type 2. Write a summary or paraphrase for completion based on the following "talk".

In many countries, especially those in tropical and sub-tropical regions, it's necessary to boil water in order to kill any infectious bacteria it may contain. Unless the boiled water can be put in a refrigerator, it'll have a flat taste, due mainly to the dissolved gases that are expelled.

Many people dislike this taste. They prefer to drink impure water out of the tap and risk infection. Indeed, I have a doctor friend who argued that by drinking water out of the tap for several years he'd probably developed an immunity to the bacteria in the water. This practice is certainly not to be recommended: you will probably end up seriously ill in the process of trying to build up an immunity in this way. If you don't like the taste of the water after it's been boiled, you can always shake the water in a bottle in order to get some air into it – or you can use it for making tea or coffee.

(3) Write a short news broadcast lasting not more than five minutes. Construct about six multiple-choice items based on the "news". (Describe fictitious incidents and characters in your news broadcast; cover several topics and try to add a touch of humour.)

SECTION 6

Section 6.1

(1) Describe briefly any method you know for testing the speaking skills. Assess the usefulness in the light of the general aims of the syllabus being followed and indicate possible backwash effects of the test on teaching and learning.

(2) The following list contains some of the components of the speaking skills. Comment briefly on each of these components and then select four or five which you consider to be of the most importance in attempting to assess oral production at any level you wish. (They are listed in alphabetical order.)

Comprehension — general understanding of what is being said to the testee

Content — ideas, etc.

General fluency — ease and speed of speaking and length of utterances

Grammar — structure and usage

Vocabulary — use of words and turn of phrase

Pronunciation — phonemic features, stress and intonation

Reciprocity — relationship with listener (contact — style of address — flexibility)

Register — kind of English suitable for subject matter

Voice and Delivery — range, clarity, use of gesture, etc.

Section 6.2

(1) The following passage has been written for inclusion in a test of reading aloud. It will appear in this version for the testees to read. Now write a copy of the passage with a key suitable for the examiner's use.

"Wait a minute!" shouted Peter. "I've got a brainwave."

"Not again," David and Tom groaned. "The last one you had got us into trouble with the police."

"Well, if you don't want to hear how we can get out of this mess, that's your look-out," said Bill.

"We're only teasing you," David laughed. "What do you suggest?"

"Do you remember the guard who was asleep when we first saw him? He asked us for a cigarette, didn't he? Now I happen to have a few packets in this bag. Let's have a go at bribing him tonight. No matter how he reacts, we can't be worse off than we are now."

(2) Adapt or write a short reading passage to test most of the following phonological features:

rising intonation, falling intonation, tonic, syllable stress, stress in compound nouns, weak forms; and the sounds and contrasts /f-v/, /p-b/, /t-d/, /l-r/, /ʃ-tʃ/, /p-t/ (final), /ð-d/ (final), /e-æ/, /iː-i/, /ɔ-ɔː/, /æ-ʌ/, /ei-ai/, and /ð/ after diphthongs.

(3) Write a short account of a humorous incident (about 150–200 words), suitable for re-telling in a test of oral production. Outline briefly some of the elements you are attempting to test by means of the passage.

Section 6.3

(1) Make use of the following sentences to test phoneme discrimination, stress and intonation by means of repetition. For each sentence outline the feature you would test and rearrange the order of the sentences accordingly.

1. Sit down on this seat if you're feeling sick.
2. What's wrong with part of the large cottage?
3. I didn't do it: it was John.
4. Is Ted still searching for his dirty, red shirt?
5. Don't blame Bill for arriving very late at the Bank.
6. It certainly is a lovely day, isn't it?
7. Tom didn't dare to ride fast up the dusty road.
8. Be careful or you'll hurt yourself.
9. Will you be able to come as well?
10. These two huge tubes of toothpaste will be suitable.
11. You're going to the party, aren't you?
12. I looked a long time for a cushion to put my foot on.

(2) Change the following mechanical drill into a natural one for inclusion in a test of oral production. Make sure that enough examples are given.

> People drink a lot of coffee in France.
> A lot of coffee is drunk in France.

1. People grow a lot of rice in China.
2. People play a lot of football in Brazil.
3. People make tyres in Malaysia.
4. People speak Spanish in Argentina.
5. People drink a lot of tea in England.
6. People teach English in most schools in Hong Kong.
7. People eat rice with milk and sugar in that country.
8. People sell a lot of fresh fish in that town.
9. People grow coconuts on those islands.
10. People often hold demonstrations in the United States.

(3) Write two drills, each one designed to test either the use of *must* and *have to* or *if only* (= I wish); the first drill should be a structural one and the second should be based on a series of situations.

(4) Refer to Situational Drills (Types 1 and 2) on Page 89 and construct six items suitable for inclusion in a class test.

Section 6.4

(1) Construct models of three different grammatical or structural items which each of the following pictures can be used to test. Write out six

.brief conversational exchanges between the tester and the testee (according to the pictures) for each of the three structural items.

(2) The following books contain picture stories, many of which are suitable for inclusion in oral production tests. Select the most appropriate story for your test from any (one) of these books:

"Composition through Pictures", J. B. Heaton (Longman).
"Picture Composition Book", L. A. Hill (Longman).
"Progressive Picture Compositions", Donn Byrne (Longman).
"Guided Composition", Fleming and Fougasse (U.L.P.).

(3) Now select the following pictures from any newspapers, magazines or comics you possess.

  (i) a picture for description
 (ii) two pictures for comparison
(iii) a picture story

Section 6.5

(1) Write questions suitable for assisting an interviewer when talking about each of the following topics:

      Transport and travel
      Health
      Careers
      Films
      Current events

(2) Discuss briefly how you would plan and score an oral interview for your students in the light of what you have read in the corresponding section. Draw up a scheme for assessment of the oral production skills.

Section 6.6

(1) Prepare a list of ten topics, each suitable for your students to give as a short talk in a test of oral production.

(2) Assign roles to students for each of the following situations:

(1) something lost in a cinema
(2) a road accident
(3) looking for books in a library
(4) an argument over articles bought in a big department store
(5) a travel agent's office
(6) complaining to a neighbour about his radio

Section 6.7

(1) Construct test items similar to either Type 1(a) or Type 1(b) to test sound/symbol association of the following phonemes:

1.	/ɑː/	sh*ar*p	6.	/ɔː/	c*au*ght
2.	/ʌ/	b*u*d	7.	/ə:/	f*ur*
3.	/iː/	s*ea*t	8.	(θ)	*th*ought
4.	/uə/	t*ou*r	9.	/au/	d*ow*n
5.	/ɛə/	h*ai*r	10.	/z/	hou*s*es

(2) Construct a test of rhyme (see Types 2(a) and 2(b)), using each of the following words.

1.	zoo	6.	tooth
2.	fish	7.	poor
3.	chain	8.	fear
4.	fair	9.	yacht
5.	word	10.	bud

SECTION 7

Section 7.2

A. Construct word-matching items for the following words. (See Page 105)

fast	real	pens	pleasant	am swimming
note	master	aloud	is crossing	has met

B. Now construct sentence-matching items for the following sentences:

(1) The bus will stop near the school.
(2) Take a cup of tea to Bill.
(3) How many windows are open?
(4) That was a foolish thing to do.
(5) It was not possible to answer all the questions.
(6) Can you swim as well as Mary?
(7) There are twenty boys and twelve girls in my class.
(8) Peter doesn't want to leave his uncle's house.
(9) We went to the beach last night.
(10) My brother is ill but I feel well.

C. Construct items for each of the following pictures. For each picture write four sentences, only one of which is about the picture.

D. Write ten sentences about the picture on Page 225: only five of the sentences must actually agree with what is shown in the picture.

Section 7.3

A. Construct twelve true/false items based on any appropriate reading extract (of about 250 words) from a magazine. The items should be at a lower reading difficulty level than the text.

B. Now select any reading text which is slightly below the reading difficulty level of the students for whom your test is intended. Construct at least twelve true/false items which are at a *higher* level of difficulty than the reading passage.

Section 7.4

A. Use the following short reading extracts to construct test items similar to those described and shown under Type 1 in this section. Write distractors for the word underlined in each extract.

(1) If you ever go into a house in Japan, you must take off your <u>shoes</u> or else they will damage the fine straw mats which cover the floor.

(2) Have you ever noticed how <u>busy</u> our roads are becoming? Every year more and more cars are using them: in some countries almost every family owns a car.

(3) In ancient times people used to worship the Moon as a goddess, and even after such practices had stopped, their <u>superstitions</u> continued for a long time.

(4) It cannot be claimed that technology has always proved <u>beneficial</u>: a great deal of harm has been done because of a lack of thought for the possible consequences of certain inventions and processes.

(5) Soon the guitar and guitar music spread among music lovers throughout the country: nothing could check its <u>popularity</u>.

(6) It is possible to find women engaged in almost as many diversified occupations as men. However, when a girl is employed as a jockey, she lays claim to a <u>vocation</u> shared by few other women.

(7) When filled, the air-cushion provides an effective protection against blows to the motorist's head and body. Half a second later, it <u>deflates</u> to allow quick exit from the car.

(8) The judge said of the victim's injuries that no one wished to <u>minimise</u> the sufferings of others but this was, in any view, a very slight injury.

B. Use each of the following statements as the basis for the construction of Type 2 test items. The following rubric has been written to introduce the test.

> "Each of the following sentences is followed by four statements A, B, C and D. These four statements are about the sentence but only one of them is true. Draw a circle round the letter of the true statement."

(1) Mary was crying when John entered the room.
(2) Peter gave Ann a new pen.
(3) Mr White was very tall but the window was too high for him to reach.
(4) Ann used to walk to school.
(5) You needn't bring anything to eat.
(6) Where's Bill? He can't have come to the party.
(7) I wish I'd told John the news.
(8) You can try to mend the radio, but I don't think you'll be successful.

C. Construct eight reading comprehension items according to the following rubric.

> "Each of the following passages is followed by one question. Each question consists of an incomplete sentence, followed by four possible ways of completing it, labelled A, B, C and D. Choose the answer which you think best completes the sentence according to the passage."

(1) My brother goes every week to see my old grandmother but I go only once a month. When he goes by himself he travels by train but when he goes with me we travel by taxi.

(2) Tom generally tries hard to get on well with David but David never makes the slightest effort to get on with Tom. Their meetings always end in an argument or quarrel.

(3) One morning Robert Tsakpo was walking past some big shops in the centre of Lagos when he saw a large, black car a few yards in front of him. Further on was the red building where he was going to post his parcel.

(4) Before setting off on the picnic, Ann looked at a map of the route. Then she put a compass in her rucksack and, after picking up a hand-kerchief, said goodbye to her mother and joined her friends outside.

(5) A burst water-pipe caused long queues of cars early in the evening today near the city centre. If it had been a hundred yards away opposite the Bus Station, chaos would have resulted. As it was, water shot several feet into the air just outside the main entrance of the City Library, and the whole of Church Street was flooded.

(6) According to a recent report published in Great Britain, the chances of an unskilled manual worker's child (Social Class V) being a poor reader at the age of seven are six times greater than those of a profes-sional worker's child (Social Class 1). The chances of a Social Class V child being a non-reader at this age are fifteen times greater than those of a Social Class 1 child.

(7) All over the world, the computer is transforming the nature of work and the relations between people and their work, and the nature of the transformation needs to be faced if the computer itself is to be properly managed.

(8) Computerisation has been frequently compared with the industrial revolution, but the crucial difference is that, whereas the industrial revolution amputated people by taking over manual and craft skills, the computer revolution decapitates people.

Section 7.5

A. Read the following passage[1] and complete each of the five test items after it by constructing *four* options (A, B, C, D): one of the options should be correct and the other three should be incorrect (i.e. distrac-tors).

One sunny morning in summer I left my sister's house and went for a walk along a hilly path. It was a warm day and there was no one on the path. At the end of the path I was sitting down to rest when a big black dog suddenly appeared. It ran up to me barking and lay down at my feet. I touched its head. When I started to walk home, it followed me and it would not go away. It had a collar round its neck but there was no name on the collar. When I got home, I rang up the nearest police-station. I told the police that I had found a big black dog. I said that I would keep it until its owner called for it. I gave the police my name and address. Two days later an old gentleman came to my home to ask about the dog. He said he had lost his dog because it hated riding in cars. One day it jumped out of the open window of his car. He offered me ten dollars, but I did not take the money. Then he gave me his name and address and invited me to visit him.

1. While I was out for a walk, ...
2. When I began to walk home, ...
3. I told the police about the dog because........................
4. The owner said he had lost his dog because.....................
5. The old gentleman asked me to ....

B. Read the following passage[2] and the test questions immediately after it. Write one multiple-choice item (consisting of four options) for each of the six questions immediately following the passage. (Note that parts of the text and certain of the questions may require some re-writing, etc.)

When we think of space, we imagine rockets and space-ships. The first man to attempt to travel in space was a Swiss, Auguste Piccard. He did not ascend in a space-ship but in something quite different!

In 1931 Piccard built a large balloon more than thirty yards wide. It was made of cotton and rubber. Beneath the balloon he hung an air-tight aluminium sphere. When the balloon rose into the air, it lifted the sphere. Piccard and his assistant, who were inside, were lifted off the ground and carried up into space. Piccard discovered many interesting things about the atmosphere high above the earth's surface.

Twenty-two years later Piccard made another voyage. He did not go up into space because by this time scientists were sending up complex spacecraft. These cost too much money for Piccard, and so space research was too expensive for him. Instead he decided to go down – to explore the depths of the sea.

He built a steel sphere which could be lowered to the deepest parts of the sea. In 1953 he went down in his sphere deeper than any man had gone before. He touched the bottom of the Challenger Deep, more than six miles under the ocean.

1. How did Auguste Piccard travel in space?
2. What was the sphere made of?
3. What did Piccard discover a lot about?
4. Where did he explore in 1953?
5. Why couldn't he go up in space again?
6. What was he the first man to do?

Section 7.6

A. Construct a reading comprehension test using the completion techniques described in this section. Construct one Type 1 test (Page 120) and one Type 2 test (Pages 120–1), using the same extract for both types of reading test.

The elephant is the only animal in the world with a trunk. It uses its trunk in many ways. It pulls leaves off trees with its trunk and then puts them into its mouth. It can even use its trunk to pull up trees when it wants to make a path through the jungle. It also uses its trunk to get water. The trunk can hold a lot of water, as an elephant needs to drink more than three hundred pints of water every day.

When an elephant is angry, its tusks can be very dangerous. The tusks of an elephant are really its front teeth. People pay a lot of money for the ivory of an elephant's tusks. In Africa men have hunted elephants for their tusks. The ivory from the tusks is made into many beautiful things.

It has been easy for men to train elephants in Asia. They use elephants to carry heavy things for long distances.

Many people say that the kings of Siam used to give white elephants to people they did not like. These white elephants were sacred and they could not be made to work. They could not be killed or given away. A person who owned a white elephant had to pay a lot of money to keep it properly. After a certain time, he usually became very poor. Nowadays people in England call a useless thing "a white elephant".

B. The following "text" is based on an extract from a telephone directory. Attempt to construct Type 1 completion items based on the information given in the extract.

Boston Tyre Co, 113 West Street	66421
Bosworth, Dr. G. R., 15 Station Parade	2300
Boulton, Frank E., 24 Belmont Ave.	86758
Bowen Private Hotel, 6 High Street	65222
Boyd National Bank, 2 Main Road	3167
Bracken, D. C. (Plumber), 217 York Place	77088
Bradley Photographers, 52 West Point	65296
Bradshaw Cafe, 7 High Street	2023
Brewer Taxi Service, 3 Station Square	4774
Briggs, Helena, Hairdresser, 5 Main Road	6566
Britain Garage, 28 Station Parade	2091

E.g. If you want a . . . ., phone 4774.

Section 7.7

Select a reading extract appropriate in difficulty level for a group of students whom you teach. Construct a cloze test from the reading passage.

SECTION 8
Sections 8.1/8.2

1. The following essay topics are far too vague. Extend the title of each topic and provide a context or situation where you consider necessary.

(1) Reservoirs.
(2) The advantages and disadvantages that would follow the introduction of a universal language.
(3) Describe a hotel you know.
(4) Road-mending.
(5) Shopping expeditions.
(6) Write a letter to a relative inviting him to stay with you.

2. Write the titles and instructions for four situational compositions. The four compositions should be based on each of the following:

(1) a letter to which a reply should be written
(2) a dialogue concerning a rescue (used to provide the basis for a report of the rescue)
(3) statistics concerning either
  (a) damage in various places resulting from natural causes: flooding, hurricanes, typhoons, storms
or (b) the various ways in which 3 people spend their wages each week
or (c) increase in population in various countries
(4) notes on any transport problems in a city you know

Section 8.3

Enlist the assistance of two colleagues and attempt the scoring of at least thirty compositions, using the impression-marking procedure. (It is helpful if you can score compositions of students with whom you are not familiar. Later, ask their class teacher to assign a mark to each composition based on the analytic method or on any other method used in the school or college.)

Section 8.5

1. Using each of the following sentences, construct twelve multiple-choice items to test those areas of reference and linkage denoted by the underlining. (The words underlined should be used as the correct options.)

(1) Tom and Dick scored 90% in the test. <u>Both</u> are extremely intelligent.

(2) Our car is that big saloon over there; <u>theirs</u> is the small sports car next to it.

(3) The old cottage with the broken windows and walls covered with ivy attracted John, but his wife would not consider buying <u>such a</u> house.

(4) We enjoyed the film, and our friends <u>did</u>, too.

(5) Although most people think Gordon is the best goalkeeper in the world, there are still a few who don't think <u>so</u>.

(6) I'm going to the beach tomorrow and <u>so is John</u>.

(7) Charles is an excellent singer. <u>Moreover</u>, he can play the piano very well.

(8) The sky still appeared dark <u>even though</u> the sun began to shine.

(9) I don't usually agree with everything John says. <u>On the other hand</u>, I agree with him about co-education.

(10) <u>In spite of</u> breaking his leg, Bill managed to continue his studies.

(11) <u>By the time</u> you read this letter, I shall be in Africa.

(12) Helen stopped working and stayed at home <u>until</u> her children were old enough to go to school.

2. Construct completion items to test each of the following areas.

(1) so (and so do I)
(2) (not only) . . . but
(3) mine/yours/ours
(4) such
(5) so (that)
(6) although

(7) neither
(8) whereas/while
(9) however/nevertheless
(10) despite
(11) because (of)
(12) -ing form of verb

Section 8.6

1. Use the following dialogue to write a punctuation test in which you are chiefly interested in testing the student's ability to use inverted commas, commas and apostrophes

> "Joe Green isn't very tall, is he?" Mrs Knight said.
> "Well, he's taller than Tony Black," Mr Smith replied.
> "But he isn't as strong as Tony," Mrs Knight said.
> "Good heavens!" I said. "Joe's as strong as any other boy in his class."
> "But Tony's a strong, healthy, good-looking boy," Mrs Knight argued.

2. Now write a passage which is suitable for use as a punctuation test. The passage should occupy no more than six lines, and you should indicate the chief punctuation marks you are interested in testing.

3. Construct a multiple-choice item to test the spelling of each of the following words.

> honour, gaol, friend, occurring, picnicking, eligible, manageable, mischievous, inoculate, innocent, forty, personal, deceive, beautifully, desirable, dissimilar, dialling, chief, handicapped, accommodation

4. Select for a spelling test twenty words from any textbook or reader

which your class is using. (Include also a number of words used by certain students in their free written work.)

(i) Write multiple-choice items for ten and
(ii) write blanks (giving only some of the letters in each word) for the other ten.

Section 8.7

1. Using a dictionary, find two examples of each of the following:

   (i)   words which are archaic
  (ii) words which are literary
 (iii) scientific terms
 (iv) newspaper jargon
  (v) commonly used words
 (vi) colloquialisms
(vii) slang words

2. Construct a test of register, using each of the following words together with any other word you select in the corresponding register:

    ignoble, dashboard, sit-in, lousy, foe, charabanc

3. Select sentences from six of the following sources so as to form the basis for a test of register (similar to Type 2(b) on pages 146–7).

    Instructions
    Legal documents (e.g. car licences)
    Children's literature
    Comics
    Detective stories
    Classics (e.g. Jane Austen)
    Humorous, light fiction
    Formal (business) letters
    Scientific reports and surveys
    Newspapers
    Advertisements
    Sports reports

4. Use the following reading text to construct a test of paragraph organisation and ordering. Select *only part of the text* (i.e. five or six sentences), scrambling the sentences so that the testee is required to reassemble them in the correct order.

    Earliest human societies lived by hunting wild animals, fishing and collecting fruits, berries, nuts, leaves and roots. Women probably did most of this primitive type of farming while the men hunted. The next stage in the early development of agriculture was the realisation that particular fruits or roots were more abundant in certain places than in other places. And so, after about 8000 B.C., a large number of tribes gradually began to settle down in certain areas. They became increasingly familiar with methods of exploiting the plant and animal resources of the particular region where they had settled. Their interest in roots and seeds led directly to early attempts at cultivation. Seeds were collected, stored and then planted in the ground. At first furrows were made in the ground with a stick. Next crude digging sticks and hoes were used. Later, about 3000 B.C., the plough was invented.

About the same time, primitive man began to domesticate animals and to keep cattle, sheep, goats and pigs. By keeping livestock of this kind, he was no longer dependent on hunting as the only source of meat. Many tribes wandered from place to place in order to obtain fresh grazing land for their herds. These tribes were the first nomads. Even in the present century several hundreds of nomadic tribes still wander over parts of Asia and Africa in search of new pastures for their herds.

Section 8.8

1. Either write or select a passage of suitable difficulty level on which the following types of exercises can be based:

   (i) copying with changes of person and/or tense
   (ii) changing the point of view
   (iii) changing the style or register
   (iv) re-writing, adding further information

   State in detail the instructions required for each type of exercise.

2. Construct sentence-joining exercises from each of the following complex sentences. The number given in brackets after each sentence indicates the number of simple sentences which you should use in each set.

E.g. One of the chief methods of propaganda is to change attitudes by emphasising certain facts which are important to the desired situation. (3)

One of the chief methods of propaganda is to change attitudes.	
It emphasises certain facts.	(by -ing)
They are important to the desired situation.	(which)

(1) The oxygen which is taken from the lungs to the body is carried by the red blood cells. (2)

(2) When the war was over, he went to live in Salem and studied law. (3)

(3) Lincoln was elected President for a second time in 1864, but unfortunately he was murdered in the following year while he was watching a play. (3)

(4) Immediately Scott and his party reached Australia, they found a telegram from Amundsen, informing them of his change of plans. (3)

(5) The Canal will be closed to shipping for at least a week until the *Hoshibo*, which is out of control and blocking the Canal, can be towed away. (4)

(6) Although it increased the costs of production, the plan which everyone agreed upon appeared the only successful solution to the problem. (3)

3. Write the instructions and parts of the first paragraph of a composition based on an exciting discovery two boys made while camping in the country. (Students should be instructed to complete the sentences in the first paragraph and then complete the composition by themselves.)

SECTION 9

Section 9.5

Without consulting any of the rubrics or instructions given in the relevant sections in the book, write suitable instructions (together with examples, where appropriate) for the following types of sub-tests.

Grammar: Multiple-choice items (with four options)
                     Error-recognition items
                     Word-order items
                     Completion items
                     Transformation items

Vocabulary: Multiple-choice items (with four options)
                     Sets (Associated words)
                     Matching items

Listening   Phoneme discrimination items (each item
Comprehension: containing three words in sentences)
                     Picture completion test
                     Dialogues

Oral Production: Picture description

Reading   True/false reading tests
Comprehension: Multiple-choice intensive reading
                     Cloze tests
                     Tests of cursory reading

Writing: Replacement items (testing reference, linkage and expansion)
                     Multiple-choice tests of style
                     Tests of register (using matching items)
                     Ordering (items dealing with sentence order at an elementary level)

SECTION 10

Sections 10.1/10.2

1. Write out the following results in order of merit, compiling a frequency distribution table. (The test was administered to a class of 40 students.)

Alan	58	Ethel	53	John	54	Oswald	56
Betty	42	Frank	60	Joyce	53	Paul	60
Bill	48	Freda	55	Kim	57	Paula	62
Charles	47	George	54	Leonard	62	Pauline	55
Christine	68	Gwenda	54	Lilly	58	Robert	48
Colin	57	Helen	64	Linda	55	Sam	47
David	74	Henry	63	Maureen	57	Sarah	52
Doreen	55	Hilda	54	Michael	60	Tina	62
Douglas	64	Jim	66	Noreen	58	Tom	51
Eric	69	Joan	55	Norman	61	Victor	50

2. Calculate the means and standard deviations of the following two tests.

(1) Mark	Frequency	(2)	Mark	Frequency
10	1		44	1
9	2		43	–
8	5		42	1
7	10		41	1
6	16		40	2
5	14		39	4
4	8		38	3
3	3		37	5
2	–		36	7
1	1		35	6
(Max = 10)	Total 60		34	5
			33	3
			32	2
			31	2
			30	–
			29	1
			28	1
		(Max = 50)	Total 44

Sections 10.1/10.3

From the results shown on Page 236, calculate the Facility Value (F.V.) and the Index of Discrimination (D) for each of the following items in a test administered to 40 students.

(U = Upper Half; L = Lower Half)

Item No.	1	2	3	4	5	6	7	8	9	10	11	12	13	14	15	16	17	18	19	20
U	15	16	14	10	15	14	9	12	13	11	9	13	12	13	5	14	10	4	12	9
L	14	12	5	4	8	7	4	4	7	5	2	9	7	10	3	11	3	1	6	8

Calculate also the mean score on the test as a whole.

NOTES
1 This reading comprehension test appeared in the Hong Kong Secondary Schools Entrance Examination (1968).
2 Extracted from *Reading with Understanding*, Intermediate Book 3 (J. B. Heaton & K. Methold), Longman.